MY YEARS IN PUBLIC SERVICE

AN ECOLOGIST'S VENTURE INTO GOVERNMENT

ARTHUR W. COOPER

authorHOUSE®

AuthorHouse™
1663 Liberty Drive
Bloomington, IN 47403
www.authorhouse.com
Phone: 1 (800) 839-8640

Published by AuthorHouse   07/31/2017

ISBN: 978-1-5462-0003-1 (sc)
ISBN: 978-1-5462-0002-4 (e)

Library of Congress Control Number: 2017911052

Print information available on the last page.

Table of Contents

Preface

This retrospective on my years in the public service arena had a modest original purpose. It began as a discussion of my years as a state government administrator from 1971 to 1976. The intent then was to document the most significant, most interesting, and sometimes amusing episodes that occurred during my five-plus years in state government. I wanted to do this because these experiences were important to me and because I thought they might be important, perhaps useful, and even interesting to others. These chapters form the core of this retrospective. After reading the material on the state government years, I realized that my experiences after those years involving the Committee of Scientists and the Coastal Resources Commission were equally important to me and, potentially, fully as important to others so I decided to include them.

As I got deeper into the writing I sensed that there might be other reasons for documenting these experiences. First, their context is important. They took place during a period of major change in the organization of North Carolina state government and during a period when environmental concerns became important considerations in government decision-making at both the state and federal levels. Discussion of these experiences offered the opportunity to reflect on the changes that have taken place in natural resource management agencies and policies both in North Carolina and nationally since the 1970s. In addition, there are "lessons" to be learned from each experience, lessons about how important decisions of the period were made and what the major influences on those decisions were. Finally, this discussion offered me an opportunity to reflect and editorialize both on the matter of how science and its findings, in this case mostly ecology, can be integrated into government policy and decision-making and how a scientist can be effective, or not, in a political environment.

Unfortunately, I did not keep a diary during the time about which I am writing. Now I wish I had. The absence of record leaves much, but not all, of this narrative to my memory, which time has inexorably faded, and to whatever other sources I could find. It also leaves open the temptation to engage in revisionist history, a problem that besets everyone who writes about, and interprets, life experiences. I have tried not to allow either of these possibilities to color what I say.

I have used the first person (I, we) throughout since I believe writing in the first person is clearer and more succinct. I use "I" when an action or issue directly involved me as an individual and "we" when the Department or individuals with whom I worked closely were involved. The reader will understand this distinction from the context of the discussion.

My discussion of each experience in North Carolina state government begins with introductory material that sets the stage for each episode. Most chapters end with a summary of "what can be learned" from that experience. Obviously, what I judge can be learned from an experience is my opinion and is colored by my own involvement in the episode. Others may view the experience entirely differently. The reader will find portions of the text repetitious. This is because each chapter is a stand-alone discussion, with chapters not leading one to another. Thus some material is discussed more than once, but each time in the context of a specific issue. Rather than constant cross-referencing, I felt this to be a better approach.

Any errors in describing events or their ramifications are mine as are any opinions expressed. Except where doing so would be clearly derogatory, I have used the real names of persons involved to tie the narrative more closely to the personalities, some of whom may be known to the reader.

I wish to thank my wife, Jean, for her support throughout my professional career and especially during my years of governmental work. I like to think she was a part of whatever good work I did. I absolve her of the "not-so-good" work!

Part I

State Government—1971-1976

Chapter 1

The State Government Years: How It All Began

When I came to North Carolina State University[1] (then North Carolina State College) in 1958 after completing my doctoral degree in plant ecology at the University of Michigan my responsibilities involved teaching undergraduate and graduate courses in ecology as well as teaching basic courses (general botany, dendrology) and doing research. The years between the late 1950s and early 1960s marked the very beginning of what came to be called the "environmental movement." Because ecology is the branch of science that deals most directly with environmental relationships, ecologists inevitably became involved in this important social movement. Until then ecology had been a branch of biology that attracted few students and was generally regarded as marginally significant with a body of knowledge that some other biologists regarded as obvious or trivial and of little real scientific value.

All of this changed with the publication of Rachel Carson's "Silent Spring", with the application of the newly-articulated ecosystem concept to major societal issues such as documenting the movement and bio-accumulation of radioactive fallout from nuclear bomb testing, and with similar problems involving movement of pesticides through natural systems. At the same time, it became evident that the United States was losing many of its important natural areas to the rapid growth that followed World War II. The Nature Conservancy, arising from needs articulated by the Ecological Society of America, stimulated a rapidly-increasing concern with preservation of natural areas.

My interests as an ecologist led me quickly to become involved in several North Carolina "environmental" issues such as expansion of the local Raleigh-Durham Airport, protection of nearby William B. Umstead State Park, and the preservation of Bald Head Island, a unique, essentially uninhabited island off the state's southeastern coast. I also was appointed

---

[1] North Carolina State University at Raleigh is the correct full name. It is known colloquially by several names and acronyms—NC State, NCSU, State. These are used interchangeably in my text.

to the Conservation Committee of the North Carolina Academy of Science, and to a similar committee of the Association of Southeastern Biologists. These activities brought extensive involvement that put me in the public eye and by the mid- to late 1960s I had become one of a small number of those regarded as spokespersons for the conservation community in North Carolina.

By the late 1960s I had also become involved with state government, having been appointed by the governor to the newly-created State Mining Commission and to an Environmental Education Study Committee created by the legislature. I also had the fascinating experience one spring in the late 1960s of developing a seminar on ecology and related sciences (water management and geology) for members of the legislature;[2] I had also given at least one talk on the science of ecology to a legislative orientation program run by the Institute of Government at Chapel Hill. The legislative seminar was organized by state Representative Norwood Bryan. It afforded me and my fellow presenters the unique opportunity for a discussion of natural resource management issues with a dozen or so legislators. Following the election of Robert W. Scott as governor in the fall of 1968, I had several formal discussions with members of the Department of Conservation and Development. So, I become reasonably well-known as a spokesperson about what had come to be called "environmental" issues. I was also comfortable talking with politicians on their terms about issues with which I was familiar.

*****

My involvement in state government began innocently enough. I was working in my office in the ecology suite on the third floor of Gardner Hall on the NC State campus in late March 1971 when my assistant, Louise Hube, rushed into my office with her eyes as big as saucers to tell me that "the governor is on the phone and he wants to talk to you." My first instinct was to suspect some hoax involving my graduate students—who were prone to do that on occasion—but fortunately I answered in my normal, gruff tone of voice. And sure enough, it was Governor Bob Scott. He got

---

[2]   Although the proper name of North Carolina's legislative body is The General Assembly the term legislature is often used in referring to it. The terms are used interchangeably throughout.

right to the point of his call which was that a vacancy had opened in the top administration of the Department of Conservation and Development (C&D) and that he and Roy Sowers (director of the department) thought I would be the ideal person to fill the vacancy. He added that Roy would be calling in about half an hour and that he (Scott) hoped that I would accept Sowers' offer. I was dumbstruck by this, and I managed only a few, probably trite, responses to Scott.

Sure enough, within a half hour Sowers called. Sowers message was short and blunt. Jim Glenn, one of the deputy directors of C&D with responsibilities in economic development, had resigned. The governor and Sowers had decided that it would be a wise move to appoint as a replacement someone with a conservation (meaning environmental) background to the job and they hoped I would accept. Sowers, in his usual straight manner, ended the conversation by advising me that "if I didn't accept the offer it was doubtful they would pay much attention to any of my suggestions in the future." In other words, put up or shut up when it came to influencing the direction of state government vis-à-vis environmental and natural resource management issues.

I told Sowers that I would certainly consider the offer very seriously but that I needed a day or so to talk to my wife, my administrative superiors, and someone in C&D about the details of leaving the university and moving into state government. One thing I was dead set on if I made this move was that, somehow, I would retain my tenure at the university. I felt I needed that cushion in the event this turned out to be an unwise or unworkable move or that I could not work effectively in a political environment. Sowers suggested that I talk with Vic Barfield, his other deputy about these matters. So, I called Barfield and arranged to have lunch with him the next day. The lunch went fine and Barfield dealt with all the questions I had, even though I dropped a container of salad dressing on his shoe while we were getting our meals! Great start!

That lunch turned out to be the first in a long series of helpful and collegial discussions I had with Barfield. He felt there was no impediment from state government's perspective to resolving my reservations and that, if necessary, Sowers or the governor probably could iron out any other issues with the university administration. It turned out to be so and quickly an agreement was struck that I would take a two-year leave

3

without pay from the university to serve with pay as deputy director for programs and plans of the Department of Conservation and Development. It turned out that the move resulted in about a $2,000 raise in salary to about $19,000. Later, to my embarrassment I found out that even the somewhat smaller salary I left behind at the university was significantly greater than that of most of the division directors in C&D. To say these men were underpaid considering the nature and breadth of their responsibilities was an understatement. This was the first of many discoveries that life "downtown" was very different from life on the campus.

As I recall the announcement was made by C&D on a Friday to appear in Saturday's papers. Of course, I was expecting a glaring headline and story about what was, to me, a major change in my life, and what was in fact a major departure from years of past practice for state government. I was chagrined to discover the announcement about two inches long and buried on the obituary page! That was my first lesson in the timing of news announcements, at least before the advent of television. Make them late Friday afternoon and you can sneak by with almost anything!

There really isn't any take home lesson from the story of how I became involved in state government except the obvious—if you are vocal enough about things you believe in deeply somebody may be listening. And if they are, you may be confronted with what amounts to an ultimatum to "put up or shut up" about what you believe in. Furthermore, you must be willing to intrude yourself into a new, unfamiliar, and most likely career-altering environment, all without any clear certainty of success. However, opportunities such as these must be seized as that is the way one grows, learns, and makes contributions to society. Teddy Roosevelt's statements about "………credit belongs to the man who is actually in the arena………" are relevant here. Carpe diem or you may forever regret it.

Another point deserves mention. The job I was taking by any reasonable standard could be described as "political." I would obviously be a political appointee and the issues with which I would have to deal would virtually all have political overtones. However, my discussions with Sowers made it clear I was being hired to provide my professional expertise in ecology to assist C&D in making decisions about issues with environmental dimensions. I had the same understanding with all the subsequent directors/secretaries for whom I worked. However, every decision at the top level of a state agency inevitably involves political considerations and one ignores these at one's own peril. So, in practice my job was to ensure that when my agency made a decision with environmental dimensions the ecological consequences of each alternative being considered were fully factored into the discussion. The final decision was, of course, always political as it inevitably is in a democratic form of government.

Because of the clearly political nature of my appointment I was concerned that, in the event I did not do well in a governmental environment or that political changes dictated that I leave, I had the option of returning to the university. Thus, as pointed out, I asked for and was granted a two-year leave without pay from NC State University. I also retained my tenure-track position in the Department of Botany. I was not privy to the discussions among the administrators at NC State who approved my leave under those terms. However, I always felt that they supported me and that they were very generous in their dealings with me. I will always be grateful for their kindness.

In retrospect, another consideration is important. Although I doubt that it influenced my decision much at the time, it had a profound impact on the rest of my career. As a member of a democratic society, each of us must make contributions to that society for it to function. Therefore, when one is offered an opportunity for public service one should, if circumstances permit, accept it. If called to public service, the call should be answered. There is no greater contribution that one can make to society than to be a public servant with all that implies. During my time in state government, I worked with public servants many of whom could have made more money and achieved greater recognition outside of government. The citizens of North Carolina owe these dedicated individuals, who illustrated the best in public service, a deep debt of gratitude.

Chapter 2

The Department of Conservation and Development
in 1971 and Its Cast of Characters

In 1971 North Carolina state government was sprawling and rich with agencies, many quasi-independent, offering limited opportunity for control by the governor. This pattern had existed for years and reflected both the antipathy of the General Assembly and the state's citizens for centralization of power and the growth in number and size of governmental agencies that took place following World War II. In addition, in many agencies with management and regulatory responsibilities the actual delegation of legislative power, rather than to an agency head, was to a board or commission composed of citizens largely appointed by the governor. Thus, many departments, in addition to being separate and independent, were marked by the potential for a struggle for power between the head of the agency and the agency's governing board or commission. Politically astute agency heads and board/commission members were often able to make this arrangement work smoothly. Other departments were often marked by internal divisions that minimized their effectiveness. In 1971, North Carolina was not unique in this regard; many other states had an equally cumbersome governmental structure. Recognizing the need to reorganize this outdated governmental structure, during 1970-71 both the governor and legislature devoted much time to reorganization of state government. Legislation to accomplish this objective was taking final form at the time I began work in Conservation and Development in May 1971. However, at the time I entered state government the final reorganization legislation had not passed and the agency in which I would work reflected the old structure of state government.

*****

The Department of Conservation and Development (C&D) was one of three major state agencies responsible for management of the state's natural resources, the others being the Wildlife Resources Commission and the Department of Water and Air Resources. As the name implies C&D also was responsible for promotion of economic development. The department had existed since 1925 and was responsible for management of the state's

6

forest, mineral, and marine resources as well as state parks, economic development, and the tourism promotion program. Wildlife resources and inland fisheries had been split out from C&D in 1947 and were the responsibility of the Wildlife Resources Commission. Management and development of water and air resources, including what pollution control programs the state had, were vested in the Department of Water and Air Resources and, to a lesser extent, the State Board of Health.

As indicated earlier, Roy G. Sowers was director of C&D. Sowers, a graduate of Wake Forest University, was a close political ally of Governor Bob Scott. Consequently, the department had Scott's confidence and thus a degree of flexibility in its operation that other agencies might not have had. Because of his lack of background in many of the resources he was responsible for, and because of his lack of interest in the details of managerial issues with which the department dealt, Sowers allowed his subordinates and division directors considerable latitude. As all C&D directors before him, Sowers background was most closely attuned to economic development. Early in the legislative session of 1971, when restructuring of state government was being considered, I remember discussing with Sowers whether economic development and conservation of natural resources should be in the same department. My feeling then was that they should be separated because economic development always seemed to hold the trump cards in any situation where it and conservation came into conflict. Sowers advised me that they should remain together because in that way it was possible to attract persons of political influence to the department, some of whom became strong supporters of, and proponents of, conservation programs. In a later chapter I discuss this argument in more detail but suffice it to say that even before I had entered state government I had come to agree with Sowers' views.[3]

Sowers came from Sanford and his favorite ploy when something came up with which he did not want to deal was to call to the young fellow who drove him and tell him "let's go to Sanford, Charles Lee," thus leaving the handling of some important issues to his subordinates. Sowers resigned

---

[3]   At the end of this retrospective I will discuss this matter further. Suffice it to say here that, given changes that have occurred since 1971 it is clearly unrealistic to expect these two functions to exist in the same department.

as director in early 1972[4] to run for lieutenant governor and was replaced by Raleigh real estate man Charles W. Bradshaw. Although Sowers was well-financed and appeared to be a strong candidate, he was opposed by Margaret Harper of Southport, black candidate Reginald Frazier of New Bern, and the young Democrat who came to dominate North Carolina politics for much of the last quarter of the 20th century, James B. Hunt of Rock Ridge. Hunt won the first primary with forty-four percent of the vote and Sowers chose not to call for a run-off. Shortly thereafter he was appointed a deputy secretary of the Department of Transportation and held that position until the end of the Scott administration in early 1973. Sowers faded from the state government scene, appearing from time to time as a supporter of someone who sought favor with one or another state agency. He worked in marketing and died in early March of 2002 at the age of 73.

Conservation and Development's activities were overseen by a board of political appointees, the Board of Conservation and Development. The board was comprised of 27 members[5] who served at the pleasure of the governor who, in making his appointments, was to "give proportionate representation to each function and activity of the Department." In practice, this meant that persons appointed to the board virtually all had political ties to Scott. Some had backgrounds that reflected one or more of the department's duties (i.e., industrial development, tourism promotion, forestry) and some before appointment had no discernible knowledge of the activities of the department. The board met four times a year and its duties were to oversee the functioning of the department and to provide citizen input into the department's operation. In this regard, Conservation and Development was a typical North Carolina state agency with the ultimate responsibility for the department's duties vested in citizens rather than bureaucrats. The bureaucrats ran the department and the board, with rare (but often exciting) exceptions, acquiesced to the recommendations and

---

[4]   By this time, the Department had been reorganized and was the Department of Natural and Economic Resources. Implementation of that legislative decision will be the subject of chapters four and seven.

[5]   When the Department was created in 1925 the board consisted of only 6 members plus the governor as ex officio chairman. The number gradually increased to its 27 members in 1971. The governor served as Chairman of the Board from 1925 until 1961.

decisions of the department's staff. Cultivating and satisfying the Board of Conservation and Development was an art one had to learn quickly. The chairman of the board in 1971 was Gilliam K. Horton, a scrap metal dealer from Wilmington who had a strong concern for conservation and management of natural resources, especially those of the coast. Horton and Sowers, to put it mildly, often did not see eye to eye on the affairs of the department, despite their loyalty to Governor Scott, leading to some strong disagreements which Sowers generally won.

The department had two deputy directors. Victor W. Barfield was Deputy Director for Administration; the position I filled was Deputy Director for Programs and Plans. As the position titles imply, the deputies had responsibility for department wide program oversight, one in administrative matters and the other in programmatic areas. Barfield, born in Wheat Swamp, NC, was a graduate of Duke University and a career state government employee. He was the consummate assistant to a political appointee—able to get things done when they needed to be done in a way that did not attract attention and with a minimal amount of feather ruffling. An apocryphal story was told about Barfield that when Hargrove (Skipper) Bowles became C&D Director in 1961 he was looking for someone to head the accounting office. The story has it that Bowles asked who that young fellow was who smoked the same brand of cigarettes as he (Bowles) did, that he seemed like a bright young man, and that he would like to interview him. During the interview, Bowles was reputed to have asked Barfield what "2 + 2 was" and Vic replied, "How much do you want it to be, boss?" Bowles is said to have hired him on the spot. This story was a compliment to Barfield because it explained his uncanny ability to accomplish what departmental leadership wanted and what the department needed but in a way that was not unduly visible, and in a way that was always within the bounds imposed by statutes and a highly visible governmental position.

At this point I need to elaborate on my relationship with Vic Barfield. He and I served as the two deputy directors of C&D from May to September 1971 and then he as the deputy secretary and me as the assistant secretary of the (newly created by the 1971 legislature's restructuring of state government) Department of Natural and Economic Resources until my departure in August of 1976. Barfield continued in his position until 1977 when he was transferred to the newly-restructured Department of Commerce as its deputy secretary. Vic and I had entirely different backgrounds. He had come up through the ranks of state government from an accountant in C&D to become its deputy director in charge of administration (budgets, personnel, etc.) and I, of course, had come from 13 years' academic experience at NC State. Vic and I became close, partly because we got along well together, but more importantly because we often had to deal together with matters delegated to us by Sowers and subsequent secretaries that were either very difficult procedurally or politically. We both also spent a great deal of time representing the department in the legislature. In addition, we ultimately served together under two different administrations, one Democrat and the other Republican, and thus had to serve two entirely different sets of political "masters." We complemented each other and consequently never minded each other's business. I will always respect Vic for the help he gave me during the five and one-half years we worked together and will always appreciate the guidance he gave, particularly in the early months, to a political novice.

The man who had preceded me as Deputy Director for Programs and Plans was James Glenn. Glenn had come into the department specifically to work with economic development and thus his purview was not that of the entire department. Glenn stayed in the job for less than two years and left for a position with industry. In making the decision to replace Glenn, Sowers and the governor were convinced of the need to hire someone with an "environmental" background, largely because of the political significance of making such a hire (remember the first Earth Day was in April 1970) and because they felt a need for an upper level manager whose experience ranged widely across the responsibilities of the department.

It turns out that the man who had as much to do with hiring me as anyone was Adrian King, Sowers' public relations man/speech writer. Adrian was a true man of the seventies. He wore mod clothes with ruffled shirts, bell-bottom trousers, and had hair that hung well below his shirt collar. Rumor had it that every couple of weeks he got a hand-written note from Governor Scott with the message," Adrian: isn't it about time to get a haircut. Bob." To put it mildly, Adrian stood out among the other buttoned-down employees of the department. However, he understood, in a way that few others in the department did, how important it was that its natural resource responsibilities be given attention and visibility. As best I could figure out, Adrian played a major role in convincing the governor and Sowers that hiring a person with my background would not only be politically wise but also important to the proper functioning of the department. In a little over a year King was succeeded by Steve Meehan who remained the department's PR man during my entire tenure.

Conservation and Development had 7 constituent divisions: Commerce and Industry, Forestry, Geodetic Survey, Marine Fisheries, Mineral Resources, Travel and Promotion, and State Parks[6]. Each division had a different history and each had a clear mission. They are described here roughly in their order of creation.

The Division of Mineral Resources could trace its roots back farther than any other division, having originated in 1823 with the creation of the State Geological Survey. In 1971, the State Geological Survey was contained within the Division of Mineral Resources. Stephen G. Conrad was the director of the division and held the title of State Geologist. He was named to that position in 1964, held it until retirement in 1990, and died in 2012. The division was responsible for geologic investigations into, and development of, the state's mineral resources, mapping those resources, and regulating (together with the Mining Commission) the mining industry through a mining act passed in 1968. The division had a small, highly professional staff located primarily in Raleigh and with an outlying office in Asheville.

The Division of Forestry contained the North Carolina Forest Service, which was created in 1908, whose leader was the State Forester. In 1971 Ralph C. Winkworth was director of the division and State Forester. He had held that position since 1966 and died of cancer in the early 1980's. Forestry was the largest division in C&D, having field foresters in virtually every county plus staff foresters in its Raleigh and regional offices. In addition, it had an "air force" consisting of a variety of planes, mostly used for fire-fighting. In the early 1970s Forestry was an old-line organization, primarily involved in providing advice to citizens regarding forestry

---

[6] The following paragraphs are not intended to be a full history of each of the department's divisions; enough is provided to understand where each division came from and its duties as of 1971.

practices and in firefighting. Its internal organization was para-military and this showed up nowhere better than during firefighting season. We used to say that fire-fighting was the glue that held forestry together—their eyes seemed to gleam a little brighter during the spring and fall fire seasons. The division was characterized by a high esprit de corps and professionalism throughout its ranks.

The Division of Commercial and Sports Fisheries was created in 1927, shortly after C&D itself, as the Division of Commercial Fisheries. Its responsibilities involved regulation and management of marine fish species caught for commercial sale and those that were of importance to saltwater sports fishermen. In addition, in 1969 it had just received, because of passage of a state dredge and fill law, a legislative mandate to regulate coastal wetlands and submerged bottoms. Implementation of this responsibility was a difficult task for the division since it received no additional funding or personnel because of the legislation. In 1971 the division was still struggling to develop a smooth implementation of its new regulatory authority. The director of the division was Dr. Thomas L. Linton, who had come to the department from the University of Georgia Marine Lab on Sapelo Island. Linton was a trained marine scientist and a character in his own right. Linton's appointment continued a step taken during governor Terry Sanford's administration when he appointed Dr. David A. Adams (oddly, my first graduate student) to succeed C. Gehrmann Holland, whose background was in law enforcement. Sanford declared, at the time of Adams' appointment, that the division must expand beyond law enforcement to include "research, education, advertising, industrialization, and market development." Sanford saw Adams' background as a professional scientist essential to achieving these objectives. Linton's appointment followed Adams resignation and established a professional background as essential to the director's position.[7] Linton remained in state government until 1975 when he moved to a marine resource job in Australia, returning two years after to the Sea Grant Program at Texas A & M University at Galveston. He is an emeritus faculty member there today. The division had many

---

[7]   While being interviewed for the position Adams expressed concern about the political elements of the job. Sanford responded by telling Adams that "once you lose your boyhood fascination with women there is nothing more exciting than politics."

employees, including fisheries inspectors deployed along the coast and a professional staff in its laboratory at Morehead City.

The Division of Commerce and Industry was, as its name suggests, charged with promoting economic development in North Carolina by assisting new industries to locate in the state and existing industries to expand. Although not an original component of C&D, the promotion of development in North Carolina was always part of the mission of the department. By 1928 a Division of Commerce and Industry had been created and was described in the second biennial report of the department as functioning "in the nature of a State Chamber of Commerce." By the early 1970s it had grown well beyond that mission and had become both the promoter of industrial development in North Carolina and the source of information for others as they sought to locate or expand in the state. Although not the largest division in the department, it was certainly the most politically important because of its duties related to economic development. The director of the division was Robert Leak. He had come up through the ranks of the division and was well-respected in the department, the legislature, and the economic development community. Leak was a central figure in the department, a good administrator, and a sometimes-colorful personality. When the occasion warranted, he could become quite the raconteur. Some of his jokes were legends not only in the department but also among other state economic development directors. Leak remained with industrial development when the division was moved to the Department of Commerce in 1977. He is now retired and living in Raleigh. The division had three sections, dealing with industrial development, food industries, and international development. This latter program was in its infancy in the early 1970s and was North Carolina's first tentative effort at internationalizing its economic sector.

The Division of Travel and Promotion was the descendent of the State Advertising Division, created in 1937 as the result of a request by the then Governor Hoey for a $250,000 appropriation for the 1937-39 biennium to create a state advertising program. This program was responsible for developing programs and materials that served to promote North Carolina as a destination tourism site. In 1971, Charles Heatherly was the division director and he had a small technical staff to assist in disseminating materials developed by the division itself or through contracts with outside entities. I have lost track of Heatherly.

In 1939 the Legislature authorized an agency to make surveys and computations to complete the North Carolina Coordinate System and to carry to completion as soon as possible the monumentation of that system. It was not until 1960, motivated by further amendments from the legislature, that the Geodetic Survey Division was created within the department. It was responsible for establishing precisely located monuments on the North Carolina Grid System and Bench Marks referenced to a vertical datum. The division had a small staff and its director was Wilbur Fuller, who is now dead.

North Carolina's state parks were managed by the Division of State Parks, created in 1948 when it was split out of the Division of Forestry. The state's few parks acquired since Mt. Mitchell in 1915, together with the state-owned lakes, were originally managed as a unit of the Division of Forestry. The Division of State Parks first director was Thomas W. Morse. Its director in 1971 was Thomas C. Ellis, a career division employee who had begun as a ranger and had risen through the ranks to succeed Morse. Ellis was a quiet, gentle, Christian gentleman in the best sense of the word. He was a pleasure to work with but was not, by nature, a hard driver who pushed for expansion of the Park system. In the early 1970s the state park system was small, containing less than a dozen very high-quality units, and poorly funded. That it had such a high degree of dedication to its programs was a tribute both to Ellis and to his employees. It turned out that one of the major objectives of my tenure at C&D was to begin an expansion and development of the park system, necessitating that Ellis and I work closely together. Ellis was cautious and he viewed expansion in the size, mission, and character of North Carolina's state parks as a mixed blessing. In short, he supported the objective but feared that resources would not be made available to achieve it. In the short run, at least, his fears proved to be partly correct. Ellis remained as director through the 1980s when he retired. He remained active in supporting the state park program for the rest of his life and died in the early 2000s.

From 1957 to 1969 the Department had a Division of Community Planning with the mission of aiding counties, cities, and towns across the state to carry out planning for their growth and development. This work was largely funded through federal grants. The division's original name was "Community Planning and Hurricane Rehabilitation" obviously reflecting the effect of Hurricane Hazel in 1954. "Hurricane Rehabilitation" was dropped from the name after two years. In 1969 the division was moved to a newly-created Department of Local Affairs. As we shall see, because of serious political difficulties (described by a play on the words of its name), this department was eliminated in the state government reorganization of 1971 and included, together with C&D's functions and those of other agencies, in a new Department of Natural and Economic Resources.

Two programs that were original parts of C&D, but which were no longer in the department in 1971, deserve comment. From 1925 until the late 1950s the department had a division concerned with water resource management (other than water pollution control which was vested first in the State Board of Health and later in the Stream Sanitation Committee). It had various names, all relating to use and development of water resources, particularly those of the coast. In 1959 the functions of this division, together with those relating to pollution control in other departments, were transferred to a new Department of Water Resources. The 1967 legislature combined this department with other water pollution control functions and responsibility for air pollution into the Department of Water and Air Resources.

In 1927 what were then separate programs in Game Management and Inland Fisheries Management were moved into C&D. They remained there until the mid-1940s when hunters and fishermen became increasingly critical of C&D because of alleged mismanagement of dedicated game and fish management funds. The status of these programs became a major political issue in 1945 with intense pressure developing to put game and inland fisheries management into a separate autonomous department. That change occurred in 1947 when the programs were removed from C&D and placed in the newly-created North Carolina Wildlife Resources Commission. The autonomy of management of inland fish and game was still a simmering cause in 1971 and, as we shall see, was a major issue in the reorganization of state government.

The Department had many support functions, including personnel and finance. These reported directly to Vic Barfield through his assistant

Bill Bradshaw. Of interest was the assignment of the state's executive aircraft to the department for management. In 1971 the state-owned two aircraft, a propeller Grumman Gulfstream 1 that seated about a dozen and a Cessna 402 that seated four to five, that were used extensively by the governor's office and in industrial recruitment. Later the state replaced the Cessna with a 6-seat Beech King Air. Three pilots flew these aircraft, Don Gunter, Floyd "Brownie" Brown, and Earl Gower. The aircraft and pilots were assigned to C&D because of their use in industrial recruitment and because C&D at that time had the reputation, largely due to Vic Barfield, of being one of the best managed state agencies and managing the airplanes was a sensitive job. The governor's office clearly had top priority and industrial development and the C&D director came next. After that, the planes were available for use, at cost, to any state agency. There was a temptation to use the aircraft for all sorts of purposes, some legitimate and others much less so. Barfield and Bradshaw were the primary referees of requests for use of the planes. Those of us in the administration of C&D and its successor agency Natural and Economic Resources did use the aircraft a great deal. To my knowledge, the criterion that guided all our uses was whether the use was essential to the operation of the department's programs and/or whether it allowed department personnel to be present in parts of the state at times when it was technically or politically important and it would be difficult to get there otherwise. The governor and upper department administration warranted a pilot and copilot. When I flew I generally rated only a pilot and try as I might I never was able to hint strongly enough that I would like to learn to fly the plane. None of the pilots ever took the bait. In retrospect, this was not an idle whim on my part, as the pilot with whom I flew alone the most, Earl Gower, died at home of a heart attack at thirty-nine about two months after I left state government in 1976!

Although it was about to undergo dramatic change, the C&D I joined was a well-run, smoothly functioning operation. From the minute I stepped into the department I felt welcomed and was always treated with the greatest courtesy by all the division directors over whom I had authority. As we will see, all of us went through many stressful events between 1971 and 1976 and the members of the department from the front office down to the division clerical staffs all felt like part of my family by the time I left. They were capable and dedicated and the citizens of the state were fortunate to have them working for them.

If there is any lesson to be learned from the structure and operation of the Department of Conservation and Development which I joined, it is the importance of understanding the culture of the agency within which one works. Conservation & Development was one of the long-standing, most important departments of state government. Since its creation in 1925 it had added new responsibilities and had lost old ones (wildlife and inland fisheries and water planning). To function efficiently at the level of department administrator, and to bring about change if that is one's goal (as it was mine), one must learn quickly how the department operates, where power really resides, and how each individual program operates. Although on an organization chart each division of C&D was "equal", it was clearly known and well understood that industrial development got the lion's share of attention from the director and the front office. The fact that the deputy director I replaced spent virtually all his time working with industrial development illustrates this reality. Some divisions were happy to work free of regular involvement from the front office; others badly needed the attention of the departmental leadership. When I began work, it was clear that I intended to be involved with all aspects of the department's operation. Most divisions did not regard this as any benefit as far as they were concerned. Others, State Parks and Marine Fisheries for example, welcomed the fact that they had an advocate in the front office and, consequently, came to me for help with some of their more difficult managerial issues.

The limited size of the staff in the front office meant that the department had little capability to deal with complex, interdisciplinary issues. Such issues were becoming more and more common in the early 1970s. For example, the first environmental impact statements were just beginning to arrive for comment by state agencies. Although coordination of the state response to EIS's was the responsibility of the Department of Administration, development of a "coordinated environmental response" lay largely with C&D, the Wildlife Resources Commission, and the Department of Water and Air Resources. It was clear that the only person at an appropriate level to coordinate C&D's responses was the occupant of the deputy director position that I held. Given my duties related to the operation of the department I was hard-pressed to give sufficient attention to development of a departmental response to each EIS. The sheer volume of some of the documents made the task even more daunting. I will comment on this problem at length in Chapter 5.

It became painfully clear very quickly that neither C&D nor state government was organized appropriately to deal with the environmental dimensions of issues with which they were regularly faced. Only time would tell whether the reorganization being debated by the General Assembly would alleviate this problem.

Chapter 3

My First Few Months on The Job

Needless to say, I was apprehensive about working in state government. It was one thing to advise what should be done by the department, yet another to be faced with the responsibility for doing it. I had not had a great deal of time to think about how I would approach the new job as the month and one-half that passed since I had been hired was occupied almost entirely with ending up the spring academic semester and working with my graduate students to ensure that they would be able to continue and complete work toward their degrees. Fortunately, we could do that and I do not believe that any of them suffered by my absence from the faculty.[8]

*****

My first day on my new job was Monday, May 17, 1971. I can remember clearly riding up in the elevator to our third-floor offices at 116 West Jones Street, in what was then called the Administration Building with, among others, Clyde Chesney, a forestry student I had taught in ecology a year or two before. I asked Clyde what he was doing there and he said he was starting an internship with the State Forest Service. Then he asked me what I was doing there and I replied that "I am a new deputy director of the department and I am not at all sure what I do." This undoubtedly did not raise his confidence or that of anyone else in the elevator about the ability of the newest member of the C&D leadership team.

When I arrived in the office I was greeted by my new secretary, Mrs. Martha Liles. I had met Martha before in the month and a half since

---

[8]   Recall that when I agreed to work for C&D I did so with the proviso that I could honor an agreement that I had made to teach for one month at the University of Michigan Biological Station. I was allowed to do this and from roughly July 15 to August 15, 1971, I was not physically present in the department, although I was on call (and was called regularly) in Michigan. All but one of the events recounted in this chapter occurred before I went to Michigan.

my appointment so we knew each other reasonably well. She brightly informed me that I had one appointment that day—at eleven o'clock with a department employee I will not name. I asked what in the world it was about and she told me I was his boss. It turned out that this gentleman was a purely political appointment who had rattled around the department for several years while a job was being found for him. Finally, it was decided he would be the responsibility of the Deputy Director for Programs and Plans. He reported to me once a week to provide an update on his accomplishments which, as I recall, were modest. He was a fine person and a good example of the sort of thing that happens to people who are appointed into a department where a job must be manufactured to meet what minimal talents they have in the areas of expertise of the department in question.

Until my appointment arrived I thought I would orient myself by looking at the files on the assumption that would give me some idea of the issues and people with whom I would soon enough be dealing. Surprise! There was, in the battery of filing cabinets in my office, only one folder and it was the folder outlining my appointment's travels through the department's various agencies. By this point, I was beginning to wonder what my predecessor had done. Even Martha couldn't give me a real clear picture of his work.

So, it was clear that I was in both the best and the worst of all situations. I could develop my own activities within the scope of what was implied by my position title, which seemed broad enough to encompass about anything, or I could wait and see what landed on my desk. What happened was a bit of both. Much of the time during my first two months on the job was spent in trips to the legislature following up on issues in which the department had an interest. In addition, the department had accumulated several important issues requiring resolution at the departmental level and they immediately became my responsibility. In addition, I had brought with me a rather full list of items to tackle, all stemming from projects I had been involved in while dealing with conservation issues during my tenure at the university. The most urgent of all these issues was expansion of the Raleigh-Durham Airport (RDU). At that time, the Airport Authority had on the books a plan for expansion that involved construction of a new runway to the east of the existing main runway, the use of which would involve direct overflight of William B. Umstead State Park by planes landing from and departing to the northwest. The impact of these flights would have been greatest on the picnic and camping areas of the park. The entire conservation community, including virtually all the small number of conservation organizations that existed at that time, opposed this runway and had managed to make it a major issue of concern in the local press and in C&D, which was involved because its Division of State Parks managed Umstead State Park and because an adequate RDU was clearly an economic development issue.

Expansion of RDU was one of the first issues that Director Sowers discussed with me after I agreed to take the deputy director job. C&D, in its capacity as the state's economic development agency, wanted the airport expanded yet also realized its responsibility to protect the parks that it managed. Sowers hoped that some means could be worked out to allow the airport to expand without impacting the park. My second day on the job involved traveling to Washington, DC to meet with various federal officials about the airport-park conflict. So, with a ticket in hand provided me by the department, I was off to Washington on Tuesday.

A digression about traveling out of RDU in those days. If one was going to Washington for a day's work, one took Eastern Airlines Flight 398 which left at 7 AM. That necessitated leaving home at 6:30 AM, driving to the airport out brand-new I-40 and parking in a special spot reserved for C&D use immediately next to the terminal. A walk of two-three minutes got one to the Eastern departure gates and, without seat assignments or security inspection, one boarded immediately, usually with five to ten minutes to spare before 7 AM departure. The flight arrived in Washington at 7:45 so, with a quick breakfast at the airport and a cab ride into the city (the Metro was under construction in 1971) one could easily make a 9 AM meeting. An early evening flight, Eastern 375 I think, would allow one to be home for dinner after a full day of appointments in Washington. Such pleasant and convenient travel arrangements long ago disappeared, along with Eastern Airlines, from RDU. I got to know Eastern 398 very well in the next ten years. One inevitably met several government or university employees on that flight.

My appointments in Washington dealing with the airport involved the very newly created and still "feeling-its-way-along" Council on

Environmental Quality, the Department of the Interior, and the Department of Transportation. My main purpose in these visits was to determine if the RDU Airport Authority, or one of the federal agencies whose interests were impacted (Interior and Transportation), was required under the terms of the National Environmental Policy Act (NEPA) that became effective January 1, 1970, to prepare an environmental impact statement on the environmental effects of proposed expansion. History has shown NEPA to be a powerful tool for exposing the environmental impacts of proposed federal actions. However, in May 1971, barely a year after it came into effect, administration of the law was mixed and confused. None of the litigation that helped define the scope and intent of the law had yet been decided, let alone filed. Thus, the answers I got to my question as to what was required of the Airport Authority under NEPA were confused and unclear. My reading of these answers, plus my own personal prejudices on the matter, led me to tell Sowers on my return that an environmental impact statement was required but that it was unclear who was responsible for preparing it. The net effect of this advice was that it stopped any immediate approval of expansion and led to an extended period during which alternatives to the location of the new runway were explored by the Airport Authority (see a fuller discussion of this issue in Chapter 5).

Toward the end of that first week I got a stark lesson in politics. Tom Linton, director of the Division of Marine Fisheries, and I rode the same bus to work as we lived fairly near each other. One afternoon late in that first week he stopped by my office and asked if I wanted to accompany him on a visit to New Hanover county Senator John Burney's office in the legislative building on the way to the bus stop. Linton had promoted development of a bill that would allow one-quarter of one-percent of the unrebated motorboat fuel tax[9] to be assigned to his program for research and development. Burney was handling the bill in the Senate. The door was open to Burney's office and he was standing with his back to us as we walked in. Linton, in his usual "hail-fellow-well-met" manner asked Burney how his (Linton's) motor boat fuel tax bill was faring. Burney did

---

[9]   Motor boat fuel purchasers paid the state highway tax on fuel and, on application, were entitled to a refund of the tax. Large numbers of boaters never applied for the rebate, thus there was a significant amount of "unrebated motor boat fuel tax."

not respond for what seemed an eternity. Then he slowly turned, faced Linton, stuck his finger at Linton's chest and said, "Doctor, I asked you for a favor on a permit 10 days ago, you have done nothing with my request, and your motor boat fuel tax bill will rot in hell." Linton was taken aback and Burney turned back to shuffling papers on his desk. Then he turned again and, with a sly grin, growled, "Politics is hell, Doctor." We both backed out of Burney's office and walked to the bus stop in silence except for Linton's one statement, "I guess I won't get my motor boat fuel tax bill this year, will I." He didn't.

Oddly enough, barely two months later, when one of Linton's fisheries inspectors was charged with first degree murder for shooting a man who attacked him with a clam fork, the department engaged Burney to defend the man in Onslow Superior Court. Burney was persuasive enough to have the entire case against the inspector dismissed, as it should have been, since he was clearly in the act of defending himself. Furthermore, the sheriff who arrested our inspector was a friend of the slain man. Burney obviously held no personal grudge against Linton and was merely informing him in no uncertain terms that favors don't come free in the world where politics and resource management meet, a good lesson to learn early on in a job in which politics were an important consideration.

The situation just mentioned involving one of our fisheries inspectors brought up a long-running issue in the fisheries program as to whether inspectors should be armed. At the time of the shooting inspectors could carry side-arms if they desired; some did and some didn't. Clearly, their job involved considerable danger and situations not infrequently arose where there was a need for an inspector to defend himself. Despite this, many inspectors felt that carrying weapons would invite armed retaliation when confrontations occurred. Furthermore, allowing some men to carry weapons and others not raised questions about the degree of training in weapons use required of inspectors. Clearly, the issue needed to be resolved.

There was disagreement within the division as to what should be done. Director Linton personally favored arming his men but felt that if he alone made the decision it would lead to a serious split among his field personnel. So, he sought guidance from "the front office", in this case meaning me. I was about to learn one of the first realities of government decision-making, that difficult issues often gravitate to the highest level of administration available. After all, that was one of the principal reasons for having deputy directors in the department. I heard arguments from proponents and opponents of arming inspectors in my office and quickly decided that it would be departmental policy that fisheries inspectors would be armed. One of the strongest arguments in favor, I felt, was that Wildlife Resources officers were armed without any of the dangers feared by opponents of arming. My decision involved several consequent actions, including a decision as to which weapon the department would purchase and how each inspector would be trained (it turned out by the Highway Patrol) in the proper use of weapons and guidelines for their use. In the end this was not a difficult decision for me because of the clear potential danger to which fisheries inspectors were regularly exposed, but I had to make it in the face of my own strong dislike of firearms and the idea of being armed.

Another very different issue arose during my first few months on the job, this one involving economic development. In July of 1971, President Nixon announced that he would visit Communist China the following winter. This step was preceded by numerous contacts with China, many involving increased trade. As North Carolina's lead economic development agency, C&D was asked for an opinion as to whether the state should begin making trade overtures to the Chinese. Director Sowers called his deputies and several of the economic development staff into his office and put the question to us. When it was my turn to comment, I said something to the effect that "I saw no reason not to do it as better ties with China were inevitable and we might as well take advantage of the situation sooner rather than later." Sowers grunted and commented wryly that was about what he expected from a "pinko college professor." However, it was unanimously agreed that the state should undertake such overtures as soon as possible.

Before that was done, however, it was necessary to inform the legislature of what we proposed to do and to get, if not their open approval, at least an unspoken agreement that we should do what we proposed. Several key legislators were invited to the department for a briefing given by the economic development staff. After the presentation had been made, there was a long, seemingly ominous silence. Finally, one notoriously-conservative legislator spoke up that "when he was in China right after

World War II he got the best damn whiskey he ever had in Shanghai so, yes, go ahead, I have no problem with it." The remaining discussion was along the same lines so the department was obviously free to pursue trade with China on behalf of the state of North Carolina.

One of the more complicated issues that hung on for resolution at the department level involved White Lake, one of the State Lakes. Among the responsibilities assigned to the Division of State Parks was management of the State Lakes, a duty made infinitely more difficult because by statute the state owned only the water in each lake and its shoreline, except where it had been bought by the state, was private property. Thus, management of State Lakes boiled down to refereeing conflicts in the use of the water largely without being able to control access to the water.

Nowhere was this oddity a greater problem than at White Lake, a popular recreation and vacation site in Bladen county. Here the state was responsible for controlling uses of the water and bottom of the lake but had only a small public access area on a shoreline that was essentially privately-owned and controlled, largely by many owners of small segments of shoreline. (The state also managed adjacent Jones Lake and its shore line, a recreation area that had originally been acquired as one of three state parks for "negroes.") One of the uses of White Lake that created continued difficulty was construction of piers by private shoreline owners. Since White Lake was an oval and piers were required to be built perpendicular to the shore, as piers proliferated and grew longer to escape neighboring piers, adjacent pier owners would come into conflict. Pier owners' source of redress against a pier problem with a neighbor was an appeal to the Division of State Parks.

Shortly after I joined C&D Tom Ellis, Director of State Parks, appealed to me for help in refereeing a squabble between several pier owners who were disputing the length of their adjacent piers, arguing that the newer, longer piers that were being built were essentially cutting off water access to shorter, older piers. Ellis indicated that the Department was required to hold a hearing which he wanted me to chair. At the hearing pier owners could argue their respective cases and, based on evidence gathered at the hearing, state parks would attempt to devise a solution that would satisfy all parties. That solution, of course, could be appealed to the courts. It is important to note at this point that in 1971 the state had no administrative procedures law that would prescribe the ground rules for such a hearing, including requirements for public announcement, rules for conduct of the hearing, and guidelines for resolving issues.[10] Each agency flew by the seat of its pants, making up its own rules as it went along, with guidance from attorneys assigned to the department by the attorney general.

A first hearing was held in Raleigh. Most of the pier owners involved showed up together with their lawyers. I represented C&D, together with Tom Ellis, and we were assisted by one of the two lawyers assigned by the attorney general to C&D. To put it mildly, the hearing was chaotic. At one point attorneys from both contesting parties objected to a statement made by a witness. Not having the vaguest idea what to do I turned to C&D's attorney and asked him what I should do. His answer was "Do what you want, it's your hearing." I cannot remember what the outcome was but it became clear that the parks people had to develop some clearer guidelines for pier construction at White Lake. This conclusion required the department to hold an open hearing at White Lake at which any interested party could testify on what the new rules should specify.

This second hearing was held in the town hall at White Lake on a very hot July evening. The town hall was about forty feet square and seated less than two dozen people. The hearing was well attended with the town hall filled and numbers of people gathered outside the open windows. The business of the hearing droned on until about dark. By then Tom Ellis and I had heard all we cared to hear about pier length, the nastiness of neighbors, and life in general at White Lake. As Tom and I packed up and prepared to drive back to Raleigh, I was accosted by an elderly man who announced "that he had a problem that I needed to fix." When I asked him what the problem was he announced that he wouldn't tell me but that "he (Tom Ellis) knew what it was." I looked at Tom and he gave me an "I don't have the foggiest idea what he's talking about" look. So, I again asked the man what his problem was and he again said he wouldn't tell me. With that, I told him that if he wouldn't tell me what his problem was there was nothing I could do to help him and I was going back to Raleigh.

---

[10] The legislature was in the process of developing North Carolina's first administrative procedures act during its 1971 session.

I was eager to get back to Raleigh anyway as my wife and I were leaving the next day for a month to teach at the University of Michigan Biological Station to which I had committed myself well before the opportunity to join state government arose.

Under the conditions that existed in 1971-72 administration of the State Lakes was difficult if not impossible. However, the advent of the State Administrative Code and reorganization of state government brought about a much more effective means of management. State Parks authorities developed a set of regulations for administration of State Lakes. These were initially approved in February of 1976, finally bringing order to the difficult task of regulating development on or adjacent to any State Lake.

It is worth pointing out here that none of the issues involving State Lakes existed at the numerous impounded lakes in North Carolina such as Kerr Scott, Kerr, Lake Gaston, Lake Tillery, and Lake Lure to name a few. At those lakes, the shore line was controlled by the entity that created the lake and that entity had control over development on the shore. At Kerr Scott and Kerr Reservoirs the U.S. Army Corps of Engineers, the constructing agency, controlled shore line development under terms of the congressional legislation that authorized the impoundment. Kerr Reservoir, and later impoundments, such as Falls Lake and Jordan Lake, however was constructed under legislation that required state participation in development and management of recreation facilities (more about this later). Thus, the department I was in did eventually become involved in management of some of these artificial lakes.

The take-home message from the first few months was not much different than the message one would take home from the first week on any new job. If one is faced with a job in which the duties are unclear, yet the position is one with significant authority, one is faced with the opportunity to effect change by his decisions as to where to place work emphasis. My opportunity was not entirely that free, as I inherited several issues that had devolved on the department's front office and which were no one's clear responsibility. Thus, my work was in a sense defined not by a job description but by issues. As it turned out, this was to be the pattern that defined much of my work during the five-plus years I spent in state government. The issues with which I dealt were largely complex ones, involving numerous disciplines that lay outside and above the responsibilities of individual departmental divisions. My job was to broker the views of the divisions, organize them into a coherent position for the department, to explain and clear them with departmental leadership, and then to represent them in discussions with other state and federal agencies and with members of the General Assembly or the public.

The difficulties with management of White Lake were but one small example of how outmoded much of North Carolina's resource management law and policy was in the late 1960s and early 1970s. The general policies under which the state's resources were managed were permissive, in that use could take place with minimal intrusion from the state. Regulations relating to water and air pollution were in the early stages of development. Federal legislation dealing with water and air pollution was under intensive study by Congress; landmark legislation requiring significant responses by the states would pass in the early 1970s. State legislation dealing with mining had passed in the late 1960s and was just being implemented. The state Dredge and Fill Act had been passed in 1969 and was also slowly being implemented. In short, the state's legislative and administrative machinery was slowly responding to the rapidly-intensifying development that was occurring in the last third of the twentieth century. Much of the work that C&D and its successor agency, and I as a principal administrator, did during the early 1970s was implement newly- passed legislation and propose other legislation to deal with clear and pressing resource management issues.

The other obvious feature of my job was the wide variety and complexity of subjects with which I would have to deal. Furthermore, although a few of them, such as the airport-Umstead park issue, related to matters in which my training and background would be useful, others such as weapons and trade with China involved subjects about which I had no personal familiarity. Dealing with those involved common sense and what is called "gut-instinct"—how I personally felt about the subject at hand. As I got deeper into my job, it became painfully obvious that most issues that I would deal with fell into this latter category. The fact that I was a trained ecologist brought precious little to bear on resolving the issues with which the department was faced. My background as a scientist did give me an ability to view issues with an organized, systematic approach. However, in the end my decisions frequently were based on simply what my gut told me was the right thing to do.

I learned several other things early on. First was the importance of being consistent and always, always telling the truth. In dealing with department personnel, with legislators, and with the media it was essential to be consistent when discussing an issue in different venues and never to fall in the trap of bending the truth, no matter how difficult it was to speak it. That does not imply that one must always tell the full truth with all its gory details. But what one says, even if it only part of the story, must be true and consistent from telling to telling. Furthermore, one must never lose one's sense of humor; sometimes the most disarming way to deal with an issue is to tell the truth accompanied by a bit of humor, particularly if the humor is at your own expense. Never be afraid to admit a mistake. Admission to an error is often the best way to deal with a mistake. After all, when one admits to being wrong and having made a mistake, what response makes any sense?

Chapter 4

Reorganization of State Government—1971-72 Phase—
and Its Impact on Conservation and Development

During the late 1960s a State Constitutional Study Commission recommended restructuring the North Carolina Constitution as well as adding new and deleting outdated provisions. One addition was a recommended amendment calling for restructuring of state government. This recommendation stemmed from the cumbersome structure of North Carolina's government pointed out earlier (see introduction to Chapter 2). The amendment (now Section 11 of Article III) was approved by the voters in November 1970 and required that "Not later than July 1, 1975, all administrative departments, agencies, and offices of the State and their respective, functions, powers, and duties shall be allocated by law among and within not more than 25 principal administrative departments........." During the 1971 legislative session, the General Assembly, with the support of Governor Bob Scott, approved the Executive Reorganization Act creating 17 state departments, some of which were perpetuations of existing agencies and others were newly-created agencies. Conservation and Development was placed in a new Department of Natural and Economic Resources. As fate would have it, I was deeply involved in the early implementation of reorganization of C&D as it related to the structure and organization of the new department into which it was placed by the reorganization legislation.

*****

Unquestionably, the most important and far-reaching issue in which I was involved during my first year in C&D was reorganization of the department, which took place as a part of the general reorganization of state government in the early 1970s. This effort was fraught with all sorts of pitfalls, some technical, some administrative, and some purely political. As a newcomer to state government (I had been in C&D for barely three months) I ended up with an inordinate amount of responsibility for shaping the new department into which C&D was placed.

Discussions of the need to reorganize state government began in the early days of the Scott administration and during the 1969 session of the legislature. In a message of March 27, 1969, Governor Scott urged creation of a Department of Local Affairs and, in addition, recommended several other changes to the organization of state government, including changes in the Department of Conservation and Development recommended by a Study Commission in 1967. Governor Scott created the Department of Local Affairs himself in 1969 but the legislature took no action on the other recommendations.

At the same time reorganization of state government was being considered, reorganization of higher education in North Carolina was also being debated. This move was a response to the efforts of several institutions, most notably East Carolina College, to be recognized as "universities" by a change in their name. Addition of the name "university" to an institution's name was initiated by the change of North Carolina State's name to North Carolina State University at Raleigh, a change that consumed over 4 years and an enormous amount of public and legislative debate. Although the 1971 legislature was considering reorganization of both the executive branch of state government and the university system, debate over the two reorganizations was conducted separately. Reorganization of state government was initiated by legislation (Session Laws 1971-864) passed on July 14, 1971 whereas reorganization of the university system was dealt with separately in a bill passed in special session on October 30, 1971.

The 1971 Executive Organization Act responded to the constitutional amendment passed in 1970[11] by cutting the total number of executive agencies from over 300 to "17 principal departments", thus meeting the requirement that there be no more than 25 "principal

---

[11] Much of the following discussion leans heavily on a research paper "The Reorganization of the North Carolina Department of Natural and Economic Resources: A Case Study" written by Charlotte R. Gantt (an intern in the Department) in partial fulfillment of requirements for the Master of Public Administration at UNC-Chapel Hill.

administrative departments."[12] The bill also gave more power to the governor by spelling out his various general and specific authorities with respect to reorganization.[13] Two top-level managerial positions, secretary and deputy secretary, were provided for in each department and the powers and duties of the secretary were also spelled out. A central requirement specified the conditions applying to each transferred agency. Those moved by a type I transfer had their statutory authority and all associated duties and functions that went with those powers surrendered directly to the secretary of the department into which they were transferred. Those moved by a type II transfer retained their statutory powers and were thus not under the policy control of their new secretary. Nonetheless, all their management functions were the direct responsibility of the secretary. Thus, type-II transfers were statutorily departments within a department but managerially one department. The type II transfer presented numerous management issues and created problems as further reorganization unfolded. Finally, the statute provided for reorganization to take place in three steps: an initial phase to be completed in 1971 that consolidated the executive branch into the 17 principal agencies (consistent with the 1970 constitutional amendment); a second phase to be completed by the 1973 legislature that would finalize the composition and policy-making functions of each principal department; a third phase, also to be completed by 1973, that would make any necessary final refinements. This phased process, although logical, also created problems in implementation which were, in some ways, exacerbated by the election of 1972 which placed the requirement to fine tune the reorganization process in the hands of

---

[12]   The departments were the 8 constitutional departments with elected heads (Agriculture, Auditor, Insurance, Justice, Labor, Public Instruction, State, Treasurer) and those with heads appointed by the governor, the Departments of Administration; Art, Culture, and History; Commerce; Culture and History; Human Resources; Military and Veterans Affairs; Natural and Economic Resources; Social Rehabilitation and Control; Transportation and Highway Safety. Subsequent legislatures and governors have restructured and renamed these agencies. Despite these changes the total number of departments has never approached 25.

[13]   It is important to note that these powers related only to the 9 new departments created by the reorganization act and not to the 8 previously existing agencies headed by popularly-elected officials.

Republicans rather than in the hands of Democrats who were the authors of the legislation and of the initial changes in reorganization.

Two models were considered for reorganization of the state's natural resource agencies. One called for separate Departments of Natural Resources and Economic Development and the other, championed by C&D director Roy Sowers, envisioned a single agency (essentially an expanded Conservation and Development) with natural resource, environmental protection, and economic development functions swept together in a single department. Sowers argument for the second alternative was interesting and instructive. It was his view that it was essential that environmental agencies be combined with economic development functions because economic development programs would attract persons of political influence to the agency's oversight board. Those persons, being charged with oversight of all departmental functions, would become supporters of environmental programs. Sowers claimed that this wide-based support existed on the Board of Conservation and Development (a contention about which he was right) and that it would also exist on the board of whatever agency become Conservation and Development's successor. Incidentally, he did not argue that Conservation and Development should simply be expanded and retain its name; he argued for a new and expanded agency with a new name.[14]

Benefits of the two-department structure included: disagreements between interests were more likely to be aired publicly raising public confidence in decisions; reflecting the tenor of the times by giving environmental protection a highly visible position in state government; freeing environmental decisions from the "control" of developmental interests; and raising controversial environment/development decisions to the level of the governor for resolution. On the other hand, an overwhelmingly important benefit of the single agency structure was the potential for coordinated decision-making on complex environment/development issues by a professional staff where benefits and costs could initially be weighed in a theoretically less political environment. Equally important, it allowed for an early identification of environmental limitations

---

[14] Time showed that Sowers' views were not workable, in part because the board created by the legislation never really functioned. See Chapter 17 for further discussion of how reorganization of NER has played out.

of which prospective industries and development proposals needed to take account. This meant that, at least in theory, the governor would be presented a balanced proposal for dealing with such conflicts and would not be faced with doing the balancing act himself. My suspicion is that this final point probably weighed heavily in Governor Scott's decision to support the single agency alternative.

With the support of Governor Scott, the reorganization legislation consolidated the natural resource and economic development functions of state government into a new Department of Natural and Economic Resources (NER). Six entities, mostly committees or commissions, were transferred to NER by type I transfer. The Department of Local Affairs, which had fallen into disfavor with the General Assembly, was transferred to the Department of Conservation and Development also by a type I transfer. Twelve agencies, including the Department of Conservation and Development, the Department of Water and Air Resources, the boards of both departments, and several commissions, councils, and committees, were transferred into NER by type II transfer. The Wildlife Resources Commission was also transferred to NER but by a special transfer that maintained its policy and management functions intact. Interestingly, the composition of the new NER was like that of the old Department of Conservation and Development as it existed in the 1930s and 40s.

Governor Scott chose NER to be a test for the implementation of reorganization. Shortly after July 1, 1971, he named Sowers as secretary of NER. Sowers, in turn, chose Vic Barfield to serve as his deputy secretary. A new position, assistant secretary for resource management, was created and I was appointed to it. Although NER did not have to come into existence until 1972, Scott and Sowers decided that NER would serve as the prototype for departmental organization and that it would come into existence on October 1, 1971. Scott's decision to make Sowers the new secretary reflected his political alliance with Sowers and his desire to create a new department that was closer to the governor and more sensitive to the governor's policies and direction, objectives that he understood to be an important goal of reorganization.

The agencies that had been placed into NER came to the new department with varying degrees of baggage and, in some cases, considerable reluctance. Some even refused to believe that the words of the reorganization statute meant they were no longer a free standing, independent agency. The (previous) Department of Water and Air Resources had paid little attention to what was going on in the General Assembly during the spring of 1971. When that department's leadership finally crashed through, due to the alertness of a staff member, that they were scheduled to be rolled into another department and lose their autonomy they tried to resist but the decision had been too long made for them to change it. In addition, they had little influence either with Governor Scott or the General Assembly and almost no constituency to make a case that they should remain independent. With reluctance, Water and Air Resources joined NER and ultimately became one of the most important, if not dominant, parts of the department. At the other extreme, the North Carolina Park, Parkway, and Forest Development Commission, a type I transfer with one employee and an office in Waynesville, refused to believe it had been made part of NER even when advised of the fact over the telephone by Secretary Sowers. Vic Barfield had to take a plane, fly to Asheville, meet the Haywood county sheriff and together travel to their offices and physically seize their records. The reaction of most other agencies included in the new NER ranged somewhere between these two extremes.

Sowers' first instruction to Barfield and me was to develop an internal structure for the new department that would satisfy the initial need for management direction from the secretary without unreasonably infringing on the authority of the agencies that had been placed in NER by type II transfer. That proved to be far easier said than done. On the one hand, the objective of reorganization to make agencies that were more responsive to the state's chief executive and were more efficiently managed clashed with the continued political independence of all the agencies transferred into NER by type II transfer. The statutory delay that was built into the phased implementation of reorganization gave agencies that wished to retain their independence the time to gather political support for that objective. Whatever Barfield and I were to come up with could not possibly satisfy all the boards, commissions, committees, and agency personnel that had been assigned to NER. At best, what we were to come up with had to provide the administrative and managerial authority that reorganization conferred on the Secretary while maintaining the policy

35

authority of the agencies that had not lost it because of the nature of their transfer to NER.

Vic and I worked through the late summer and most of September to put together what seemed to us to be a scheme that reasonably satisfied both objectives. Much of our final proposal was fleshed out on a trip he and I took to Hyde county to look at a proposed development on the shore of Albemarle Sound.[15] We proposed 6 administrative units designated as Offices:

Forest Resources consisting of the North Carolina Forest Service from C&D;

Recreation Resources comprised of State Parks from C&D, the Division of Recreation from Local Affairs, and the previously independent Kerr Reservoir Development Commission;

Industrial, Tourist, and Community Resources made up of Commerce and Industry and Travel and Promotion from C&D, the remainder of the Department of Local Affairs, the Board of Science and Technology, and the Park, Parkway, and Forest Development Commission;

Earth Resources consisting of Earth Resources and Geodetic Survey from C&D, the Mining Commission, and the State Soil and Water Conservation Committee;

Water and Air Resources composed entirely of the old Department of Water and Air Resources and its constituent boards; and;

---

[15] The proposed development turned out to be ill-advised to say the least. Vic and I were flown over the site to observe it from the air. At one point, Vic asked me "what was all that silver down there between the plants." My answer that it was water, in which the development was to be built, essentially killed any support he and I would have for the proposal before the plane landed.

Fisheries and Wildlife Resources made up of Commercial and Sport Fisheries from C&D and the essentially-independent Wildlife Resources Commission.

The Offices of Forest Resources, Industrial, Tourist, and Community Resources, and Earth Resources were to be directed by their respective directors from C&D. The director of the Department of Water and Air Resources became the director of the Office of Water and Air Resources. The Office of Recreation Resources was directed by the director of the Division of Recreation from the Department of Local Affairs. Initially, there was no director appointed for the Office of Fisheries and Wildlife Resources as that position was essentially a box on the organization chart with no real duties (because of the essentially independent status of the Wildlife Resources Commission). Unfortunately, political systems do not like empty boxes and, to the dismay of everyone from Sowers on down, Orville Woodhouse, a politician from Currituck county was appointed by the governor as director about a month after the organization was announced.

This initial organization of NER was publicly announced by Sowers on October 1, 1971, and illustrated on an organization chart that Barfield and I developed. Unfortunately, and to our great chagrin, the first organization chart was intended to explain the managerial structure of the department and never showed any of the boards and commissions that had been moved into the department, implying by omission that they no longer exercised their statutory authority. This oversight quickly led to strong negative reactions, expressed all the way to the governor's office, from the missing boards and commissions and from others who did not favor reorganization to begin with. Barfield and I hastened back to the drawing board and within a day produced another chart showing not only what was on the first chart but also the lines of authority of the department's boards and commissions. Although we explained the discrepancy between the two charts by indicating that the first showed only the administrative and managerial lines of authority conferred on the secretary by the reorganization statute and that the second showed the "full functional" organization of the department, the skeptics of reorganization were hardly mollified.

37

The flap over the two organizational charts was far from the only indication of political concern for creation of NER. A major dispute between Sowers as NER secretary and the Board of Conservation and Development arose over the seemingly innocuous decision to consolidate the department's field offices in the mountains by closing the office in Sylva and moving it to Asheville. We in the department considered this well within the secretary's managerial authority, particularly given that achieving financial savings was one objective of reorganization. The Board of C&D, however, objected strenuously all the way to the governor's office. This dispute was followed shortly by a debate over filling the position of Director of Conservation and Development—another one of those dangerous empty boxes. Again, we in the administration of NER felt that Sowers could fill this position as well as his position as secretary and there was no need to pay two persons to do what was essentially one job. The board objected strongly and again the matter ended up in the governor's office. This time Scott responded to the board in December 1971 by appointing W. Eugene Simmons as C&D Director (more on this later in this chapter) and issuing a strongly-worded statement explaining that the Board and Department of C&D did indeed still exist and that the position of Director needed to be filled. The governor's statement also referenced the organization charts that, in his opinion, had been issued contrary to law. Barfield and I wondered many times afterward how close we came to being fired over the "reorganization chart" episode.

The board's objections were rooted in more than just a concern for its authority. They reflected the feeling among many that reorganization was moving too fast and that it needed to be rethought. It also reflected the fact that most members of state boards and commissions had not really followed closely the reorganization as it moved through the General Assembly and thus did not fully appreciate the significant effect it would have on them and their appointments. This point was driven home to me when, at the height of the gubernatorial campaign in October 1972 I gave a talk in Asheville that was largely a discussion of how NER was structured and my perception of the benefits that would flow from that new structure. Hargrove "Skipper" Bowles, the Democrat candidate for governor and hands-down favorite to win, was present and spoke to me briefly afterward. He essentially warned me that I should not spend so much time talking about reorganization, and implied that it might all change after he was elected.

With Sowers' resignation in December 1971 to run for Lieutenant Governor and his replacement as secretary by Raleigh realtor Charles W. Bradshaw the pace of reorganization slowed dramatically. Bradshaw was essentially instructed by Scott that his job was to maintain the status quo and to concentrate on making the structure of NER work successfully. Bradshaw was an interesting appointment. One might have expected that with his background in real estate appraisal and development he might be disinterested in the natural resource functions of NER. Bradshaw's approach to running the department was very even handed and all functions of the department benefited from the "light touch" he exerted as secretary. Bradshaw treated the front office staff very well and we all got along together. In fact, he would occasionally invite us all to lunch and we would tool off together out Downtown Boulevard and Wake Forest Road in his black Mercedes to the Hangchow Restaurant for a long, big Chinese lunch. About 1:30 we would head back to the office and arrive nearly asleep, particularly if Charlie had provided us each a small bottle of his favorite German Underberg bitters.

Mrs. Bradshaw, when visiting the Department's offices shortly after her husband was sworn it, decided that redecorating was in order. Mrs. Bradshaw's tastes were, to put it mildly, at great variance from the usual sheet rock-beige paint-cheap carpet décor of state agency offices. She had the Secretary's office painted a dull navy blue with dark red accents and decorated it with a gold plaster eagle, a china dog, and other odds and ends of decoration. In addition, a deep pile, bright red carpet was laid throughout the entire administrative office complex. She even undertook to redecorate the ladies "powder" room which (although I never saw it except when the door was held open for everyone to view the entrance) was decorated with plastic hanging flower baskets and trim around the mirror. Although we were never sure who paid for all the decorations we always suspected that the Bradshaw's themselves did. I was asked once to describe the décor in the administrative offices and the only description I could come up with was "early French something." Although these comments about redecoration of the departmental offices may sound critical of Mrs. Bradshaw, they are not meant that way. She was a sweet woman who had different tastes than the rest of us. The changes in décor she made remained through the rest of the time the department occupied offices in the Administration building and they certainly presented a more "elegant" and welcoming image than that of most state offices.

Bradshaw served out the remainder of the Scott administration. During that time, no major changes were made in the structure of the department. We all suspected that when the Democrats won the gubernatorial election, the new governor Hargrove "Skipper" Bowles would either undo or radically alter the reorganization changes that had already been made. However, as I point out in a subsequent chapter the Democrats did not win and an entirely new set of Republican appointees was handed the job of completing reorganization. Without discussing the details of what was done (discussed in later chapters), suffice it to say that the Republicans built the Department based on the structure that was implemented in the fall of 1971. The fundamental structure of the department, although different in detail, remained built on the design Barfield and I laid out in September 1971 until 2011 when the legislature began transferring units to other departments. I think things might have turned out entirely differently, with the composition of NER being changed somewhat, if the Democrats had won the 1972 election.

Implementation of the first phase of state government reorganization had some interesting and convoluted implications. As I indicated, the Department of Conservation and Development did not cease to exist on September 1, 1971; it merely became part of a larger Department of Natural and Economic Resources (DNER). That meant that all of C&D's statutory authority and its constituent agencies still existed and still carried on business but under the umbrella of a larger department that exercised only management authority over these component parts. When the second phase of reorganization took place, scheduled for 1973 (but not occurring until 1974), C&D would form a large part of NER and would pass out of existence. Thus, C&D was eliminated in a two-step process. In a nutshell that is how it happened. The actual events associated the C&D's demise are more complicated.

The reorganization legislation of 1971 transferred certain previously-independent agencies into C&D by type I transfer and then transferred C&D, together with those agencies, into the new Department of Natural and Economic Resources by a type II transfer. To repeat, this meant that C&D's constituent agencies came under the management authority of the secretary of NER but retained their statutory authority. In practice, this meant that the Board of Conservation and Development still existed and still exercised its statutory authority with respect to the agencies that were in the department at the time of transfer. It also meant that the position of Director of Conservation and Development still existed. In addition, there were certain duties assigned to C&D agencies by statute, such as cooperative fire control programs with counties, dredge and fill permits, and the authority to close coastal waters to shell fishing due to pollution. These actions required recommendations from the appropriate division of C&D and the signature of the director. Although Vic Barfield and I felt that logic dictated that these duties be assigned to the Secretary of NER, we found that this was not only statutorily impossible but, as we learned from the "organization chart" escapade, also politically infeasible.

The Board of Conservation and Development made it clear that it must stay in existence (as the reorganization statute required), continue to meet, and continue to discharge its statutory responsibilities. It pressed its position vigorously with Governor Scott's office. Although awkward, this situation really posed no managerial problems except the necessity to remember always that the board continued to exist and that it should be consulted when making decisions not only about the work of the old C&D agencies but also about the future administrative and statutory structure of the department.

The board also made clear to the governor its belief that someone must be named as the Director of Conservation and Development. Because the statutory duties that were required of the director were minimal, Sowers, Barfield, and I felt it made sense to designate the Secretary of NER as C&D Director and that it would be wasting money to fill a position with such minimal duties with another person. However, the Board of C&D pressed the case for a separate director, insisting that reorganization was moving too rapidly and that they (the board) were being ignored. The governor's office ultimately came down on the side of the board and decided to appoint someone to the position.

The person chosen by the governor's office was W. Eugene Simmons of Tarboro, a political associate of the governor's, and Chairman of the North Carolina Democratic Party. Simmons had previous experience with C&D through service on the board during the governorship of Luther Hodges. Simmons' appointment on November 26, 1971, evoked numerous critical articles and editorials from newspapers statewide, the tone of which was "why appoint someone to a job that had at best minimal duties." Some went so far as to say the appointment was inconsistent with the purpose of government reorganization. Criticism of the appointment reached such a level that Governor Scott felt compelled to explain his appointment of Simmons. On December 13, 1971, he issued a lengthy statement explaining and vigorously defending the appointment. Scott's statement pointed out that C&D was indeed not "defunct" as one newspaper had put it and that the criticism of Simmons' appointment was largely based on a misunderstanding of the reorganization statutes. Scott also referenced the organization charts of NER that left out lines of statutory authority (the original diagram Barfield and I drew) by omitting the board and director. Scott pointed out that later diagrams did show the board and director and were correct whereas the "earlier ones should have [shown them]." In short, Scott never referred to the director's limited duties but emphasized that the reorganization act by transferring C&D intact and leaving its statutory powers unaffected required C&D "to exercise its prescribed statutory powers independently of the head of the principle department" (in this case NER). Scott's statement did not dwell at length on what actual duties the director would perform. As I recall, Barfield, Adrian King, and I provided a good bit of the argument included by the governor's staff in the statement.

Although the controversy surrounding Simmons appointment never abated completely, he assumed his duties as Director of C&D, doing those few things that directly required his attention. Simmons was a fine, decent man and those of us who worked with him enjoyed doing so. However, it was clear that Simmons was never completely comfortable in his job, largely due to the taint applied to his appointment in the press. He resigned effective July 1, 1972 about six months after being appointed. At the time of his resignation, a statement circulated through the department purporting to be Simmons' letter of resignation to the governor. Its source was never clear but nonetheless it clearly conveyed what must have been Simmons' feeling about the whole affair. After mentioning Simmons' problems with the press, the "release" states "At all times, Sire, I have striven to be the epitome of gentlemanly deportment and composure, but,

Sire, they have raked my ass over the coals." The statement concludes with the line "Everybody gotta be someplace but this sure as hell wasn't mine." Although humorous, this "statement" would pertain fully for all appointees to jobs for which they are not at all a good fit.

The "death of C&D", however, did not end with Simmons's resignation. In early July 1972, without comment Governor Scott appointed me as Director of Conservation and Development effective July 1, 1972, and I served until the department went out of existence on June 30, 1974. One accidental but very real personal benefit of my appointment was that I took the oath of office from Justice Susie Sharp, giving me my only opportunity to meet that North Carolina icon. While I was director, the only duties I can really remember performing were the signing of occasional closings of shellfish waters due to pollution and signing five copies per county of a cooperative fire control agreement with each of the one hundred counties. I asked once if I couldn't just as well use my signature stamp on the documents but was told "no, the signatures had to be originals." So, I brought the stack home and signed them while I watched TV.

My dual office-holding status continued until the second phase of reorganization was passed in 1974. To recognize the nearly 50-year existence of C&D, my wife and I held an "end of the line" party for the C&D administration at our house on the night of June 30, 1974 where, at 11:59 PM, the department officially went out of existence.

The confusion that existed over the status of C&D was a good example of passage and implementation of a far-reaching statute that was not well understood by virtually all the people affected by it and not entirely understood even by those charged with implementing it. State government reorganization was a dramatic change in the way North Carolina's government was structured and how it did business. Although the changes were thoroughly discussed in hearings and in front of the legislature the impact of the changes embodied in the reorganization act was not at all clear. The confusion over the status of C&D is but one example of that. Few, if any, of the members of the Board of C&D realized that reorganization effectively did away with their board and the department with which it was affiliated, albeit in a delayed, two-step sort of way. The same confusion existed to a lesser extent within the department itself, with some employees (those moved by a type I transfer) in a new department with no clear lines of communication and authority and others (in agencies transferred by a type II transfer) unsure to whom they were to look for supervision and approval of proposed actions.

The organization that Barfield and I devised was supposed to resolve those insecurities within the department, and did to some extent, but clearly only made matters more confused for the members of boards and commissions and in two of the "offices" we created. Since appointments to boards and commissions originated with the governor, appointees took their concerns to him, creating further confusion. The fact that these events occurred during the last 18 months of the Scott administration probably dampened somewhat the outcry against reorganization—that it was going too fast and that changes were being made that no one anticipated. If all of this had occurred during the first 18-24 months of Scott's administration the outcome would probably have been much different. As it was, by the winter and spring of 1972 much of the frustration had been vented at the new Department of Natural and Economic Resources that, polyglot as it was, conducted business with efficiency and in a manner consistent with the intent of the reorganization statutes. By the summer of 1972, the gubernatorial and presidential campaigns were drawing heavy attention and concerns about reorganization faded. However, as we shall see, reorganization was an issue in the campaign of the Democrat candidate for governor and, had he won, the changes accomplished by reorganization up to that point would undoubtedly have been revisited.

A case can be made that the legislation implementing reorganization itself contributed in large part to the confusion with implementation. By choosing a two-step process for reorganization, with a first step involving transfer of existing agencies to new, umbrella agencies and leaving two years between this first step and the next, there was a built-in opportunity for those persons and agencies displeased with their new position and status to express that displeasure. Such a situation could have led at the very least to changes in the planned reorganization and at the worst to total failure of the process. I always strongly suspected that there was more disaffection with reorganization than we were hearing in the department front office. Because we were Scott appointees, and he was going out of office in less than a year, displeasure was probably being expressed to the candidates for governor.

The other reorganization alternative would have been to simply declare that, on a date certain, all previous agencies were to go out of existence and be replaced by new agencies with a very short time allowed for the transition—what might be called "lightning bolt" reorganization. Such an approach on a state level would have been difficult, if not chaotic, and would have led to more than a few months of confusion in the machinery of government. This latter approach is probably more effective when used with a relatively small set of persons or agencies and where personal contact with those being reorganized is possible. Barfield and I used this approach several times when organizing within NER and could pull it off because we made sure first that we had the backing of the Secretary.

The decision to include industrial development within Natural and Economic Resources was not without controversy. Some of the industrial development staff believed, and I think this belief became stronger as reorganization of the department was implemented and the reorganized structure put into effect, that their interests were being submerged by the department's more numerous and complex environmental obligations. In short, the industrial development staff and its constituency came to feel that it was not receiving the attention it deserved and the emphasis that it needed to do an effective job of growing the state's economy. This feeling later became apparent during the gubernatorial election of 1976 and, with the election of Jim Hunt, led to movement of the industrial development programs into the Department of Commerce.

Chapter 5

Dealing With The National Environmental Policy Act

The late 1960s and early 1970s saw the passage of numerous pieces of legislation, on both the state and national levels, relating to management and protection of the environment. Perhaps the most far-reaching of these was the National Environmental Policy Act (NEPA) passed into law effective January 1, 1970. NEPA was a far-reaching piece of legislation that immediately exerted profound impact on the operation of federal, state, and local agencies. It had two major requirements. First, every agency of the federal government was required to include a statement... ..."of the impact of its proposals for legislation and other major Federal action's" .....on the environment; this statement shortly came to be known as an "environmental impact statement (EIS)." Second, it established a Council on Environmental Quality to oversee implementation of the act and to advise the president on national policies to protect the environment. As Adams (1993) points out the act was not well written, was naïve in many of its directives, and immediately after its passage was not taken seriously by federal agencies. However, as Adams states, "it changed for all time the way federal agencies do business."

Federal agencies were slow to accept that the requirements of NEPA pertained to them and even slower to conform to them. The general position of most agencies that administered programs that impacted the environment was that their existing requirements and procedures were consistent with NEPA and thus needed no real change. Consequently, they proceeded with their programs with no acknowledgement that NEPA might apply to them. It took court decisions, deriving from cases brought by environmental or citizen groups, to establish that virtually any action of an agency that had, or might have, a significant impact on the environment fell under the requirements of NEPA and that agencies themselves must do the analyses required rather than rely on the work of others. It would be an understatement to say that initial federal agency response to these court mandates was slow to come and weak in substance.

*****

It took several years after passage for the impact of NEPA to be felt at the state agency level. Regulations for implementation of NEPA required that an environmental impact statement (EIS) be reviewed and commented on by affected agencies and be available for public review. North Carolina used its State Clearing House for federal documents, managed by the Department of Administration, as the entity through which comments would be solicited, summarized, and returned to the originating federal agency. Although comment was required within 30 days, extensions of the comment period could be requested. However, because of time lags incurred in circulating and summarizing comments, an agency usually had no more than 14 days in which to develop its own comments. This frequently led to hurried, superficial reviews by personnel whose work was fully committed to other tasks. The result in the first days of NEPA implementation was state comments that were of little substance and with little impact. Within another year or so, impact statements changed dramatically as federal agencies tried to meet court mandates for more complete analyses by literally cramming every piece of information that appeared even remotely relevant to a project into a long document that frequently showed little effort to relate the information contained to the project being analyzed. A classic example of this was an early EIS for a nuclear power plant sent to NER for review that consisted of two volumes each nearly a foot thick that was wheeled into my secretary's office on a freight cart. Under existing conditions of time and available personnel a meaningful and useful analysis of such a document was impossible. By the time I left NER preparation of EISs by federal agencies had become more institutionalized with documents usually containing at least a pro forma effort at analyzing the real environmental impacts of projects. The review and comment process had also evolved into discussions among NER agencies and with their federal counterparts that often led to project revisions that altered or reduced negative impacts on the environment. Less often, but in several cases involving highly controversial projects, they resulted in an outright abandonment of the proposed work.

Conservation and Development (later Natural and Economic Resources) contained almost all the agencies of state government with expertise in analysis of environmental impacts. Thus, it was the agency that virtually always had the job of analyzing and commenting on the complex environmental consequences of projects that might be of large or small impact but often were large in both scope and/or political importance. Since my duties involved coordination of the programs of our constituent agencies, the work of coordinating responses to environmental statements fell to me. Because it quickly became clear to me that my other duties would prevent me from doing a competent job of coordinating our responses to EISs I prevailed on Vic Barfield to allow us to hire a person whose specific duties were to deal with EISs. The young man we hired, Robert Finch, proved to be an excellent hire for the job. As I will show, he played a major role in developing our response to a number of projects, several of which were politically volatile.

It is important to note here that North Carolina passed its own Environmental Policy Act (SEPA) in 1971. This legislation resembled the national act in that it contained statements of policy regarding protection of the environment and required an environmental impact statement for major projects affecting the environment that involved state money. Final decision regarding acceptance of an EIS and approval of a project was vested in the governor or in a body to which he might delegate that authority. The SEPA covered projects only involving the expenditure of state funds or involving state land and thus usually were not subject to NEPA analysis. Because most projects requiring environmental analysis did involve federal funds in some way, virtually all the EISs with which we dealt were from federal agencies. However, there were a few prepared by state agencies that we did review and the first of these proved to be an important test for the fledgling concept of environmental impact analysis where state funds were involved.

Shortly after Finch began work in the late spring of 1972, the first SEPA EIS landed in our "inbox" for review. The project involved widening of Oberlin Road in Raleigh, oddly enough a road that I used regularly if I drove home. The part of Oberlin Road singled out for widening was a narrow stretch that ran through the black Oberlin settlement north of Cameron Village and between wider sections to the south and north. The widening would have required the demolition of several small homes owned by blacks and possibly a black church. The project was being promoted by the city of Raleigh and was opposed by several persons who would be directly and negatively impacted as well as by several citizen's groups. Finch and I had discussed the project briefly before all comments were in and we had not come to an agreement as to how the Department should respond. Driving home one night, I took the section of Oberlin Road in question. While stopped there for a turning car, a noticed an elderly black lady sitting in a rocking chair on the porch of a house that certainly would have been demolished if the road were widened. The thought flashed through my mind that I might be about to be part of the approval of a project that would evict that lady from a home that she might well have lived in her entire life, to enable me to get home thirty seconds earlier. The inequity of this stuck with me and when Finch and I discussed NER's response we agreed that we should find the EIS deficient (which it clearly was) and oppose the project. The state had no established mechanism to adjudicate such a dispute between a state agency and a local government and the matter was referred to the Council on State Goals and Policy at its July 1972 meeting. The Council discussed the matter and heard comments from Finch. No final decision was made and Raleigh decided not to pursue the matter. To this day (2017), the disputed section of Oberlin Road has never been widened!

Perhaps the best example of the inadequacies of early EISs was the one prepared in late 1971 by the U. S. Army Corps of Engineers for the proposed Falls Lake project that, at that time, would cost tens of millions of dollars and was viewed by the city of Raleigh as essential to its future water supply and thus to its growth. It was, as I recall, about fifteen pages long, described in general terms the project, enumerated its benefits, and concluded it would have no negative impacts. Because this was one of the first that Finch dealt with, he was unsure how to proceed. In discussion with me, he pointed out that it was a totally inadequate piece of work, and knowing its political significance, asked for guidance. Together we agreed that we had no choice but to send a response to the Clearinghouse that spelled out NER's objections to the document, that it failed to provide any real analysis of the project's impacts, and that it was completely unacceptable. These comments, together with those of several citizen organizations and a court case brought by one of them in which the judge ordered a hearing on the adequacy of the EIS sent the Corps back to the drawing board. Eventually, it produced a larger (and better), 2000-page document that at least laid out the positive and negative features of the project thus bringing into clear focus the merits and demerits of the proposed dam and lake.

My first direct contact with NEPA requirements came on my second day on the job when I went to Washington, DC, to determine, among other things, whether the Raleigh-Durham Airport Authority was required to prepare an environmental EIS for its proposed expansion (see Chapter 3 also). The option on the table in May 1971 proposed a new runway, to the southeast of the existing main runway, which would be significantly closer to William B. Umstead State Park and would have caused planes landing from, or taking off toward, the north to directly overfly the picnic and group camp areas of the park. Although no physical encroachment on the park was proposed, conservation and citizen's groups strongly opposed this alternative arguing that the noise created by overflights would essentially ruin the recreational value of the park. Some even argued that the overflights constituted a taking of the affected section of the park and would, under the terms of the deed by which the land was transferred to the state, cause it to revert to the federal government.

Director of C&D Sowers was in a quandary as to what to do. On the one hand, he recognized the importance of the airport to the economy of the Triangle region, but on the other he recognized his obligation to protect the integrity of the parks program in his department. Consequently, his first instruction to me when I accepted the job at C&D was to recommend how the department should deal with the dilemma of airport expansion. I left with a clear understanding of the problem but no clear plan as to how to resolve it. After a visit to the Department of Interior, I learned that it was deeply concerned about the impact of the proposed changes on the park, but got no clear answer from it as to whether the changes would be sufficient to trigger the reverter clause in the deed of gift. A visit to the Council on Environmental Quality was more productive and did lead to a clear understanding that the proposed expansion (because the Airport received federal funds) would trigger the environmental impact requirements of NEPA. Of course, who would write the statement remained unresolved. I reported my findings to Sowers and the department shortly announced that before it would make any decision concerning the Airport Authority's plan for expansion it would have to see an analysis of the environmental impact of the plan. This had the effect of sending the issue of airport expansion back to the planning table and it did not re-appear as an issue until a draft of a new plan, proposing a second runway oriented perpendicular to the existing runway, appeared. Ironically, NER found the new proposal met its concerns about impacts on Umstead park. On the other hand, this second proposed runway would lead to take-offs and landings directly over Research Triangle Park and RTP objected strenuously to the new plan. Since NER's Division of Industrial, Tourist, and Community Resources objected to this proposal on grounds of its negative impact on the Research Triangle Park, the department found itself back in the position of rejecting a plan for airport expansion but because of a negative impact on a different one of its responsibilities. The matter was not entirely resolved until the early 1980s when a second runway northwest of the original runway was proposed and built without any significant objection. The Airport Authority had rejected this proposal when NER made it during discussions concerning the original alignment but, when it became clear their other alternatives were not acceptable the northern second runway suddenly became feasible.

Undoubtedly the case where an EIS played the greatest role in determining the outcome of a controversial project was the lengthy debate over the proposal to create a pumped-storage hydroelectric project on the New River.[16] In this case, the EIS prepared by the Federal Power Commission, with assistance from Appalachian Power, served as the focal point for debate over approval of the project. Opponents of the project, other federal agencies and NER found the EIS to be totally unacceptable because of its failure to deal substantively with the most controversial aspects of the project. The EIS strongly resembled one drafted earlier by the power companies and, even as the document was re-written in response to criticisms from opponents and the courts, it never became more than an affirmation of the importance of building the Blue Ridge Project. In fact, acceptance of the EIS by the Federal Power Commission was a crucial step leading up to its, and the courts, approval of the project. In the last analysis, the New River was saved from being dammed not by disapproval of an EIS but by raw politics in the Congress. The EIS, however, served as the vehicle to prolong and sharpen debate over the wisdom of the project long enough for the political process to develop a final decision that did "save" the river and thus prevent a very undesirable (from North Carolina's perspective) project from being built.

---

[16]   For a more detailed description of this situation see Chapter 13 discussing the entire New River controversy.

Chapter 6

The Election Of 1972

In many ways, the election of 1972 was a watershed event in North Carolina. In electing a Republican to the governor's office, it marked the first election since the turn of the century in which the Republican party was sufficiently competitive to win a major statewide office. Since 1900 the Democratic party controlled both the governorship and both houses of the General Assembly. The last Republican governor, Daniel Russell, had been defeated in 1900 in a bitter, unabashedly racist, campaign by Democrat Charles Brantley Aycock. Since then the Democratic party had controlled North Carolina politics. The most recent governors, Luther Hodges, Terry Sanford, Dan Moore, and the incumbent Bob Scott, all shared the same basic philosophy, which political observer Rob Christensen has described as moderate-conservative, business-progressive.

The Democratic candidate in 1972, Hargrove (Skipper) Bowles, certainly had that same philosophy. He had survived a contentious primary with Lieutenant Governor Pat Taylor that left the Democratic party divided. The Republican candidate, Jim Holshouser, who was in his late thirties at the time, had been a member of the legislature since 1962, was active in Republican party politics, and became state party chairman in 1966. He had upset Jim Gardner in the Republican primary. Holshouser was a populist and not at all like some other Republicans active in state politics in that he rejected racism as a part of his campaign and actively appealed to black voters. It is also important to note that the 1972 election also featured a race for U.S. Senate between Democrat U.S. Representative Nick Galifianakis and first-time conservative Republican candidate Jesse Helms. The presidential race that year pitted incumbent Richard Nixon, perhaps benefiting from the Watergate break-in, against George McGovern.

Although Bowles and Galifianakis initially had large leads both leads dwindled as the election neared and Helms and Holshouser strongly identified themselves with Nixon. By election day the state races were clearly trending Republican with Helms and Holshouser riding the coat-tails of Nixon who won North Carolina with more than seventy percent of the vote. Helms also won with fifty-four percent of the vote, beginning his long tenure as the most conservative member of the Senate. By winning just fifty-one percent of the vote, Holshouser upset Bowles to become the first Republican governor since 1900.

It is hard to understate the significance of Holshouser's victory to the future of state government reorganization generally, to NER, and to me. In my opinion, it is quite likely that had Bowles become governor, the structure of NER put in place in the fall of 1971 would have been drastically altered and, likely, I would have returned to the University. Holshouser appointed a very effective secretary of NER and was supportive of virtually all the controversial and far-reaching initiatives of the department. Many programs and initiatives that the department undertook between early 1973 and late 1976, such as the Coastal Area Management Act, major expansion of the state park system, and preservation of the New River, would have occurred differently and, in fact, might not have occurred at all if Bowles had been elected. Much of the subsequent discussion in this retrospective is devoted to these initiatives and to Jim Holshouser's support of them. I like to think that North Carolina is a better state because of NER's work during these years.

*****

To say that Holshouser's election was an upset is to put it very, very mildly. Despite the divisions in the Democratic party, most North Carolinians had expected Bowles to win and he was endorsed by most of the state's media. The confidence of Bowles campaign was illustrated by something that happened to me in early October 1972. I had been out of the office all morning and when I came back I found a woman in my office inspecting it and measuring windows and bookcases. I backed out and whispered to Martha Liles "who is that?" Martha replied "That's Gladys Gooch and she will take over your office when Bowles is elected. She is to be the new Secretary's assistant." Martha knew because the woman had told her! My reaction was "well, ok, we'll worry about that in November." I always had my tenure at the university to fall back on. My chance meeting with Bowles during a talk in Asheville mentioned earlier suggested to me that if Bowles were elected it was quite likely that much of the reorganization of the department that Barfield and I developed would be undone. Bowles' apparent negativity toward reorganization probably stemmed from close ties that many of the members of the old

Board of Conservation and Development, and perhaps even members of the department itself, had with Bowles. After all, Bowles had been Director of C&D under Governor Terry Sanford in the early 1960s, at least three members of the current board had also been appointed to it by Sanford, and many current C&D staff members had been with the department when Bowles was director. It is quite probable that there were behind-the-scenes conversations with Bowles about the merits and demerits of the changes that had occurred in C&D because of reorganization, although I was neither privy to, nor aware of, them.

Wednesday, November 8, 1972, the day after the election, was like no other day I ever experienced in state government. The building was as quiet as a tomb and one could almost smell panic in the air. Holshouser and the Republicans were a completely unknown quantity and no one had the faintest idea what Holshouser's election meant, either for state government in general or for their own job specifically. This degree of the unknown incrementally exceeded that which normally occurs following an election and had never been experienced by anyone in the department. About 10 AM my phone started ringing and it rang regularly throughout the rest of the day with virtually the same messages. The caller would ask "who is this Hillheimer, Holsburger, Hamhocker?" Do you know him? Who will be the new secretary? What does this mean for me and my appointment to "X" board or commission? Can you talk to the new governor on my behalf?" The presumption that I would know more than they knew was amusing, and the suggestion that I could talk to the new governor on their behalf even more amusing, but the uncertainty that the calls reflected was not at all amusing. My first answer always was "his name is Holshouser and it probably would be well to remember it and to learn how to spell it and how to pronounce it." To all the other questions all I could say was "I don't know" and then give as sympathetic an ear as possible to the caller. This continued for several days until the shock wore off, reality set in, and people began to cultivate their own contacts and relationships, such as they might be, with the new administration.

A word about Governor-elect Holshouser is in order. As indicated earlier, he was quite young, from Watauga county in the Mountains, and and had been active for ten years in Republican Party politics. He had graduated from Davidson College and UNC Law School and practiced law in Boone. After having served under him for nearly four years, I came to regard Holshouser as one of the most decent, honest people I ever knew in politics. He was a populist and tended to place considerable weight on the effect of governmental actions on common people. One episode he recounted to me late in his tenure illustrates this. When we were discussing why he had come to oppose a dam on the New River when favoring it was the most traditional, and certainly the easiest, route to follow, he recounted a conversation he had with an elderly gentleman in Ashe county. The gentleman pointed out that if the dam was built "the land on which he and his family lived would be forty feet under water if he (Holshouser) became governor would he help him." Holshouser instinctively felt the injustice of what was about to happen to the man and he said that, then and there, he decided to oppose the dam. In many ways, I felt Jim Holshouser was too decent a man to be governor. When he went out of office, in disfavor with the rank and file of the North Carolina Republican party for his support of Gerald Ford rather than Ronald Reagan in the 1976 primaries, I felt he had been badly treated by the party he had served for four years.

The rest of November, all of December, and January 1973 before Holshouser's inauguration were, as I recall, characterized by an eerie sort of quiet. Our contacts (at least mine) with the Holshouser transition team were minimal, Charlie Bradshaw remained as secretary, and business continued as usual. Obviously, no major policy decisions were made and hiring was limited to positions not subject to potential turnover. As November turned into December and December to January there still was no announcement as to whom the new Secretary of Natural and Economic Resources would be, even though all other cabinet administrative positions had been filled.

The announcement finally came on January 5, 1973, the day of Holshouser's inauguration, that James E. Harrington, of Banner Elk had been appointed the new secretary. Harrington was forty-five, born in New Hampshire, and had a bachelor's degree in chemistry from Virginia Military Institute. His employment background was in resort development and management in Pinehurst and most recently at Banner Elk in the mountains. He was an utterly unknown quantity both inside and outside the department. Once his appointment was announced, I again received a volley of telephone calls asking what I knew about the new Secretary and how "could the caller meet him." Since I knew as little as anyone else, my answers were evasive at best. I clearly remember that one caller, who apparently knew Harrington, referred to him as a "lightweight." The future proved that no characterization could be farther from the truth.

Harrington proved to be knowledgeable in areas relating to many of the department's programs and quick to learn in the others. His native intelligence and willingness to work extremely hard for long hours proved to make him a formidable power in the secretary's office. His first several months in office proved rocky as he did not announce immediately his decision as to who would stay and who would go from the department's management structure. Because there had been extensive firings of upper level management in most other departments, it was assumed that the same would occur in NER. I had an opportunity to determine my situation very early in Harrington's tenure. He called me into his office and told me that the governor was looking to place Ernie Carl, an UNC-CH faculty member, who had helped him compete strongly against Bowles in Orange county. I knew Ernie and I knew that his background was a good bit like mine. Harrington asked me if I knew any place in state government where Carl would fit and I responded that of all the positions I knew he was probably best qualified to replace me. Harrington was silent a moment and then said, "that wasn't what I had in mind."[17] With that simple statement, it was decided that I would continue as Assistant Secretary for Resource Management. Apparently, Harrington came to a similar conclusion concerning Barfield as he stayed on, albeit in the position of Assistant, rather than Deputy, Secretary The position of Deputy Secretary was filled on January 10, 1973 with the appointment of George W. Little. Little's duties were unabashedly political rather than programmatic (we called him the "commissar") and he proved immensely helpful in serving as a buffer between the technical programs of the department and its political constituencies.

There was no formal public announcement that Barfield and I would stay on as two of the top administrators in the department. The uncertainty of the status of the other office directors in the department, and of some of their direct assistants, quickly became a major concern that had a negative effect on the morale of the department. In fact, I was asked

---

[17]   Carl did go on to become an administrator in NER's successor department under the next Republican governor, Jim Martin.

by Ralph Winkworth, Director of the Office of Forest Resources, to attend a February, 1973, meeting of his managerial staff at Southern Pines. At the meeting, I was asked into Winkworth's motel room and confronted by many of his staff with the direct question "where do we stand with the new administration?" and with the statement "we have heard that you and all of us are going to be fired." Although I knew the answer—that they were to continue in office if they so desired—I could not say so as it was clearly a decision that the secretary had made and that should be announced by him, and certainly not by me in a motel room. I parried the question by telling them I did not feel their fears were well-grounded and by saying that I had been informed I would continue. I also promised to relay the question of the status of the forestry administrative staff to the secretary and try to get a quick answer. On returning to Raleigh I told Barfield about my conversation and found that he had encountered similar fears. We agreed that we must tell Harrington and urge him to make a public announcement of his plans. When Barfield and I reported the deep concerns about their status among the "troops" Harrington was puzzled and allowed as how they ought to realize that if they were to have been let go it would have been done very early in his tenure. Nonetheless we urged him to make an announcement quickly to the department staff which he did. His announcement clarifying the status of the department's administration allowed everyone to carry on their duties free from the threat, imagined or real, of a political purge.

One reason the department's administrative staff remained in office was their reputation as capable professionals who did not concern themselves greatly with the political dimensions of their decisions. Another, and perhaps equally important reason was that the Republican party in North Carolina had few if any loyal members who were technically oriented toward the work of the department. In simple terms, there were few if any Republicans to whom Holshouser could turn even if he wanted to make administrative changes in NER. Much to his credit, he apparently never considered making changes in NER simply to fill positions with Republicans. Of course, I was never privy to any conversations between Holshouser and Harrington on the subject. Nonetheless, knowing Harrington as I now do, my guess is that he would have resisted mightily appointment of "political hacks" to managerial positions in his department. Over the first six months of 1973 there were several appointments of new staff members, mostly in the front office and as a legislative liaison, some

57

of whom had strong Republican ties. All of them were fully qualified for their jobs.

By early spring, Holshouser and Harrington had their respective "teams" in place and NER was working in a totally different environment than previously existed. Harrington deeply involved himself in the details of each of the department's programs and his degree of understanding of the broad issues and details involved in programs and decisions was impressive. It took all of us a while to get used to the fact that we had a knowledgeable secretary and that we could make our cases on issues in terms of the facts as best we understood them, leaving dealing with the political dimension to Harrington and Little. Harrington relied on me primarily to deal with issues that spanned the interests of several programs, which involved making a change in procedures or previously-espoused departmental positions, or issues which were of such high visibility that they needed to be handled at the level of the secretary's office. Although Harrington could be a tough man to work for, he was fair, he listened, and his decisions were sound. All in all, from my perspective at least, it was a productive working environment. Harrington served until early 1976 when he resigned to pursue a run at the governorship. He was replaced on March 1, 1976, by George Little who continued in office until the end of the Holshouser administration. Sadly, Harrington's pursuit of the governorship went nowhere; most of us felt that it was ill-conceived from the very beginning as he was not suited by temperament or disposition to the requirements of either running for, or being, governor.

I came to know Harrington on a personal basis. As fate would have it, when he brought his family to Raleigh they moved into a house right around the corner from us. On weekends, he often would be "in charge" of his youngest son and would stop off at the house on his way to the grocery store. His son loved playing with some toy cars that my boys had outgrown so Jim would frequently end up spending several hours at our house. While there, he and I would often discuss departmental business and issues in a very informal way—mostly just sharing ideas on how to deal with the problems facing NER—sometimes while I continued to work in my yard with Jim sitting on his favorite tree stump.

It is very difficult to generalize about the periods of political transition that occur every four (or eight) years in government after elections, particularly those during which there is a change in the governing party. There was literally no precedent in North Carolina for the change that took place between November 1972 and January 1973. I had little contact with Holshouser's transition team, although I suspect Vic Barfield did. The transition of late 1972 from a Democrat to a Republican administration was even more unique in several ways. First, as mentioned previously, there was relatively little infrastructure to the Republican Party in North Carolina. Consequently, the pool from which the Holshouser transition team could find persons to fill upper-level administrative positions was small. In some departments, notably those where technical expertise was not as important as it was in NER, extensive firings occurred down into departmental infrastructure, particularly where individuals had been active in the Bowles campaign or were well-known as active Democrats. The Department of Administration, where most administrators were traditionally close to the governor, was one such department. In NER, however, there were virtually no firings, again largely due to the technical nature of the department's work. Another reason wholesale firings throughout state government were limited in number was Holshouser's nature. Although he was a Republican, he was not an extreme right-wing Republican of the kind that would take over the party in 1976. As Rob Christensen pointed out in his "Paradox of Tar Heel Politics" Holshouser was philosophically much like the moderate-conservative Democrats that had preceded him. Holshouser always seemed to me to be more interested in governing effectively with the interests of all North Carolinians at heart than he was in establishing a Republican dynasty in state government. A third reason undoubtedly had to do with the fact that the legislature was still dominated by Democrats and, as a past legislator himself, Holshouser realized that to be effective he needed to cultivate support in the legislature. Wholesale firing of established state government employees who were known and respected by legislators and were known Democrats probably would have been a quick way to the legislature's doghouse!

The impact of Holshouser's election on the implementation of state government reorganization is arguable. On the one hand, I have no idea what Bowles' plans were for implementing reorganization. As I have stated, and implied, it is my belief that Bowles was not a whole-hearted supporter of the reorganization act of 1971. Given that, it is likely that the structure of many departments, particularly the remnants of the old Department of

Conservation and Development that he had once directed, would have been treated much differently had he been elected. This is almost certainly true of NER although I cannot say how it would have been different. One thing is certain—NER's offices would have been eliminated. Bowles promised to do this during his campaign. However, Secretary Harrington kept the basic structure of NER as it was and made no major changes when he took office. Details were changed and personnel were shifted, but the basic structure of a department designed to house related functions in the same administrative unit regardless of the Department from which they had come was maintained as was the concept of providing a degree of coordination among programs at the level of the Secretary's office. However, in preparing legislation for the second phase of reorganization, Harrington did away with the offices, replacing them with a structure in which the divisions reported directly to the secretary. This change reflected NER's administrative experience with the offices—some worked well and others not at all—so the change was necessary. In sum, the NER that emerged from Holshouser's administration was basically the same NER envisioned by the reorganization statute with its internal structure altered somewhat from that which existed at the close of the Scott administration.

A tipoff to how things might have been different had Bowles been elected is the move by Jim Hunt, almost immediately upon his inauguration in 1977, of the economic development and tourism programs from NER to the Department of Commerce. Hunt undertook this move to provide greater emphasis on industrial development. As I have pointed out, the staff of the industrial development program had never made any secret of the fact that they did not occupy the pre-eminent position in NER that they had in C&D and that they felt this limited their effectiveness. It seems to me reasonable that if Bowles had been elected, there is a good chance this shift would have been made in 1973, thus shifting reorganization of the state's environmental agencies to the "two department" model. The move of economic development marked the beginning of a slow shift of NER and its successor departments from an integrated resource management and development agency to what is now, in 2017, an agency that leans heavily toward regulation. Consequently, it has few political friends and increasingly is a target of "anti-regulation" interests (see Chapter 17 for a longer discussion of this change).

As for Holshouser himself, he finished his term in office literally banned from the Republican party. Its state convention in 1976 was dominated by the radical right wing of the party led by Jesse Helms. Holshouser and the state's two Republican Congressmen, Jim Martin and Jim Broyhill, were barred from serving as delegates to the national convention because of their support of Gerald Ford, rather than Ronald Reagan, for the presidential nomination. Holshouser, although generally well-respected throughout the state, never returned to politics. He moved to Southern Pines and became active in banking and other financial ventures. His own health was poor, and he lived with kidney difficulty for many years. His wife, Pat, who had taken courses in nursing after stepping down as first lady so she could assist with his medical treatments, died in December 2006 after a three-year battle with lung cancer. Holshouser himself remained active and, among other things, served as a long-time member of The University of North Carolina Board of Governors, later as a member Emeritus. Throughout his years after serving as governor he was an outspoken supporter of the university system. The last time I saw him was September 2001 on the banks of the New River when he and I shared time on the program marking the twenty-fifth anniversary of the designation of the New as a National Scenic River. He died in June 2013 after many years of declining health. Words spoken at his funeral were a testimony to his service to North Carolina and of his dedication and decency as a public servant.

Chapter 7

Reorganization of State Government—1973-74 Phase

The Executive Organization Act of 1971, as pointed out earlier, established a two-stage process for reorganization; a first phase to be completed in 1971 and a second phase to be completed by 1973. In effect, what this legislation did was establish a two-year trial period during which the departments established in the legislation assimilated the various agencies transferred to them and allowed testing of an organizational structure. The fact that not all agencies were transferred with the same status (type I transfers lost all their administrative and statutory powers to the new department whereas type II transfers lost only their administrative powers and retained their statutory authority) made the two trial years between 1971 and 1973 awkward and led to tensions and disputes over how the intent of reorganization should be carried out. This was certainly true in NER. The fiasco involving the organizational chart (Chapter 4) that omitted several bodies that still retained statutory authority, difficulties with organization of the field offices, the problems with the C&D directorship, and difficulties with implementation of the office concept, all previously discussed, illustrate some of these problems.

*****

In many ways, the second phase of reorganization was anticlimactic and without the excitement and political furor of the first phase. This was due largely to the change in administrations from Democrat to Republican in early 1973. Because the Democrats were no longer in control of state government, most of the persons who were politically able to object to, and able to influence, further reorganization no longer were politically able to do so. In fact, most of the work of refining reorganization went on within state government itself or in consultation with key members of the legislature. In NER, the refinement of the department's structure was heavily influenced by the new secretary, Jim Harrington, and Vic Barfield.

Fortunately, a written evaluation of the initial reorganization of NER in 1971-72 was done by Charlotte Gantt, a student in the Department of Political Science at UNC-Chapel Hill, who worked as a management trainee in NER from September, 1971, to October, 1972. Her analysis and

62

conclusions provide much of the basis for the following comments on how reorganization was implemented, the deficiencies of that implementation, and the background for the structural and administrative changes that were recommended to, and approved by, the 1974 legislature. Since Vic Barfield and I were interviewed extensively by Gantt, in many ways her comments reflect our views. Her conclusions, of course, were her own.

Integration of the various administrative duties of the programs reorganized into NER took place relatively smoothly, with the major exception of organization of the field offices the department inherited, primarily from C&D and Water and Air Resources. Common sense, an intention to save operational funds, and a desire to integrate fully the new departmental functions, led Barfield to consolidate the field offices into central locations. Most such consolidations went smoothly, but the C&D Board took major exception to movement of the Sylva office to Asheville where Water and Air Resources had its office. The issue was simple— whether the reorganization legislation gave the Secretary of NER the authority to make such a move. Barfield clearly felt it did and the C&D Board felt the decision was a policy, rather than management, decision. Ultimately, Barfield's view prevailed and the office consolidation was made. However, that issue plus the dispute over whether there should be a director of C&D, served as a red-letter reminder that, because reorganization had a huge political dimension to it, we should go slowly with any changes that were not clearly and unarguably managerial in nature.

The office structure that Barfield and I recommended[18], and that was put into operation by Governor Scott, was the heart and soul of our effort to consolidate similar operational functions and bring about an integration of all the functions assigned to NER. It was our hope that the offices would serve to limit the number of administrators who reported directly to the Secretary, cause employees to identify with NER (rather than their previous home), and to introduce wider participation in decision making. To recapitulate, the concept called for the establishment of seven

---

[18] Barfield and I did try to include input into this process by establishing a series of citizen advisory committees. However, our hearts were not really in that process and the basic decisions concerning office structure and composition were made by Barfield and me.

offices, each composed of related functions and built around the framework of C&D's divisions. Three offices consisted of single units, Forest Resources and Community Resources[19] from C&D and the previously independent Water and Air Resources program. Two contained closely related programs, Fisheries and Wildlife Resources containing the marine fisheries program from C&D and the quasi-independent Wildlife Resources Commission, and Earth Resources consisting of the mineral-oriented divisions from C&D and the previously-independent State Soil and Water Conservation Committee. Two, Recreation Resources and Industrial, Tourist, and Community Resources were genuine hybrids each containing agencies with very different origins and missions.

As might be supposed, each of these offices posed a different set of management issues. Charlotte Gantt identified three major problems. Since she did so after several interviews with Barfield and me, in which we identified problems with operation of the offices, it is clear we accepted these problems as real. Most important of all was the ambiguity concerning the role of the office director. Barfield and I envisioned the office directors as the coordinators of the programs under their control, as the initiators of policy recommendations concerning those programs, and as the principal contact with the department administration concerning program activities. In some cases, directors could do this effectively; in other cases, they floundered and never could "get a handle" on the programs they administered. In retrospect, a major reason for this problem was that Barfield and I never really made a strong effort to explain to the office directors what our expectations were and how we expected them to be carried out.

Another major factor contributing to the weaknesses of the offices was the hodge-podge nature of several, particularly Recreation Resources and Industrial, Tourist, and Community Resources. In Recreation Resources, although all the units in the office had a common mission in recreation, the problems arose because of direct differences in

---

[19] The Office of Community Resources was short-lived as its director was shifted by Governor Scott to a new assignment. The units of the Office were shifted to the Office of Industrial and Tourist Resources creating an Office of Industry, Tourism, and Community Resources.

philosophy between the office director and the state park superintendent. This difference was never reconciled and continued until the office was split in 1974. In the case of Industrial, Tourist, and Community Resources the problem was in part the very wide differences in the objectives of the programs under the director's control and in part to the director's personal commitment to industrial development. In his defense, however, he did make a proposal to unite his programs with a common concentration on growth management, even going so far as to suggest his office be renamed the Office of Growth Management. However, departmental administration never developed a commitment to the idea and it died.

As pointed out earlier, the weakness of the office structure was apparent at least to the Democrat nominee for governor, Skipper Bowles, who had publicly stated during his campaign that when he was elected he would do away with the offices as an unnecessary level of middle management. Although the offices were a new level of management, they did not (except in the case of Fisheries and Wildlife) involve any new personnel. Each office director previously had been an upper-level administrator in one of the units under his director; he continued in those duties as well as serving as an office director. I always felt that Bowles' criticism was politically expedient and reflected more his dissatisfaction with reorganization generally and his dislike for the radical changes made in the department he once managed. However, realizing that problems with the offices had become painfully obvious, both externally and internally, it was necessary to take another approach when recommendations for the second phase of reorganization were being prepared for the legislature.[20]

Despite its short-comings, the office concept did have some positive features. First, it dealt with the sheer size of the department that came into being on September 1, 1971. Given the dispositions of the two men who served as secretaries between September 1971 and January 1973, managing the department with all the agencies reporting directly to the secretary would have been chaotic. The office concept limited the number of units reporting directly to the secretary and served as a sort of "holding tank"

---

[20]   Choice of the term "office" was unfortunate as it clearly carried a bureaucratic connotation. It was unpopular on that basis alone. Looking back, though, I'm not sure what other term we could have used.

that combined programs of roughly similar interest while allowing their component units to sort out their functions relative to the other programs placed in NER. It also allowed some programs to become used to the idea of reorganization—that they were no longer independent—and to learn to work effectively with a new upper level of management

When the time came to put forth proposals for the second phase of reorganization, the political supervision of the department had changed with the election of Jim Holshouser as governor and appointment of Jim Harrington as secretary. In developing recommendations for the 1973 legislature Harrington generally subscribed to the philosophy of clearly delegating greater policy-making powers to the secretary than were delegated by the first phase of reorganization. Furthermore, he was personally comfortable with having a larger number of agencies reporting directly to him. At the same time, he recognized that there were certain elements of traditional North Carolina government, the citizen boards and/or commissions with policy-making authority in clearly defined areas (e.g., water and air pollution, wildlife resources, marine resources) delegated by the legislature, that needed to be maintained. However, this bow to tradition did not extend to a board with authority for policy across the entire department; this was deemed not only unworkable but also undesirable. Although one was included in the final statutes creating NER, it consisted primarily of representatives of state agencies rather than private citizens. It never played a role in the running of the department and in 1989 was removed from the statutes.

Thus, the recommendations that Barfield, with some help from me, developed for Harrington contained only limited extensions of the secretary's power in addition to recommending the continuation of certain powerful boards and commissions such as the Board of Water and Air Resources (renamed the Environmental Management Commission), Marine Resources Commission, and the Wildlife Resources Commission. The recommendations included elimination of the offices and establishment of twelve divisions, each reporting to the secretary. Because of the inherent weaknesses in the Office of Recreation Resources and the Office of Industrial, Tourist, and Community Resources, this recommendation simply put into statute the way departmental operations had evolved since Harrington became secretary. In addition, the recommendations included creation of a position as Assistant Secretary for Economic Affairs to coordinate the department's economic development policy and to work with me to direct a "task force" approach to problems facing the department. These recommendations were submitted to the legislature in the spring of 1973, were considered in committee, but never acted on. They were, however, approved in 1974 essentially as submitted, except that the position of Assistant Secretary for Economic Affairs either was not submitted or not approved by the legislature. Departmental operations during the remaining time I worked in state government were accomplished within this new organizational framework.

There is no such thing as permanence when it comes to the structure of governmental agencies. Each new administration feels a need to tinker with and re-structure agencies to make them more "efficient" or more "responsive" generally without ever bothering to define those terms. Despite Jim Harrington's boast (to my wife) that "we" had structured NER so that it could not be taken apart, as early as the election of 1976 the structure of NER became an issue. With Jim Hunt's election, he carried out his professed intention to move economic development programs into the Department of Commerce. Literally every administration since has made changes in NER, including its name, some small and some great (see Chapter 17).

Chapter 8

Growing the State Park System

As pointed out in the discussion of the Department of Conservation and Development, North Carolina had a state park system since 1916 when Mt. Mitchell was acquired. However, from then until 1948 the system was managed by the North Carolina Forest Service, grew slowly, and was grossly under-funded. Even after being established as a free-standing division in the Department of Conservation and Development in 1948, it still grew slowly and saw no significant increases in funding. It was also managed under a highly conservative philosophy and was never able to attract sufficient funds or political support to grow commensurate with the needs of a rapidly-growing state. By the late 1960s most of the existing state parks were either the result of gifts of land or transfers of state or federal land; eighty-four percent of the land in the system had been acquired in this way. I calculated that, up to the mid-1960s, North Carolina had spent about ten cents per (then) citizen for the acquisition of park land! The legislature seemed to subscribe to the philosophy of Joe Cannon, Speaker of the U.S. House in the early nineteen-hundreds, "not one thin dime for beauty." In fairness to the legislature, this parsimony was in large part because funds had never been requested.

Nonetheless, the small park system that North Carolina had developed by the 1960s consisted of high quality, well managed areas most of which focused on preservation of areas of considerable scenic beauty or of high value for public recreation use. They included such sites as Mt. Mitchell, Fort Macon, Morrow Mountain, Hanging Rock, and William. B. Umstead. In 1963 the System incorporated natural areas with the addition by gift of Weymouth Woods. In 1929 all the natural lakes in the Coastal Plain were designated as State Lakes and assigned to the parks program for management. However, as only the water in the lakes was included in state ownership and adjacent land was owned by the state only at Jones and Pettigrew Lakes, the "State Lakes" were a substantial management problem (see Chapter 3). The philosophy under which the park system was managed was conservative with few facilities, except at Ft. Macon and Cliffs of the Neuse, designated for intensive public recreation. The state had provided little money for development at existing parks, due in no small part to the fact that management of the park system had not aggressively requested it, and that many of the public use structures that did exist had been constructed at no cost to the state by the Civilian Conservation Corps or the Work Projects Administration during the 1930s. Between 1968 and 1971 several important areas were added to the system, including Pilot Mountain, Stone Mountain, Raven Rock, and Carolina Beach State Parks and Bushy Lake Recreation Area. Despite these additions, there remained a substantial list of candidate areas for designation as parks and considerable public pressure for more development at the existing parks.

*****

By the time I joined state government in 1971 a movement had sprung up, in which I had played a role, to develop political support for growth of the state park system. The strategy envisioned was to obtain new land areas first and develop the system's existing areas and its new acquisitions as the second step. At least eight potential park areas had been identified, inventoried and studied for their potential by park system personnel and designated as appropriate areas for new parks. A booklet entitled "Now or Never" describing and explaining the potential value as additions to the state park system of these and other areas was prepared in time for the 1972 legislature. This booklet served as the basis for a budget request for $11.5 million for land acquisition and $2.4 million for facility improvement. The request was approved by the 1973 Legislature and supplemented by an additional $5.5 million for land acquisition and $3 million for capital improvements in 1975. Although obviously not planned that way, implementation of what was clearly a major land acquisition effort fell to the new Republican administration.

With some money finally in hand, NER undertook the job of acquiring land at many of the areas that had been identified as potential parks. Immediately a serious problem arose as to who would do the work of acquiring the land. The problem arose from the system that the state used to acquire and manage land. Land purchases, such as those for state parks, by law were done by the Division of Property Control in the Department of Administration. Acquired land was held by the Department of Administration which then assigned it to a specific agency for use and management. Thus, once park land was acquired by Property Control, it was assigned to NER for management as a state park. Property Control in the early 1970s had a small number of employees and simply was not staffed to undertake a major program of land acquisition. In their wisdom, they decided to use land acquisition staff from the Highway Commission in the Department of Transportation (DOT).

It had been agreed that acquisition would begin at Medoc Mountain. It was one of the more complex proposed purchases because, outside of the 2,300 acres on which the Halifax Development Commission had obtained one-year timber rights from Union Camp Company, many separate tracts were involved and none were potential donations. No sooner had the land acquisition people from DOT begun their work than serious rumbles of trouble began to come in from the area. The modus operandi the highway people used was the same that they used for acquiring land for highways— make an offer of fair market value based on appraisal (favoring the state and usually low) followed by condemnation if the offer of appraised value was not accepted. In other words, "take our offer or we'll see you in court." Needless to say this cold approach to land owners stirred up a hornet's nest of angry people and did little, if anything, to create good will toward creation of Medoc Mountain State Park.

A digression to discuss the state land acquisition process as it existed in the early 1970s. Realizing that our whole park acquisition effort was going nowhere unless we could work out a better method of land acquisition, Secretary Harrington and I discussed our problem and agreed we had to take it up with the Department of Administration. Fortunately, the Secretary of Administration, Bill Bondurant, was attuned to our desire to expand the state park system (leadership in property control was not!) and he persuaded property control to be more cooperative. The state's land acquisition system was in fact an impediment to acquisition of land for any purpose, let alone for parks. The state, of course, could not purchase land for less than appraised value and all purchases had to be approved by the Council of State. Furthermore, the notion of negotiating for land seemed to be a foreign concept to property control and negotiation was at the core of virtually all our proposed park land acquisitions.

Consequently, we had to turn elsewhere for help. The Nature Conservancy seemed our best, and only, hope. I had familiarity with the Nature Conservancy, a national organization with a mission to acquire land for preservation purposes, and had worked with several of their key people on land preservation issues in North Carolina. In the early 1970s the Conservancy was the only organization of its kind, differing from other conservation organizations in that land acquisition for preservation was its only purpose. Furthermore, it avowedly used land acquisition strategies common to the land development community. Harrington and I realized that we would have to use some practices that, although entirely legal, had not been used by the state before in land acquisition. One of the most important of these was the use of "matching funds" available from the Federal Land and Water Conservation Fund (LWCF). The fund would not only match dollar for dollar state monies spent for recreation land acquisition but would also match the appraised value of a tract, even if the state paid less for it or received it as a donation. Land and Water Conservation Funds, although subject to fluctuation at the federal level, effectively gave us a mechanism for doubling our available acquisition money. It would be fair to say that the assistance of the Nature Conservancy and the availability of land and water conservation money, together with state funds were the backbone of what turned out to be a very rapid, aggressive, and successful growth of the state park system between 1973 and 1976. How this occurred is best illustrated by the events surrounding the addition of specific new parks added between 1973 and 1976: Crowder's Mountain (1973), Eno River (1973), Medoc Mountain (1973), Merchants Millpond (1973), Dismal Swamp and Chowan Swamp State Natural Area (1974), Goose Creek (1974), Jockey's Ridge (1975), South Mountains (1975), Lake Waccamaw (1976) and Hemlock Bluffs, Masonboro Island, and Mitchell's Mill State Natural Areas (1976).

Before discussing several acquisitions in detail, it is worth mentioning two actions in the General Assembly, in which NER assisted, that have turned out to be important for the Park system. The first was a North Carolina Environmental Bill of Rights. This legislation, passed in the General Assembly and approved by the voters in 1971, added a section to Article XIV of the constitution that made it a proper function of the state to, among other things, acquire lands for park purposes. In addition, the article provides that state-owned lands can, on action of three-fifths vote of both houses of the General Assembly, be placed into the "State Nature and Historic Preserve." Perhaps more important was the provision that no land could be removed from the Preserve except by a similar three-fifths vote of both houses. In 1973, we drafted a statute to create the State Nature and Historic Preserve, to specify the ".......the conditions and procedures under which such properties or interests therein shall be dedicated for the aforementioned public purposes" (as required by the constitutional amendment), and to place all the lands of the state park system in it. The act was approved and, except for small areas and under certain special conditions, all park[21] lands remain under that protection today. This provision has proven to be powerful protection for park system lands that might otherwise be subject to development and other destructive schemes.

A second was passage, in 1972, of the State Environmental Policy Act (see Chapter 5). This legislation, patterned after the similar federal statute, required state agencies to consider the environmental consequences of actions involving the expenditure of state money. Although not extensively used, existence of this statute was most helpful in protecting park and similar lands against unwise development proposals. In addition, the General Assembly created the State Natural and Scenic Rivers System in 1972 and the North Carolina Trails System in 1973 providing additional mechanisms by which lands and waters of the state could be preserved for public use and enjoyment.

As the previous discussion of our problems with land acquisition at Medoc Mountain showed, establishment of each new park area carried with it its own special problems. Each acquisition was different and each required a different approach. One theme that seems to unite many, if not all, of them is that the area in question had long been treasured by local residents but it was not until development of some sort threatened the area that a move to create a park arose.

Back to Medoc Mountain. In the early 1970s a state park was proposed for the central northeastern county area of the state as there was none at that time. The Division of State Parks surveyed the five-county area and concluded that Medoc Mountain in Halifax county was an appropriate

---

[21]   Several other categories of state-owned land benefit from the provisions of the State Nature and Historic Preserve legislation, including State Historic Areas, State Natural and Scenic Rivers, and State Trails. Lands owned by local government units may also be placed in the Reserve by legislative action.

site for a park. The Halifax Development Commission used a one-year timber-cutting option from Union-Camp Corporation to allow the state to acquire the 2,300 acres needed to establish Medoc Mountain State Park.

Despite the initial difficulties with land acquisition for Medoc Mountain State Park[22] the rest of the initial acquisition was relatively straight-forward. During the 1800s the area around Medoc Mountain had been a vineyard but by the 1960s little trace of it could be found. A Boy Scout Camp had been built on the mountain in the 1920s and a few years later the mountain's forest was cleared. In the early 1930s molybdenum had been found near the summit and various mining explorations had disturbed the area. The site had been used by local citizens for years as an informal "public" area for hunting, horseback riding, and hiking. Establishment of the park simply clarified the status of land that had long been used as a de facto state park. It now contains 3,893 acres.

While concentrating on adding new areas we put considerable attention on the expansion of Stone Mountain State Park, established in 1969 with a gift of the mountain itself and some surrounding land by North Carolina Granite Company. An influential conservationist from Winston-Salem, Philip Hanes, had considerable interest in the park and owned some land that he offered to give to expand the park conditioned on other adjacent lands being acquired. After considerable negotiation, and with significant help from the Nature Conservancy and much arm-twisting by Hanes, the Hanes land and three other significant tracts with borders on the Blue Ridge Parkway were added. Thus, the much-enlarged Stone Mountain State Park, together with the adjacent Thurmond Chatham Game Land and Doughton Park on the Blue Ridge Parkway, created a large block of protected land between the upper Piedmont and the crest of the Blue Ridge in Wilkes and Alleghany Counties. Stone Mountain Park now contains 14,351 acres.

---

[22] This and other descriptions of the background leading up to acquisition of each site draws heavily from the "History" section for each park on the North Carolina state park web site. Initial acreage figures when cited in this narrative are only those associated with the land acquired when the park in question was created, the "core" lands which justified establishing a park. In subsequent years, all areas grew substantially in size as most recent acreage figures (also included) show.

Crowders Mountain, a large monadnock in Gaston county west of Charlotte, had long been recognized as a site important to the history of the area. Nearby Kings Mountain was the location of a major American Revolutionary War victory and in the late 1700s valuable minerals were discovered at Crowders Mountain. Large gold nuggets were found on the mountain and quantities of gold were found in other locations near the mountain. Until the California gold strike of 1849, the Charlotte region (including Crowders Mountain) made North Carolina the nation's largest gold-producing area. During the 1960s kyanite was mined in an open pit near the mountain. When exploratory drilling and excavation began in 1970, the threat it posed to Crowders Mountain prompted a local citizens group, the Gaston County Conservation Society, to organize local citizens to oppose mining and to promote Crowders Mountain as a state park. A formal proposal was made in 1971 and the site was approved as a potential state park. The core land for the park was acquired in 1973 using funds from the 1972 park land acquisition appropriation and Crowders Mountain State Park was opened in 1974. Acquisition of these lands was made relatively easy by work of local groups supporting creation of the park. The land acquired, however, did not include the summit of the mountain so the park was not viewed as complete. In addition, there was a communications tower and easement on the summit when the park was established; to my knowledge, it is still there. Other later acquisitions in 1977, 1987, and 2000 added the summit of the mountain, Kings Pinnacle, and a connection to the Kings Mountain National Military Park and Kings Mountain State Park in South Carolina. Park area now is 5,126 acres.

Eno River State Park was another story entirely. For many years, the city of Durham had regarded the Eno River as its next source of water after the Lake Michie dam on the Flat River became no longer adequate. Desiring a permanent water source, the city in 1925-26 built a dam on the Flat River, creating Lake Michie. This lake served as Durham's lone water supply until after World War II. It also provided hydroelectric power until 1960 when the generators were removed. By the mid-1960s Durham had begun serious planning for a reservoir on the Eno and was beginning acquisition of land along the river. Its initial plan was for a dam and lake in Orange county and an urban park through Durham.

When plans to impound the Eno became public in 1965, a citizen group, the Association for the Preservation of the Eno River Valley led by Margaret Nygard, with the avowed intention of keeping the Eno a free-flowing river, led a vigorous campaign to save the Eno by creating a state park along the river. During the late 1960s and early 1970s, Durham continued planning for an Eno River reservoir and the citizen's group turned to state government for help with its park effort. Margaret Nygard proved a formidable opponent for the city government and slowly public opinion shifted to the point where there was strong sympathy for creating a park on a free-flowing Eno.

When I entered state government in 1971 the Durham city administration was locked in debate with the Eno River Association over the proposed dam. In my discussions with the State Parks Committee of the Board of Conservation and Development I found considerable sympathy for creation of a park on the Eno. I also had several discussions with Harding Hughes, Durham City Manager, about the city's need to obtain an additional water supply. In early 1972 the Association and the Nature Conservancy agreed to cooperate in an effort to obtain land for a park. In May of 1972 the Board of Conservation and Development approved the concept of a park on the Eno. Shortly thereafter, a gift of ninety acres provided the first land specifically devoted to a park. The state also acquired several small tracts along the river thus creating a hodge-podge of small tracts of land with three different owners. Discussions with the city during the ensuing year revealed that the planned reservoir on the Eno did not have the capacity originally thought and that the city was amenable to a park. Accordingly, a deal was struck whereby the city sold its property along the Eno to the state and in spring 1973 Governor Holshouser declared Eno River State Park to be a reality. With the help of the Association and the Nature Conservancy additional lands were added over the next few years and in 1975 the park, then containing over 1,000 acres, became a full-blown park. Master plan development began in 1975. The plan contained two basic proposals, one for a narrow, linear park concentrated on the river and the other for a larger park containing the river. Since the latter concept involved acquiring considerable land in Orange county as well as in Durham county, it led to resistance from upstream land owners in Orange county. I left state government before the plan was completed but over the years the Eno River State Park has slowly continued to acquire additional land and has been accepted as an important addition to the region's recreational opportunities. The park now comprises 4,200 acres running almost continuously from Guess Road on the east to near Hillsborough on the west with the Eno flowing freely through. Although Margaret Nygard died in 1995, Eno River State Park exists as a tribute to her hard work toward its creation.

My role in creation of Eno River State Park was conflicted. On the one hand, I had supported creation of the park before I came into state government and had done so in front of the Board of Conservation and Development at the time the board declared itself in favor of a park on the Eno. On the other hand, once I became assistant secretary of Natural and Economic Resources I had to deal with the reality that the city of Durham had planned for years to use the Eno as a water source; in fact, Durham was one of the few cities in the state that had done a good job of long-range water resource planning. In addition, one major alternative source of water Durham turned to after opposition to the Eno arose was raising the height of the dam at Lake Michie to increase the storage capacity of its impoundment. The proposed increase in height of water in Lake Michie would have backed water up into NC State University's Hill Forest, flooding many of the richest coves along the river and making the summer camp site nearly a lake-side facility. The School of Forest Resources let me know that they did not think this a good idea and that they hoped I would oppose it. After further analysis Durham concluded that the amount of water produced by raising the level of the Michie dam would not meet its needs. After briefly considering another dam site on the Flat just above the northern boundary of Hill Forest, Durham settled on a site on the Little River and a new reservoir was completed there in 1987. Thus, Durham ultimately ended up with both the new reservoir it needed and the Eno River State Park which has turned into one of the better multiuse facilities in the state park system. It is the site of an annual 4th of July Festival of the Eno, a highly popular, heavily attended, event. Despite, or because of, a lot of sweat and tears the outcome that ended in the park and the Little River reservoir was to everyone's benefit.

Acquisition of <u>Merchants Millpond State Park</u> illustrated the importance of a generous donor and of the ability to cooperate with the Nature Conservancy. Although millponds had existed on Bennett's Creek in Gates county since pre-revolutionary days, they fell out of use before

World War II. Mr. A. B. Coleman bought the 1,900 acres on which the 190-year old Merchants Millpond was located and donated it to the state in 1973 enabling establishment of Merchants Millpond State Park. The Nature Conservancy acquired 925 acres of adjacent timberland from Georgia-Pacific Corporation, also in 1973, and sold this land to the state thus expanding the park. It now contains 3,447 acres. Coleman pushed the state hard to accept his land and to create a park at Merchants Millpond, insisting always that the natural features of the area be preserved by the park. His love of the deep quiet of the cypress swamp that occupied the millpond area was obvious as was his generosity in offering the land to the state. The area offered unique opportunities for combining canoeing and camping, an experience not available in other state parks at the time. Mr. Coleman was an interesting personality, as were the dozen or so other dedicated and often headstrong personalities that contributed through their work, their personal wealth, or both, to the rapid growth of the state park system. North Carolina owes them a debt of gratitude.

Creation of Dismal Swamp State Park was in some ways the effort least likely to succeed of all the state parks created while I worked for NER. The Dismal Swamp, long a prospective site for various development schemes, starting with George Washington, by the late 1960s had become a target of the land preservation community. Its sheer size and value as a unique, regional wetland had led the Nature Conservancy and the U.S. Fish and Wildlife Service to look on the area as a possible wildlife preserve and management area. North Carolina had joined in this effort and part of the park acquisition money appropriated in 1973 was to be directed to the Dismal Swamp as described in the booklet justifying the appropriation. The problem was making the Dismal Swamp sound like a good place for a state park. Even though North Carolina's proposed acquisition was for only about 14,000 acres, all located in North Carolina, there remained the questions as to how the area would be used and what would happen to the much larger portion in Virginia. In short, a deep swamp with dense vegetation and numerous forms of wildlife dangerous to humans did not seem to lend itself to development for conventional public recreation.

The Nature Conservancy had acquired the tract that North Carolina proposed to buy with the agreement that North Carolina would purchase it when state funds became available. These events came to a head in

January-February of 1973 right after Jim Harrington became secretary of NER. It fell to me to explain the "deal" to Harrington and to convince him buying 14,000 acres of deep swamp for a park was a good idea. I had known Jim less than a month and I felt going into my meeting with him to discuss the Dismal Swamp that there was a good likelihood that he would not like the idea at all and that it might get him and me off on the wrong foot. However, after listening to my pitch, which leaned heavily on the commitment, which of course could not be binding, that North Carolina had made to buy the land, Harrington agreed with little adverse argument that we should go ahead with the purchase. Thus, the Dismal Swamp State Park came into existence. Since its acquisition public access facilities, largely oriented to boating along the canals and streams in the area, have been constructed. It now is 14,432 acres in size. Most of the rest of the Dismal Swamp in North Carolina and Virginia was bought by the federal government and now comprises the 112,000-acre Great Dismal Swamp National Wildlife Refuge.

The Dismal Swamp acquisition illustrates how important the working relationship between the state and the Nature Conservancy was to efforts to grow the state park system. Frequently, opportunities to acquire highly desired tracts of land arose quickly and had to be capitalized on quickly, often before state funds were available. Under these circumstances the Conservancy could agree to acquire the land with a handshake understanding that the state would purchase it at the price the Conservancy paid for it when funds became available. The arrangement involved a gamble for the Conservancy because there was never any guarantee that state funds would materialize. However, the Conservancy's view was that the land could always be sold to another buyer; thus, it considered the gamble a good one. This arrangement allowed us to move ahead with several park land acquisitions while at the same time working to obtain funds from the General Assembly or some other source. There were times when this "cozy" arrangement between the state and the Conservancy raised eyebrows in the legislature. Questions came up as to who was driving the land acquisition program and whose interests were really being served. We were able to satisfy most legislators by explaining each effort as part of state-driven effort to expand its park system for the benefit of all the state's citizens.

Establishment of <u>Goose Creek State Park</u> involved yet another different set of circumstances. The land in question lay on the north side of the Pamlico River just east of Washington and was wholly owned by Weyerhaeuser Corporation. Although the land did not figure heavily in the company's future timber operations it was regarded as a potential site for a recreational housing development. Thus, our negotiations were with Weyerhaeuser exclusively and had to consider the potential value of the land for private recreational development. In addition, there existed the possibility of recoverable minerals (such as phosphate) and the even more remote possibility of oil or natural gas on or under the property.

The initiative for creation of Goose Creek State Park, as in most cases, came from a local citizens group. At their instigation, state park personnel studied the area and determined that Goose Creek was the most suitable site for a state park among several areas along the northern shore of the Pamlico River east of Washington. A resolution to the Governor indicated strong local interest in a park so the department began the process of acquiring the desired land. To start negotiations, I called the person in Weyerhaeuser's home office in Tacoma, Washington, responsible for land purchases and sales. Naturally, my first approach was to ask that the company make a gift of the land or at least consider a bargain sale. The response was that "Weyerhaeuser regards its land as its most valuable commodity and it wasn't in the business of giving it away." From that point on we negotiated until a sale price acceptable to both parties was established. The question of mineral leases remained. The state would not accept, nor would the state parks staff wish to administer, land on which the threat of mineral exploration and/or exploitation existed. The real issue was the potential for gas and oil, however remote that possibility seemed. Finally, we agreed that Weyerhaeuser would retain a right to slant drill under the state park land if the drilling was done from outside the park and with no damage to the surface. With this agreement reached, the state purchased 1,208 acres from Weyerhaeuser and Goose Creek State Park was opened in September 1974. With acquisition of additional tracts of land, the park now totals 1,672 acres.

One of the most contentious acquisitions of land for a new state park was at <u>Jockey's Ridge</u> in the town of Nags Head. The land involved was widely known and highly visible since it was a huge, unvegetated, live (moving) sand dune that happened to be the largest dune on the east coast of the United States and one of the best-known land features of the outer banks. This acquisition almost certainly would be difficult and very expensive due to the presence of extensive second home development near the ridge itself.

Creation of the Cape Hatteras National Seashore in the late 1930s placed a seventy-mile, 30,000-acre portion of the Dare county outer banks in federal ownership. The creation of the seashore was strongly supported by local citizens, particularly when it was accompanied by a federal program to build and stabilize dunes along the outer banks. The shoreline had become badly eroded during the early 1930s; in fact, the Cape Hatteras light house was in danger of being swept away. Despite a brief flirtation with oil prospecting and development in the early 1950s, the formal dedication of the seashore in 1954 was widely hailed as the basis for growth in the Dare county tourist economy. Despite the acceptance of the seashore, there was a strong feeling in Dare and Currituck counties that enough of the northern outer banks had been protected from development. The opinion was that to capitalize on the tourist potential of the seashore the remainder of the land, particularly in Nags Head, Kill Devil Hills, and Kitty Hawk, should be developed.

Nonetheless, there were two areas, Jockey's Ridge and Nags Head Woods, noted for their natural beauty and uniqueness, that many citizens thought should not be developed. Jockey's Ridge was famous as the highest active dune (at nearly 100 feet) on the outer banks. Immediately to its north lay Nags Head woods, an area of old, stable dunes heavily forested with live and other oaks, beech, pine, and hornbeam; there was no other similar place on the outer banks. The sheer uniqueness of these areas argued for their protection from development. However, all the land in both areas was privately-owned and, since the owners had plans for development of both, it was highly unlikely that without active citizen support government action to protect these areas would take place. The importance of both areas was recognized when they were declared National Natural Landmarks in 1974.

Active citizen support for preservation did arise during the early 1970s, particularly around Jockey's Ridge which was the most directly threatened by development. A local citizen activist, Carolista Baum, who happened to be a member of an old, well-respected outer banks family, became the leader of Citizens to Save Jockey's Ridge. Ms. Baum was an outspoken, direct, and formidable proponent of saving Jockey's Ridge. She also had the respect and support of local government which recognized the potential of the dune as a tourist attraction. Although there was no similar local proponent of saving Nags Head woods, the Nature Conservancy became interested in that cause, and quietly began an effort on behalf of the woods. Saving Jockey's Ridge, however, came first. The history of Jockey's Ridge State Park, as outlined on its web page, provides a much-simplified version of what happened:

> "On a summer morning in 1973, a couple of Baum's children were playing on the dunes. When they saw a bulldozer flattening out part of Jockey's Ridge, they went running home to tell their mother. Carolista Baum went to investigate and found that an earth-moving machine was preparing a residential development site at the base of Jockey's Ridge. For years, local groups had talked of protecting the large dune from encroaching development, but no substantial steps had been taken. This destruction, however, forced Carolista into action. She planted herself in the path of the bulldozer, forcing the operator to shut the equipment down. From that point on, the effort to "save our sand dune" took on new determination. The People to Preserve Jockey's Ridge was organized. Appeals, backed by a petition, were made to local and state governments. The state's Division of Parks and Recreation was asked to study the feasibility of making Jockey's Ridge a state park. In 1973, the Division of Parks and Recreation issued a report in favor of the park, and a year later the dune was declared a National Natural Landmark. In 1975, the General Assembly appropriated funds to create Jockey's Ridge State Park. With this money and matching federal funds, the state bought 152 acres. An additional purchase from the Nature Conservancy brought the size of the park to 266.8 acres. Today, the park encompasses 420 acres."

As the summary tells, Carolista Baum was the driving force behind the effort to save Jockey's Ridge as a state park. She became well known in the department and, to put it mildly, would not let us ever forget how important Jockey's Ridge was to the people of the outer banks and what a significant move it would be to save it.

With the appropriation of money in 1975 directly earmarked for a park at Jockey's Ridge, the department had no choice but to enter negotiations to make it happen. Secretary Harrington was conflicted about what to do. On the one hand, there was intense pressure to buy the area and to create a state park. On the other, because residential development had begun around the base of the dune (in fact some units had already been built), the asking price per acre for the land was far more than the state had ever paid for park land. Harrington and I discussed the matter several times; he was deeply concerned about spending close to a $1million to acquire what was, in reality, a "pile of loose sand." At one point, I remember telling him that I did not think either he or the Holshouser administration would want to go down in history as the "people who failed to save Jockey's Ridge when they had the chance." Because we were actively involved in creation of several other parks, and because the funds appropriated by the General Assembly were insufficient to meet the owner's demands for the land we would have to use Federal matching dollars from the Bureau of Outdoor Recreation that we had "earned" as matching funds from other park acquisitions. After lengthy discussion, we decided to proceed. The acquisition effort was two-parted. The Nature Conservancy bought the tract on the north nearest the road, which had already been prepared for development by a group from Virginia Beach, while the state began purchase of the largest (152 acres) tract that contained the peak of the dune proper at a negotiated price that turned out to be $900,000.

As with all land acquisitions, final approval by the Council of [23]State was required. Although approval of the purchase of land for parks was usually easily given by the Council, Jockey's Ridge was different. The proposed purchase had received much publicity and the price per acre, which approached $6,000 for what detractors derisively called a "pile of sand", was controversial. Jim Graham, the Commissioner of Agriculture, was

---

[23]   The Council of State consists of the governor, the lieutenant governor, and the elected state agency heads. During Holshouser's administration the Council was split with a Republican governor and all other members Democrats.

clearly ready to make an issue of the purchase as was the Commissioner of Labor, Billy Creel, an associate of Graham's. I drew the short straw and was responsible for appearing in front of the Council to make the department's case. To say it did not go well was an understatement. No sooner had I begun to make my argument as to why this purchase was both symbolic and important, Graham began to interrupt with a series of questions clearly designed to win points in the political arena. He was joined by his friend, Creel, who supported Graham's arguments with evidence he claimed to have gathered on the outer banks. During the "ass-chewing" Graham was giving me, which in retrospect was amusing, I noticed Phil Kirk, the governor's assistant, reach over, tear a sheet of paper from the note pad in front of the governor, and very obviously begin writing a note. When done, he got up while I was in the midst of defending myself, walked over, and handed me the note. Figuring that it was an instruction from the governor to the effect that "you're dying, try some other approach", I opened the note and read it. It said "aren't you about ready to become a Republican?" There was nothing I could do but refold the note, put it in my pocket, and ignore Kirk who by this time was smiling broadly. I knew if I even caught his eye it would be impossible to continue with my defense, which was becoming lamer and lamer as the meeting went on. Finally, I was dismissed and the Council continued its discussion, eventually voting to support the purchase of Jockey's Ridge. I still have Kirk's note as a souvenir of what it was like to be in the middle of a political argument with Jim Graham on the offensive and me the object of attack. In retrospect, I concluded that although Graham may have been serious in his concerns, a good bit of his argument was just a chance to make political hay at Republican expense.

The land was purchased and the park formally created in late 1975. Since that time, with the assistance of the Nature Conservancy, the state has added 113 acres and other adjacent lands so that the Park now encompasses 426 acres. The Park is adjoined on the north by one of the Nature Conservancy's premier North Carolina natural areas, the 1,100-acre Nags Head Woods Ecological Preserve. Jockey's Ridge State Park and the Nags Head Woods Preserve together protect over 1,500 acres of natural dunes, swales, ponds, and maritime forest amid one of the most heavily utilized tourist areas on the outer banks.

The Nags Head Woods Preserve is a testimony to the foresight and the willingness to take financial risk of the North Carolina Chapter of the Nature Conservancy during its early days. Nags Head woods was its second acquisition. When it became known that the woods were for sale and that the town of Kill Devil Hills favored its development, the Conservancy Chapter, then no more than a year old and with virtually nothing in the bank, put earnest money on the woods through an un-disclosed second-party attorney from Elizabeth City (who happened to be a member of the Chapter Board). This action secured the land but only for a period during which the executive director of the Chapter, Tom Massengale, went on a frantic fund-raising effort to secure the money necessary to make the purchase. He was successful and, together with major generous gifts of land from John and Rhoda Calfee and Diane St. Clair, and subsequent cooperative efforts between the towns of Nags Head and Kill Devil Hills and the state, the Nags Head Wood Ecological Preserve now stands as a 1,111-acre testimony to Massengale's work. It also stands as an important adjunct to Jockey's Ridge State Park and as an ecological treasure protected for the enjoyment of all North Carolinians.

Any examination of the state park system as it existed in the early 1970s, and as it had been enlarged by the previously-discussed areas, clearly showed that greatest attention had been paid to areas in the Piedmont and Coastal Plain. The western-most addition at the time Jockey's Ridge was acquired was Crowders Mountain in the western Piedmont. Mt. Mitchell (1915), Mt. Jefferson (1956), and Stone Mountain (1969) were the only state parks in or close to the mountains. Of course, this situation reflected, in large part, the major areas of federal land (two National Forests and the Great Smoky Mountains National Park) existing in the mountains as well as the concentration of population to be served by new parks east of the mountains.

Representations from citizen's groups in the mountains led us to realize that there was need for, and interest in, new state parks in the mountains. We began filling this major gap with an effort that led to creation of South Mountains State Park. This area had long been identified as a desirable site for a park. In fact, during the 1930s a Civilian Conservation Corps camp (Camp Dryer) was located in the region and CCC men constructed roads, cleaned stream beds, and built an observation tower.

Several of the roads are still used as trails in the park today. Although a study done in the 1940s identified the South Mountains as a desirable site for a park, it was not until funds became available in 1974 that land was acquired.

As with many other units acquired during the early 1970s, the threat of second-home development, primarily on the north slopes of the mountains, galvanized action by the state and local support groups. Secretary Harrington and I attended a meeting of local park enthusiasts in late August, 1974. At one point, Harrington was pushed to state exactly when the group could expect a park to be announced for the area. His answer was "this summer." On the flight home I asked Jim if he realized that he had made a commitment to complete acquisition of the land and announce creation of South Mountains State Park "this summer" and that it was already almost Labor Day. He ruminated a moment and responded with "summer lasts until September 21." We made his deadline but just! The initial purchase was of 5,579 acres and substantial land has been added since, bringing South Mountains State Park to its current size of 19,830 acres, making it the largest unit in the North Carolina State Park System.

Lake Waccamaw is one of the State Lakes located in southeastern North Carolina. There had been a state park at Jones Lake since 1939 when the federal government leased land acquired by the Resettlement Administration to the state. In 1954 title to the land was turned over to the state and Jones Lake State Park, the first state park for blacks, was created. Singletary Lake State Park was created in a similar way. However, no state land existed on Lake Waccamaw, one of the largest of the southeastern North Carolina lakes. The fact that the state managed the water in Lake Waccamaw combined with the pressures of heavy public use to create a demand for a state park on Lake Waccamaw. As early as October of 1964 the Board of Conservation and Development tried to obtain land on the lake shore but failed. However, in May of 1976 we were able to purchase 273 acres to create Lake Waccamaw State Park. Other lands have been added since, particularly from holdings of Federal Paper Company and Georgia-Pacific Corporation, bringing the current total land to 2,201 acres.

A state park was created on the New River[24] in 1976 after the state in 1975 and the federal government in 1976 designated a 26-mile portion of the New River a State and National Wild and Scenic River.

In addition to State Parks, State Natural Areas and State Recreation Areas were added to the system in the early 1970s. The State Natural Area System had been created in 1963 with the addition of Weymouth Woods near Southern Pines and Bushy Lake State Natural Area, near Singletary Lake State Park, had been added in 1971 by administrative transfer of authority. Several new Natural Areas were added between 1971 and 1976. The Theodore Roosevelt Natural Area, in Pine Knoll Shores on Bogue Banks, was added in 1972 and became the site of the central coast State Aquarium. The 265-acre Roosevelt Natural Area contained a large stand of maritime forest and is virtually the only tract of any size like it remaining on Bogue Banks. During 1976 three Natural Areas were added: Hemlock Bluffs, Masonboro Island, and Mitchell Mill. Hemlock Bluffs, where the only stand of Canadian hemlock east of the Blue Ridge occurs, was a site that had been identified for preservation since the early 1960s. The land containing the hemlock bluffs was eventually leased to the town of Cary to administer. Masonboro Island was a slender barrier island between Wrightsville Beach and Carolina Beach with no permanent human settlement. Because of the doubtful fate of Bald Head Island to the south, there was considerable local support for preservation of Masonboro Island. Acquisition proved to be a virtual nightmare as there were literally hundreds of individual parcels, some with multiple owners, scattered widely throughout the United States. Although enough ownerships were acquired to establish Masonboro Island State Natural Area, many others proved so difficult that it eventually became necessary to condemn the land through the courts. Masonboro Island is now not only a State Natural Area but is also a National Estuarine Research Reserve. Mitchells Mill is a granite flat rock area near Rolesville northeast of Raleigh. It was also an area that had been identified for years as a desirable site for preservation; funds finally became available to acquire ninety-three acres in 1976.

---

[24] The story of the New River is so important and complex that it is the subject of an entire chapter (14).

The first unit was added to the State Recreation Area system in 1971 and a set of principles to guide management and development of recreation areas was adopted in 1974. The Kerr Reservoir Commission was transferred to NER by reorganization in 1971. Thus, the lands that the commission managed essentially became the first State Recreation Area in 1971 although they were not formally transferred and named Kerr Lake State Recreation Area until 1981. Recreation areas were also established as parts of Corps of Engineer projects at Jordan Lake and Falls Lake when construction of these projects was authorized. Project recreation lands came under control of the state park system in the early 1980s.

Even though virtually every state park created when I worked in NER was stimulated by a local citizens group and land had usually been identified, acquisitions were frequently complex and difficult. The easiest (relatively) acquisitions were those in which the Nature Conservancy bought the required land, or a part of it, often at a bargain price and held the land until the state could buy it from them. Negotiations with land owners were often protracted and frustrating necessitating the involvement of real estate and legal expertise. Despite the legislative appropriations of 1972, 1974, and 1975 money was almost always an issue. The cost of the areas identified for acquisition exceeded the state funds available, and had these appropriations been the only source of money several areas could not have been purchased. Although gifts of land, with consequent tax benefits to the donor, figured in several acquisitions, the most significant additional source of funds was the Federal Land and Water Conservation Fund administered by the Department of the Interior mentioned previously. Because this program made dollar-for-dollar matching funds available for purchase of land and development for recreational purposes, it essentially doubled the amount of money available for acquisition of park land. Although funds had to be authorized anew by Congress every year, meaning there was always a degree of uncertainty as to exactly how much money would be available, appropriations during the early 1970s were sufficient to support NER's program of land acquisition.

Administration of the Land and Water Conservation Fund (LWCF) money at the state level was a complex matter. The money came from Washington to the Department of Administration. Some of it was directed to local governments and the remainder was designated for state use and administered by the Department of Administration (DOA) in its role as the state's land acquisition agency. In practice, when the state made a land purchase it had to pay for it and then apply for reimbursement from the LWCF. Reimbursed funds were then supposed to be deposited in the park land acquisition account. Secretary Harrington and I had continual difficulty in finding out exactly how much money, state and federal, was available to spend at any point in time. In fact, this difficulty became so great that Harrington instructed me to keep records of the status of park land acquisition money, including expenditures and reimbursements from the LWCF. My records consisted of a single sheet that I kept in my top desk drawer with "minuses" for expenditures, "pluses" for reimbursements, and a running balance—primitive accounting but it turned out to be more accurate than the Department of Administration's accounting. By 1974 we were getting close to the end of our available funds so it was critical that we knew exactly how much we had left and that all reimbursements had been deposited. Finally, one acquisition (South Mountains, as I recall) came up and I warned the Secretary that this one "would break the bank" if DOA had not placed the last LWCF reimbursement in our land acquisition fund. He told me to go ahead with the acquisition and, sure enough, the answer came back from DOA that we did not have adequate funds. A hasty meeting with their financial people convinced them that our land acquisition effort was owed money and DOA then had to go to Washington to the LWCF administrator hat in hand and ask for permission to make a transfer of federal funds at the state level to cover our shortfall. It turned out that the reimbursements were being spent in a way that matched federal dollars with federal dollars violating a major constraint of revenue-sharing. Making the retroactive transfer was not an easy matter, but to our benefit both administrations involved were Republican and the matter was resolved. The episode finally convinced DOA that we needed to have more accurate financial records in order properly to manage our land acquisition program.

Although the state park system has grown much larger since I left state government with the addition of some truly magnificent areas, prime examples being Chimney Rock, Gorges, Grandfather Mountain, and New River I would like to think that the spark that began this growth was struck during the time I served in NER. Growth of the park system, a project that clearly would benefit all the citizens of the state, was one of my personal objectives when I joined state government. It became a major activity of the department, and is a source of pride to me and I am sure to all of us who were involved.

However, there is much more to the story of growth of the state park system. One of the major concerns about a rapid program of land acquisition voiced by superintendent Tom Ellis was a fear that funds to administer the lands properly would not be appropriated. To a degree, he was correct as no significant increase in management funds occurred while I was in NER; it was not until the late 1970s and 1980s that significant appropriation of funds for development and management occurred.

Growth of the state park system continues to the present. Several important acquisitions have been made since the big burst of additions in the early 1970s. These include such significant additions as Gorges acquired in 1999, which when combined with an adjacent 2,900-acre State Gameland, constitutes a 10,000-acre public recreation area on the Blue Ridge escarpment west of Brevard, and two well-known tourist attractions, Chimney Rock in 2005, and Grandfather Mountain in 2008. Other areas added include Lake James in 1987, Lumber River in 1989, Elk Knob, Haw River, and Mayo River in 2003, and Carvers Creek in 2005. Fourteen new State Natural Areas have been added, five new river segments have been named State Rivers, and four State Trails have been designated, all since the mid-1970s. The State Parks Act of 1987 named six kinds of areas for administration by the North Carolina Division of Parks and Recreation: State Parks, State Rivers, State Trails, State Recreation Areas, State Natural Areas, and State Lakes.

Despite the growth of state-owned natural and recreation lands, and the fact that virtually all these lands are designated as part of the State Nature and Historic Preserve, periodic threats to the integrity of the system have arisen. For example, in February 1990, sale of most of William B. Umstead State Park was proposed as a result of a study of the potential for sale of all lands in the state park system. The concept underlying the proposal was to use the money realized from the sale to set up a perpetual endowment for development and operation of the state park system. The proposal ran into a fire storm of opposition, as well as failing to consider the federal reverter clause on the land, and was quickly put to rest. Nonetheless, as funds become tighter and all operations of state government are studied for potential savings, those with interests in maintaining and enlarging a vibrant state park system must remain forever vigilant against such proposals.

At one point or another during our efforts to expand the state park system, we were questioned by members of the General Assembly, in committee meetings or alone, about the role of the Nature Conservancy. Somehow, the Conservancy's involvement in our land acquisition program had come to be viewed by some as a subterfuge to "force" the state to acquire lands that it might not otherwise have acquired and to do so without full legislative authorization. This was, of course, an exact reversal of the real roles of the two parties. In all cases, the Conservancy purchased lands that the state had identified for acquisition in presentations made to the legislature. The Conservancy was often able to negotiate a purchase at a price well below fair-market value, thus reducing the state's cost when it purchased the land from the Conservancy. This also allowed the state to apply for LWCF money using the actual fair-market value of the land as the state's part of the match. Usually, we could convince legislative skeptics as to the importance of the Nature Conservancy's involvement to the state, particularly when they came to understand that with their help we could increase the amount of money available for state park land acquisition.

The whole state park land acquisition effort illustrated the difficulties of being successful while working in a governmental environment. The difficulties centered on the number of steps, agencies, and persons involved. Approval of the proposed program of acquisition first had to be approved by the legislature through appropriation of funds. However, funds were sometimes appropriated and dedicated to a specific acquisition either by direct legislative language or by an informal "understanding" with a specific legislator. This meant that the flexibility to move money from one proposed purchase, where difficulty with negotiations had cropped up, to another where circumstances demanded immediate acquisition, was difficult. The fact that state law required the Property Control Office of the Department of Administration to be the state's land acquisition agency required an extraordinary degree of cooperation, and agreement in philosophy, between Property Control and NER. As I have indicated, this philosophical agreement and cooperation did not exist in the early stages of our park land acquisition program and it took direct personal coordination at the level of the two departmental secretaries for it to be resolved. The statutes also required that all state lands be acquired by the Department of Administration and then, as appropriate, assigned to another agency for management. As we will see in conjunction with another case, the Cape Lookout National Seashore (Chapter 9), this statutory requirement occasionally became a genuine impediment to responsible management of state lands. Finally, the difficulty with management of reimbursement for state park land purchases from the LWCF by the Department of Administration proved nearly fatal in at least one case to a politically-important acquisition. This convoluted system probably served to ensure that no state agency became involved in land acquisitions that were contrary either to the interests of the state or state law. On the other hand, it lacked the degree of flexibility that was needed to insure acquisition of park land in a timely and politically responsive way.

Chapter 9

Cape Lookout National Seashore

As the following narrative makes clear, NER became involved in the Cape Lookout National Seashore very late in the long history of the Seashore's creation. However, the task of completing transfer of land to the federal government for the Seashore fell to NER, and to me by assignment from the secretary, at a crucial point in the process. The state agencies that had been dealing with the issue since authorization of the Seashore in 1966 were incapable of carrying out the work of assuring that the land to be transferred was in a condition that the National Park Service would accept. I always felt that NER ended up with the job because no other state agency wanted to become involved and because the governor's office was satisfied that if NER took on the job we would see it through to completion. Because NER became involved so late, much of this chapter deals with the background leading up to NER's involvement. I have chosen to discuss it at some length because it is an excellent example of the cumbersome, inefficient way state government dealt with land transactions during the 1970s. The reader of the Cape Lookout saga will be left to wonder that the Seashore ever did come into existence.

*****

The land ("outer banks") that is now included in the Cape Lookout National Seashore consists of Core and Shackleford Banks in Carteret county as well as a small administrative and access area on the mainland at Harker's Island. The area was relatively well populated in the 1800s with the thriving community of Portsmouth Village located at the extreme north end of Core Banks. However, a series of storms led to a slow decrease in population and the great hurricane of 1933 virtually wiped the banks clean, cutting numerous inlets through them. Efforts were made to stabilize the islands but these met with failure and it quickly became obvious that, as with the northern outer banks in Dare county, the only entity with the resources to manage the area properly was the federal government. Much of the land on Core Banks was privately-owned with a few widely-scattered fishing camps used by both commercial and sports fishermen. The resident population at Portsmouth Village declined until in the early

1960s only three residents, two elderly white women and one elderly black man, remained.

Recognizing that management of the banks must somehow be transferred to the federal government, an effort was begun in the early 1960s to create the Cape Lookout National Seashore. This effort was led by what was then the North Carolina Seashore Commission, a creation of the Terry Sanford administration.[25] A bill authorizing the Cape Lookout National Seashore passed Congress in 1966 with some important provisions. The state was required to buy Core Banks (it had already begun to do this in the early 1960s) and donate it to the federal government. With this done, the Secretary of the Interior would then establish the Seashore and begin acquisition of Shackleford Banks. Fishing and hunting were declared uses compatible with the proposed seashore and were to be perpetuated. The Corps of Engineers would be allowed to build a protective dike but only in a manner mutually agreed to by the Department of Interior and the Corps. This was a controversial provision, reflecting what was then accepted practice with respect to hurricane protection. However, there was serious disagreement in Carteret county as to whether a protective dike would be a wise move. Finally, an area of about 250 acres at Lookout Bight, belonging to Sanford businessman Charles Reaves, was "mysteriously" excluded from the Seashore and another interesting provision entitled any property owner owning property as of January 1, 1966, developed for non-commercial, residential purposes on July 1, 1963, to a twenty-five year right of use and occupancy.

---

[25] The Seashore Commission was composed of a mix of politically influential Sanford supporters and persons with deep interests in the coast (the two groups were not mutually exclusive). Many of the commission members were genuine characters and collectively they constituted a truly unique body. Together with Dr. Bill Woodhouse of the North Carolina State University Department of Soil Science, I served as one of two "advisors" to the commission. The commission supported research on coastal problems and its influence played a major role in obtaining an appropriation to NCSU for such research. I was named Director of the new NCSU Coastal Research Program. In a very real way this program served as the progenitor of NCSU's entrance into marine research and ultimately to its development of a full-blown marine studies program now located in the Department of Marine, Earth, and Atmospheric Sciences.

With the Seashore authorized the State Property Office accelerated its efforts to purchase Core Banks. Early purchases were at very low values (between $30-300 an acre). No real bargaining was done and the land was either bought at the state's offer or condemned, a process that created no small amount of ill will in Carteret county. By 1966-67 about three-quarters of the needed land had been acquired. However, several influential property owners, chiefly the Core Banks Gun Club, fought condemnation with the Gun Club's case ending up in the state Supreme Court. The court ruled that the use of condemnation was invalid because there was no clear statutory basis indicating that condemnation was for a public purpose. However, the court did suggest what wording would be required if legislation were sought to remedy the situation. The 1969 legislature passed the necessary legislation but with an unfortunate proviso. It did not authorize quick-take condemnation but instead authorized condemnation by the so-called Chapter 40 process which was slow, allowed for extended bargaining, and did not permit the state to take possession of the condemned land until all negotiations were complete. As might be surmised, a member of the Core Banks Gun Club was serving in the legislature when this statute was passed.

During the early 1970s the Property Control Office continued with condemnation of land not owned by the state, land owned by Charles Reaves not excluded from the Seashore, and other privately-owned land. Little headway was made as the state was contested in court at every step. In the meantime, an increasing number of private individuals had begun "squatting" on state-owned land, constructing buildings and establishing trailer facilities. Some of these "camps" were almost luxurious, even to the extent of having generator-driven air conditioning. Some of the pre-existing fish camps were also expanded and many users of the land brought over vehicles in large numbers to use on the beach when surf fishing. In some cases, as at Portsmouth village, yearly leases were negotiated. Desultory efforts were made to remove the squatters and fish camps, but nothing substantive was done largely because the Department of Administration, in which the titles to the land resided, had no means whatsoever of enforcing its administrative authority.

By 1974-75 the situation had clearly gotten out of hand and was being widely discussed in the press. The change in administrations in

1973 proved to be immensely helpful in finally negotiating a way out of the mess. With the transition to a Republican administration Mr. Reaves lost most of his influence in Raleigh and found it in his interest to negotiate a resolution regarding his land. In addition, as a side effect of NER's negotiating for state park land, it had developed a very good working relationship with the Republican administration in the Department of Interior in Washington, specifically with one of the Assistant Secretaries of Interior, Douglas Wheeler. Wheeler and I worked closely together on several matters and this contact proved to be vital to resolving the Cape Lookout Seashore situation.

The issue of the Reaves land was finally resolved when he agreed on $1.5 million for all his land that was included in the Seashore. In addition, he agreed to donate almost all his land that had been excluded when maps of the proposed Seashore were drawn. This broke the logjam and the other properties at Cape Point were soon also acquired. Negotiations with the Core Banks Gun Club, however, were more complicated. With the help of the Nature Conservancy, and with Wheeler's assistance in the Department of Interior, an arrangement was finally worked out in which the Gun Club accepted $3 million for its property, $2 million to come from the state, and $1 million from the federal government (as reimbursement for the "extra" originally-excluded acreage obtained from Reaves). With Wheeler's assistance, the legislation authorizing the Seashore was amended in October 1974 to remove the Reaves exclusion, to allow use of federal funds for acquiring the Gun Club property, to allow the Secretary of Interior to establish the Seashore when he "shall determine enough land is available for an administerable (sic) unit," to require a wilderness study by January 1, 1978, and to increase the funding authorized for the Seashore.

Although the pathway to the Seashore was legally cleared, it remained for the state to meet its commitments with respect to transfer of the land. By this time there were nearly 400 squatters and an estimated 2,500 junked automobiles on Core Banks. Rightly, the National Park Service did not want to assume responsibility for these encroachments and, unfortunately, the state did not have the legal tools to deal with them quickly. Fear arose that pressure from the squatters on legislators might lead the legislature to reverse its approval of the Seashore and prevent the governor from transferring the land. Fruitless negotiations continued through 1975 and early 1976 until the Director of the National Park Service, Gary Everhardt, finally stated that the Service wanted the Cape Lookout National Seashore and that a means must be worked out to accomplish this.

That is where NER entered the picture as more than a participant in the various past discussions on the future of the Seashore. By an administrative stratagem through establishment of temporary regulations, responsibility for the Seashore was shifted to NER. We were required to hold a series of hearings at which citizens would express their desires with respect to creation of the Seashore even though the positions of all the interested party were well known and publicly stated. I will not say the hearings were a sham, but I can say that it was quite clear that the governor wanted the Seashore created and NER was to provide him the support he needed to do it.

In all, three hearings were held, one on the coast and two in the Piedmont in Winston-Salem and Mooresville. I was charged with arranging and chairing the hearings and Mack Riddle, the "superintendent-in-waiting" for the Seashore, was to accompany me. The Piedmont hearings were located to maximize the opportunity for squatters to have their case heard. All the hearings were tense, particularly the one in Winston-Salem, with strong expressions of opposition from the squatters and equally strong expressions of support for transfer of the land and creation of the Seashore. Almost at the beginning of the Winston-Salem hearing I was forced to interrupt and forcefully declare that if there were further outbursts against speakers I would close the hearing then and there. The atmosphere became so tense that I arranged with the State Bureau of Investigation to provide armed protection for the last hearing, in Mooresville. It turned out that no protection was needed and the final hearing went off without serious interruption. Needless to say, Mack Riddle and I were glad to see that experience behind us.

The results of the hearings were about what we expected. There were vocal demands from squatters that they be allowed to stay on the banks and keep their cars permanently and expressions from others that the squatters should go and the cars be removed. The only point of agreement among the parties was that Core Banks should remain isolated and that no structural access (i.e., a bridge) should be provided. The final resolution of the matter provided that the National Park Service would take the land

and give the squatters the equivalent of two more fishing seasons before they had to remove their structures or turn them over to the Park Service, that the cars could stay but that they had to meet minimum requirements spelled out by the Service, that the state would remove the junked cars, and that the state would retain a pipeline easement across the banks.[26]

With these terms accepted by all parties, the land was transferred to the federal government in early June 1976. The ceremony took place near the lighthouse with the governor and director of the Park Service participating. Precautions were taken to provide armed protection in event that someone tried to disrupt the proceedings but nothing unfortunate happened. It was a beautiful day, a short and harmonious ceremony, and a fittingly uneventful end to what had been a long, hotly contested, and intensely negotiated episode. The federal government quickly began purchase of Shackleford Banks and the mainland administrative site on Harker's Island. The Seashore was immediately staffed (Mack Riddle remained Superintendent during the early years of development of the Seashore) and the Park Service began its extended planning process. Thus, the Cape Lookout National Seashore came into being and is enjoyed today by thousands every year. It provides about the only thing approaching a wilderness experience anywhere on the North Carolina coast and that, alone, makes all the effort to bring it into existence worthwhile.

One of the factors making management of Core Banks difficult was its instability in the face of storms (in this regard it does not differ much from any of the other North Carolina "outer banks"). When the state began acquisition in the 1960s original Drum Inlet existed several miles south of Portsmouth Village and Okracoke Inlet. Its existence was important to both sports and commercial fishing interests as it served as the only means of egress to the ocean for eastern Carteret county. By 1971, "Old" Drum Inlet was nearly closed and, under pressure from fishing interests, the Corps of Engineers blasted and dredged a "new" Drum Inlet at the approximate center of Core Banks. New Drum Inlet rapidly shoaled,

---

[26] This easement had been included in discussions all along and was supposed to provide for a pipeline if off-shore oil were ever discovered in Lookout Bight. None of us felt it was particularly important but the governor insisted that it remain, so remain it did.

never was much used by sports fishermen, and actually never was used by commercial fishermen. Hurricane Dennis in 1999 re-opened Old Drum Inlet and in 2005 Hurricane Ophelia opened Ophelia Inlet southwest of New Drum Inlet. Despite Ophelia Inlet's merger with New Drum Inlet, neither this inlet nor the re-opened Old Drum Inlet proved to be reliable exits to the ocean. No pressure has been placed on the National Park Service to take steps to open or maintain any of the inlets on Core Banks so there now is essentially no egress to the sea via this route for eastern Carteret county.

The nearly fifteen-year effort to create Cape Lookout National Seashore is a good illustration of the complexity of such endeavors. The state's land acquisition capability was cumbersome and slow with the result that those who sold land early in the process received far lower value than did those who held out longer. And of course, in the end Charlie Reaves and the Core Banks Gun Club came out as financial winners although they did, of course, lose their permanent facilities on Core Banks. The squatter problem ended up as the factor that almost doomed the Seashore. It came into being because the Department of Administration had no "on the ground" presence to prevent such encroachment on state-owned land. Although the adverse possession rule would have given the squatters a right had the land on which they squatted been privately-owned, adverse possession cannot be established against the state and thus the squatters had no legal claim to the land on which they located. That fact, of course, became secondary to the squatters' political efforts to gain sympathy for their desire to remain on state-owned land. Some of NER's meetings with the squatters were almost ludicrous, with the squatters arguing strenuously for a "right" they did not possess. I remember one of the more vocal of the squatters was Rae Scarborough who had been a pitcher for the Washington Senators when I was a boy growing up in Washington. I saw Scarborough pitch many times and the case he made to NER was on a par with some of his pitching performances for the Senators.

In the end, however, despite state government's inability to bring the matter to quick and decisive solution, with the strong cooperation of, and some significant concessions from, the Department of Interior (the agreement to help pay for the Core Banks Gun Club property, the agreement to allow privately-owned automobiles to remain, and the amnesty to allow squatters to continue to use their camps and to fish for two more years) the Seashore was created. An undercurrent in this whole effort was the desire by the Republican administration in Washington (Gerald Ford was then President and locked in a major battle with Ronald Reagan supporters for re-nomination) to gain favor with the Republican administration in Raleigh. There is no question but the strong cooperation from the Department of Interior in this case (and particularly regarding the New River (chapter 14)) was colored by politics in Washington and Raleigh. However, the old saying that when political influence works for you it is "statesmanship", but when it works against you it is "dirty politics", certainly holds in the case of the Cape Lookout National Seashore. This valuable public recreation resource would probably never have come into being without the active help, in part politically-motivated, of the Department of Interior and National Park Service.

Chapter 10

Dams, Some Built, Some Not Built

At the time I entered state government the country was near the end of an epidemic of dam building and stream channelization. Although many dams had been built and streams channelized in the 1950s and 1960s, objections to them, centering on the validity of the economic analyses used to justify them and their demonstrably-negative environmental impacts, were increasing. The U.S. Army Corps of Engineers and what was then the Soil Conservation Service (now Natural Resource Conservation Service) viewed dams and channelization projects as the easiest and most cost-effective way to accomplish a variety of socially-desirable objectives—flood control, drainage including wetland drainage, water supply, downstream water quality improvement, fish and wildlife conservation, and public recreation. Approval of these federally-constructed projects was a highly political exercise and many a local government seized on construction of a dam or a stream channelization project as a solution to water resource management issues in its area. Furthermore, the availability of federal money made possible projects that would otherwise have been wholly beyond the means of local, and even state, governments. Construction of a given project was generally based on a favorable cost/benefit ratio for the project; i.e., the desirable benefits of the project were calculated to exceed its costs.

In many cases, however, costs that were either hidden or simply not considered brought into question the fiscal and environmental credibility of a given project. In addition, virtually all such projects required acquisition of large amounts of privately-owned land, often by condemnation, with the consequent eviction of families from land that frequently had been in the family for generations. Numerous environmental organizations had begun to raise serious questions about such projects and, because of passage of the National Wild and Scenic Rivers Act in 1968 and particularly the National Environmental Quality Act in 1969, many proposed dams and channelization projects had become the subject of bitter public debate, serious criticism, and court cases.

Generally, North Carolina had supported construction of such projects. State participation was largely coordinated by the water planning staff of the Department of Water and Air Resources (later to become the Office of Water and Air Resources and later the Division of Environmental Management in NER). Some of this support could be attributed to the fact that most of the senior Water and Air Resources staff had at one time or another been employed by the Corps of Engineers in a military or civilian capacity. North Carolina had its share of such projects. Impoundments (Lakes Lure, Nantahalah, and Tillery to name a few) built early in the twentieth century, by a variety of entities both private and public, existed on many North Carolina streams and rivers. The Corps of Engineers completed construction of John H. Kerr Dam and Reservoir on the Virginia state line north of Raleigh in 1953 and W. Kerr Scott Reservoir near Wilkesboro in 1963. Both projects were multi-purpose with the initial justification being flood prevention. Benefits of both included substantial amounts of recreational opportunities plus hydropower generation at Kerr Lake. Consequently, both projects were popular with many local interests. By 1971 the Corps was actively studying and preparing to construct two dams in the Triangle area, Hope Valley Dam (later the B. Everett Jordan Dam and Reservoir) on the upper Cape Fear and Falls Dam and Reservoir on the Neuse River north of Raleigh. In addition, other dams were on the drawing board, including the Clinchfield project west of Charlotte, one at Randleman, and several at other locations. Although these Corps projects were to be federally-authorized and constructed, they required considerable participation from the state, in terms of planning and, most important, cost sharing.

Several stream channelization projects had been constructed; one being planned for Chicot Creek near Greenville had become the subject of intense controversy and litigation. In addition to these projects at least one TVA dam was proposed for construction in the mountains, at Mills River south of Asheville. Closer to Raleigh the Soil Conservation Service had proposed a flood control dam on Crabtree Creek that would flood most of the old growth bottomland and ravine forests in William B. Umstead State Park. Duke Power Company was in the early stages of seeking approval for construction of Lakes Keowee and Toxaway in association with its Keowee Nuclear Power plant. Finally, the granddaddy of all these projects, the proposed Appalachian Power Company dams on the New River had moved to the point where North Carolina's position had to be made clear[27].

*****

In my capacity as assistant secretary for resource management coordination of the state's response to these proposed projects became my responsibility. I must admit that I was not favorably disposed toward most of them as I had come to believe that, in most cases, their costs from all sources far outweighed their benefits. This was particularly true for environmental costs as these were generally not even factored into the cost/benefit ratio, the assumption being that any destruction of natural environments, such as floodplains and wetland forest would be outweighed by the creation of wildlife habitat, improvement in water quality, and provision of public recreation facilities. In addition, I felt that the taking of private property involved in most of these projects, in some cases the destruction of entire rural communities and their associated way of life, was a serious social issue that was not given sufficient consideration. The problem that faced the department was whether to support, oppose, or seek modification of projects that had already been approved and were awaiting funding (including state funds) for construction, and to develop a position on projects that were being planned. Opposing or modifying a project that had already been approved usually meant political problems with local interests that had supported the project as it was being planned and initially approved. In some cases, opposition was made easier by the change to a Republican administration in Raleigh. When arriving at a position, in addition to considering the position of previous state administrations, we had to consider the recommendations of different agencies within NER, recommendations that frequently were directly opposed to one another. Finally, we had to consider what continued support would mean in terms of financial commitments by the state. In the case of Corps of Engineer projects state financial commitments could be stretched out over a period (like mortgage payments), but in approving such an arrangement we would

---

[27]   By all odds the most complex and controversial dam and lake project NER was involved in while I worked there were the proposed dams on the New River in Ashe and Alleghany counties. This is covered in Chapter 14. There have been several books written on the subject as well.

essentially be advising the governor (ultimate approval came from the governor on advice from the various affected agencies of state government) to agree to future financial commitments which only the General Assembly had the statutory authority to make.

Generally, my advice to the secretary and governor on projects that had already been approved by Congress was pragmatic and took the form of recommendations that state actions should be directed at insuring that ongoing projects were constructed in the least damaging way. In the case of projects that were still in the planning stage, unless there was some compelling public purpose to be served by a project or there was strong local demand for the project, my advice was that the state oppose them. Although such opposition allowed us to eliminate some clearly undesirable projects, nonetheless it did not save us from becoming involved in some projects in a deep and continuing way. Discussion of individual projects illustrates how complex were the decisions we had to make. This point was driven home by a conversation about one such project I had with Weldon Denny, one of Governor Scott's assistants, about 3 weeks before Scott's term in office ended. After outlining in depth the complexity of the issue to an obviously disinterested Denny, he asked me "how much longer will this hold" (i.e., do we have to deal with it now?). When I told him it would hold at least a couple of months, his response was "please see that it does hold for a couple of months!" As will become evident most of the discussion and opposition by the department occurred after Republican Jim Holshouser was elected governor. For various reasons, some related to personal beliefs and some related to financial impacts on the state, Holshouser and NER Secretary Jim Harrington were more inclined to oppose these projects than were their predecessors.

Mills River

The proposed TVA dam at Mills River between Asheville and Hendersonville was the culmination of nearly thirty years of planning by TVA and local economic interests. As early as the 1920s a dam was proposed near the mouth of Bent Creek creating a reservoir of over 80,000 acres that would flood many communities including Mills River. Nothing came of this proposal but after the creation of TVA in 1933 the proposal was renewed when a TVA engineer, speaking to a public hearing in November 1933, indicated that a 120-foot high dam at Bent Creek would produce

"45,000 horsepower of electricity" and would elevate water levels to as much as thirty feet at Rosman. This proposal died when TVA engineers found that costs of the project would exceed benefits.

A different proposal, a flood-control only dam on Mills River, was raised in 1943. Local interests objected to this proposal and, when a Hendersonville attorney, Monroe Redden, who owned property near the proposed dam, was elected to Congress in 1946 his opposition stymied further work. However, election of Roy Taylor, a strong supporter of TVA projects in western North Carolina, from the district served as the impetus for TVA to resume its planning. The plan that emerged in 1965 called for a system of dams on the main tributaries of the French Broad south of Asheville, including Mills River. The plan gained momentum in 1968 when Congress approved $250,000 for planning. The dam at Mills River emerged as the most cost-effective of all the proposed dams and attention become focused on that project. The proposed dam was to be 110 feet high and would impound a lake with about fourteen miles of shoreline. Claimed benefits included water supply, downstream flood protection of fields and industrial sites and, of course, recreation. This proposal was strongly opposed by interests living in the town of Mills River and by those who owned land to be affected by the impoundment. In April 1969, it was announced that no funds were included in the federal budget for construction at Mills River; this announcement spurred strong efforts by promoters of the dam to restore funds to the budget. These statements of support led to formation in September 1970 of the Upper French Broad Defense Association, which organized opposition to the project.

In October 1970 Congress approved $2 million for construction, but the Nixon administration "froze" all new federal projects until at least 1972, effectively putting Mills River in limbo. The federal budget for the next year, 1972, did not include funds for Mills River. In the meantime, goaded by the Upper French Broad Defense Association and the State of North Carolina, TVA prepared an environmental impact statement for the project. This document was weak and, when circulated for review among state agencies, was found to be totally inadequate. TVA held a hearing in August 1971 which turned out to be a fiasco as in reality it became a "virtual pep rally" for opponents. With election in November 1972 of a Republican to the Governor's office, TVA apparently recognized that state support for the project would not be forthcoming and, in mid-November 1972, terminated the project. I knew of TVA's action about two days after the election when one of the TVA officials with whom I had discussed the project (and to whom I had voiced the state's rejection of the EIS and its strong opposition to the project) called me and effectively said "you win." That was one of the more satisfying days of my tenure in state government.

Crabtree Creek

Much closer to Raleigh the Soil Conservation Service (SCS) had been working for years on a Public Law 566 flood control project for Crabtree Creek on the northern outskirts of Raleigh. As early as 1963 the SCS had issued a comprehensive plan calling for many small dams on tributaries of Crabtree Creek and two larger dams on the creek itself. One of these proposed dams was located on the main stem of the creek just outside the western park boundary and posed no real threat to Umstead Park. The other, however, was located just outside the eastern boundary of the park and was a much greater threat. It would have backed water up for the entire length of the creek in the park and to a level that would have inundated much of the tributary ravines that drained into the creek. This last dam constituted a major problem for the state park people and for all conservation organizations in the Raleigh area. I happened to be personally familiar with the impacted area as it was a place where I frequently took my ecology students; we had conducted intensive studies in one of the major ravines draining into Crabtree Creek.

The entire Crabtree Creek flood control project itself was a problem for conservation organizations, and for me. It sought to control flooding on Crabtree Creek with over twenty small dams on tributary streams and contained no recommendations whatsoever for control of development on the creek floodplain itself. In fact, the whole proposal was developed at the insistence of the city of Raleigh and its mayor who at the time owned the floodplain land along the creek that was later developed into Crabtree Valley shopping center. The proposal lacked any requirements, or even suggestions, for restraints on flood plain development and seemed to be blatantly oriented toward promoting and protecting development. Furthermore, PL 566 projects were intended to provide benefits for rural and agricultural lands and were not intended to provide flood protection for urbanized areas. In short, the proposed project was hard to defend except for owners of lands along Crabtree Creek affected by flooding.

By the time I entered state government, planning for the proposed Crabtree Creek flood control project had progressed substantially and the dam that would flood Umstead park was an integral part of the plan. I met several times with Jesse Hicks, who was then the SCS State Conservationist, each time voicing on behalf of the state parks staff the department's strong opposition to any dam that would permanently flood any part of Umstead park. Apparently Hicks and his staff either did not hear what I said or did not take it seriously as they kept coming back with the same proposal. Finally, in yet another meeting with Hicks, I closed my office door and told him in as clear terms as I could that the department did not then approve any dam that would permanently flood any part of Umstead park, nor would it ever approve such a plan in the future. In short that part of the plan was dead as far as the department was concerned. I did indicate that the department would consider a dry dam east of the park, with approval depending entirely on the extent, height, and duration of flooding that might occur.

The subsequent history of the Crabtree Creek flood control project is a mixed bag. The dam that would have flooded Umstead park was eliminated from the plan. Some other planned structures have been built, both upstream and on tributaries within the Raleigh city limits and their impoundments and associated lands are important recreational areas. The large impoundment proposed for the main stem of the creek west of Umstead park has been built and is the site of the popular Lake Crabtree county park. However, several proposed structures have never been built largely due to the inability or unwillingness of the city of Raleigh to protect the site of the structure from development.

The lands on which several proposed impoundments were to be built are now parts of housing developments. The dam construction that has been accomplished has not been sufficient to protect the main stem of Crabtree Creek through the city of Raleigh from serious flooding. Major floods occurred in 1973, 1996, and twice in 2006. In short, the Crabtree Creek flood control project is a good example of planning for flood control based on doubtful premises. Coordination with the state was never particularly effective due to weak enforcement of flood control standards by local government. It did, however, enable construction of the Crabtree Valley mall which has become one of the major shopping centers in the city even though its parking lots, and even the mall itself, are flooded during heavy rains.

B. Everett Jordan Dam and Reservoir

Although this project had been authorized and begun before I entered state government, the department nonetheless had to cope with several issues related to it.

Originally the New Hope Dam and Reservoir, this project had a long, contentious history. It was originally authorized as a flood control project in response to serious flooding on the Cape Fear River in Fayetteville resulting from a tropical storm in August 1945. Sen. B. Everett Jordan supported this project, which was authorized in 1963 and, as planned by the U.S. Army Corps of Engineers, consisted of a large dam on New Hope Creek and part of the Haw River. However, landowners in the affected area, largely in eastern Chatham county, opposed the project because of the land it would take, including the small town of Bells that would be totally inundated. An alternative consisting of many smaller dams on tributaries of the Cape Fear was proposed by the Soil Conservation Service and was advanced by Representative Harold Cooley. Eventually the Corps of Engineers proposal, now named for Senator Jordan, was approved by Congress despite considerable debate about the validity of the economic analysis underlying the project and the poor quality of water that would be impounded in the reservoir. Legal challenges to the project, based largely on water quality issues, delayed construction for many years.

Construction was begun in 1973 with the dam completed in 1974. However, problems with the dam construction were encountered and the actual filling of the impoundment was not completed until 1983. NER's involvement in this project was minimal, largely since state approval and participation had been approved well before 1971.

Although Jordan Reservoir was never planned as a water supply, its water has been allocated by the state to several western Wake county municipalities. The predicted water quality problems have come to pass and by the early two thousands were serious enough to warrant attempts

107

by the state to develop plans to alleviate them. The measures proposed by state environmental regulators sought to limit nutrient runoff by controlling watershed development in the upper part of the reservoir and on streams draining into the reservoir. The plan, which had been through public hearings and administrative review, was ready for action by the Environmental Management Commission in 2013. At this point the legislature, responding to critics of the proposed land use controls, set the plan aside and replaced it with a "study" of the effectiveness of floating "solar bees" in reducing excess nutrients in the water. The "solar bees" are floating, solar-powered pumps designed to promote water aeration and to slow growth of polluting algae. Studies completed in 2015 showed them to be ineffective. Nonetheless, the legislature chose to continue the experiment, thus postponing the day of reckoning for Jordan Reservoir water quality. In 2016 the "solar bees" were declared ineffective by the state and removed. The 2017 legislature authorized a multi-million dollar "aeration" system that, hopefully would retard algal growth. Effective means for dealing with pollution in Jordan Reservoir now rest with the Environmental Management Commission and, ultimately, the legislature.

Falls Dam and Reservoir[28]

The Falls project, located ten miles north of Raleigh, was the most technically and politically difficult dam project, outside of the New River, that we dealt with during my years in NER. The project was authorized in 1965 (PL 89-298) for flood control, water supply, water quality, recreation, and fish and wildlife. Of all these purposes, none was more important than water supply. Even though the Corps of Engineers was not authorized to construct reservoirs in which water supply was the sole purpose, the Falls project from its inception was envisioned as the major, new water source that would provide for future economic growth of the city of Raleigh. All its proponents were motivated by that benefit alone. As far as that motivation was concerned, the project has more than served its purpose. Without it, Raleigh's growth would undoubtedly have been severely limited. With it, it has been explosive.

---

[28] An excellent discussion of this extremely complex project can be found in "The Battle for Falls Lake" written by Janet Steddum and published by her in 2007.

Actually, the dam proposed by the Corps of Engineers at Falls on the Neuse River was to be the second dam at that site. The explorer John Lawson passed by the site in 1701, describing water rushing down a series of rock outcroppings. A small community developed around the area during the middle 1700s and as the community grew the flow of water over the "falls" was utilized to run a grist mill and later a saw mill and a flour mill. A low wooden dam was built across the river, backing water up as much as ten miles behind it, providing more reliable water to power the mills. The largest of the mills was purchased in 1899, converted to a textile mill, and a granite dam built to provide additional water power. The mill never prospered and last operated in the late 1950s; the granite dam slowly fell into disrepair and deteriorated.

Motivated by the history of serious downstream flooding on the Neuse River and by Raleigh's limited water supply, the Corps of Engineers conducted a study from 1958-64. The result of this planning was the Neuse River Basin Study that served as the basis for congressional authorization of the project in 1965. Planning was guided by the various congressional authorizations under which the Corps of Engineers operated. These acts authorized the Corps (and other federal agencies) to include multiple purposes in the planning of their water development projects, including flood control (the original benefit), water supply, downstream water quality improvement, fish and wildlife enhancement, and recreation. To be viable, the benefits of a project, measured by impacts on local resources and users, must exceed its costs. Thus, in planning a project the Corps must develop a plan that integrates all potential benefits in a size and manner that exceeds not only costs to the federal budget for construction but also costs in the form of negative impacts to the environment and to local citizens. The authorized project was to cost about $18 million, would reduce flood damage downstream by fifty percent, regulate low flows for water quality enhancement, provide public recreation opportunities, and serve as a major new water source for Raleigh.

Ultimately, the Falls project incorporated almost 40,000 acres of land, of which only 12,000 represented land taken for the reservoir. Another 10,000 were taken to create the flood pool (the area around the lake to store flood waters and protect downstream interests from flooding). An additional 14,000 acres were taken for "freeboard" land, land that could be impacted during extreme storm events. These 36,000 acres collectively provided the five benefits for which the project was constructed. Local interests expressed strong desire for additional recreation benefits to be built into the project and after considerable discussion an additional 4,500 acres, so-called "separable lands" were included in the project. These lands became extremely controversial as they constituted an additional taking of private land by the government for a purpose that not all parties accepted. In addition, when costs and benefits of the project were calculated, recreation provide sixty-three percent of the total benefits. Much of this figure was attributable to the separable lands and they thus became crucial to the final federal approval of the project. Ironically, the fate of Raleigh's future water supply lay on the inclusion of these recreational benefits in the project's final plan.

Although this planning had taken place prior to the time I entered state government, NER did have to deal with two important aspects of it, the environmental impact statement (EIS) for the project and the state's provision of the matching funds required by federal law for the separable recreation lands. The first EIS, written in 1971, was only fifteen pages long and, contrary to the Corps' belief, failed utterly to meet the requirements of the impact statement provisions of the newly enacted Environmental Policy Act. Robert Finch, who was responsible for coordinating review of all EIS's within NER, wrote the department's comments, which flatly stated the EIS was inadequate and forwarded these to the State Clearinghouse. In the meantime, several citizen groups, particularly the Neuse Valley Association (NVA), the League of Women Voters, and the Sierra Club, also found the EIS inadequate and one, the NVA, sought an injunction in federal court to halt the project. In April of 1973 a federal judge denied the injunction but ordered a hearing on the adequacy of the EIS. By April 1974 the Corps had produced a new EIS about 2,000 pages long. Based on this document the federal judge ruled that the Corps had met the EIS requirements of NEPA and that the project could proceed.

However, the separable recreation lands continued to be a serious problem, particularly for Senator Jesse Helms who had defeated Nick Galafianakis in the fall 1972 election to fill the seat vacated by B. Everett Jordan. Helms opposed the project largely because its cost had ballooned to well over $100 hundred million. On those grounds he urged Raleigh to find another water source and, in November 1973, introduced a bill into the Senate that would remove the separable recreation lands from the project. Many believed that this bill, if passed, would kill the project because, with the separable recreation lands removed, the lowered cost/benefit ratio would make the project harder to justify. The problems raised by Helms' bill were exacerbated by the fact that prices for the land involved in the project were escalating dramatically, due to speculation on lands designated for inclusion. Privately, in conversations with the Secretary of the Army, Helms voiced support for the water supply portion of the project and the Corps agreed to begin acquisition of land on Beaverdam Creek which would allow construction of a temporary water supply for Raleigh.

Helms bill removing the separable recreation lands was defeated in committee in July 1974 essentially clearing the way for the project to be constructed. Because the project was by then so far behind schedule Raleigh provided $2.5 million to the Corps to allow it to impound Beaverdam Creek thus providing an emergency source of water. At one point, it became necessary for the Holshouser administration to reaffirm the agreement for cost-sharing for the separable recreation lands. This discussion was unpleasant and I can recall Col. Albert Costanzo, the Wilmington District chief, arguing that the small amount of money required each year was essentially like buying a house on time—almost as if we were getting Falls Lake with a credit card. We again pointed out that any administrative commitment made could not be binding even with the governor's signature. Nonetheless, the cost-sharing agreement was reaffirmed, more land acquisition took place, and construction began in 1976. Filling of the lake began in 1981 and was completed by 1983. Raleigh had its water supply and the Triangle had a fine, new recreation facility.

As completed the earthen dam at Falls stretched over 1,900 feet and had a top elevation of 291.5 feet above mean sea level. The lake itself extends twenty-eight miles up the Neuse River to just past the confluence of the Eno and Flat Rivers in Durham county with small embayments extending into Granville county. At the top of the conservation pool the lake has a shoreline of over 175 miles and covers 12,400 acres. The portion of the lake in Wake county is generally narrow and relatively deep, reflecting the surrounding topography. In Durham county, on the other hand, the lake is relatively broad and shallow and subject to episodes of low water and poor water quality. Protection of water quality in the lake has been an issue since its completion, largely due to continued residential growth in the Wake county portion of the watershed. When NER was involved in its discussions with the Corps about the issue of water quality we suggested that the Corps should include a requirement that, in exchange for its water supply, Raleigh and Wake county must enact strict land use controls on the watershed of the lake. The Corps refused to do this, stating that it was not within their statutory authority to place such a requirement on local governments. Although the Corps' argument was probably correct, the failure to enact land use controls early in the life of the Falls project has caused great difficulties for subsequent Raleigh and Wake county governments. In addition, serious droughts, most recently in 2005 and 2008, have shown that it is difficult for Raleigh and the towns it serves to meet demand from Falls Lake alone, forcing the city to enact water conservation measures and to begin the search for another, supplemental water supply.

No issues with which we in NER were concerned while I worked there better illustrate the complex interactions of federal, state, and local governments, local economic development interests, local interest groups representing a wide range of constituencies, technical analyses of the economic and environmental impacts of development projects, and pure, raw politics than do the dams with which we were involved.

My tenure in NER coincided with the decline in construction of major public works projects by the federal government. The dramatic growth in numbers and size of public works projects began in the depth of the Great Depression of the 1930s. These projects were intended to put people to work first and develop the nation's natural resources second. This program of public works continued into the post-World War II years with a scope that reflected the general boom economies of those years. As the environmental movement developed steam during the 1960s, and as questions were raised about how long and to what degree the federal government should continue its financial involvement, questions raised about these projects became more intense.

One project on the drawing board but never seriously discussed while I worked in state government, the Randleman Dam and Lake, came back to life, so to speak, in the 1980s because of the Piedmont Triad's need for an additional water supply. Randleman Dam was originally proposed by the Corps of Engineers in 1937 with funds first authorized in 1968. Studies done through 1980 indicated an estimated cost of $135 million and in 1987 the Corps withdrew support as costs were estimated to exceed flood control benefits. Later in 1987 the Piedmont Triad Regional Water Authority proposed $57 million to construct the dam as a regional water supply Environmental impact statements were prepared and a final statement was issued in 2000. In April 2001, the Corps issued a permit for construction which began in August of that year. Construction was completed and the lake was opened to recreation in March of 2010. By 2011 drinking water was being withdrawn from the lake and treated for use at a facility built near the lake. Randleman Lake covers 3,700 surface acres with another 2,975 acres contained in a 200-foot buffer strip around the lake.

Oddly enough, I became involved with this project during my two-year tenure on the Environmental Management Commission. The commission had to approve construction of the lake and grant state permits before the Corps of Engineers would act. I served as one of three commission members who chaired hearings on plans for the dam and lake precedent to commission action. Several concerns about the proposal had been raised, one involving the relatively narrow size of the buffer and another concerning the possible impact of an abandoned Seaboard Chemical site in Jamestown. The site had been the location of a facility that treated toxic wastes and which had been closed because of numerous spills. The location of the site on the Deep River immediately above the upper limits of the proposed lake raised serious questions about impacts on drinking water quality to be withdrawn from the lake. I considered these two issues important enough to vote against approval of construction of the lake.

Randleman Lake is now serving its purpose as the major water source for the Piedmont Triad area. Traces of pollutants, probably coming from the abandoned chemical site which is now being remediated, occur in lake water. They are highest in the upper lake, but at levels that are not deemed harmful. Furthermore, they diminish downstream toward the point where drinking water is withdrawn. The lake is also an important recreation facility for the Triad region and stories on the internet indicate that the lake is a prime bass fishing site. In retrospect, perhaps I was wrong to oppose the project.

Chapter 11

Coastal Area Management Act

The 1960s were a time of rapidly growing concern with management of coastal and ocean resources. Much of this concern grew out of the destructive impact of a series of devastating storms on the east and gulf coasts of the United States as well as concern for extensive human exploitation of marine and coastal resources. The storms dealt serious damage to coastal residential and commercial development, leading to staggering economic losses. Alterations associated with human use (ditching, filling, housing developments) reduced the area of many coastal habitats such as marshlands and dunes. In addition, research was being conducted on the ecological functions of estuaries and their fringing salt marshes. This research demonstrated the importance of salt marshes as nurseries and sources of energy for fish and shellfish inhabiting estuaries. Many of these fish and shellfish species were important both for human consumption and as the base of coastal economies.

Because of these impacts considerable governmental attention began to be devoted to managing the effects of nature and to limiting human impacts on estuarine and coastal environments. The first federal legislation dealing with regulation of the coastal environment was three sections of the Rivers and Harbors Act of 1899. These dealt primarily with navigation by allowing the Corps of Engineers to regulate bridge construction, dredging and filling, and deposition of refuse in navigable waters. For sixty years, these provisions were used primarily to protect navigation with no consideration of their use to control environmental impacts. However, by the mid-1960s these authorities were enlarged by court case decisions that extended the definition of navigable waters broadly enough to allow regulation of dredging and filling to protect fish and wildlife habitat and to regulate deposit of pollutants (defined as refuse by the courts). Amendments in 1958 of the Fish and Wildlife Coordination Act of 1934 required federal agencies working in the coastal zone to include impacts on fish and wildlife in analyses of their proposed projects. A series of studies (National Estuarine Pollution Study, National Estuarine Study), an interagency committee, and the work of the Commission on Marine Resources and Engineering in the late 1960s all reached a similar recommendation that a national coastal zone management program was necessary.

By the late 1960s several northeastern states had developed regulatory programs designed to limit further destruction of marshland and California was carrying out an intense debate about creating a coastal management program. In 1969 North Carolina had passed its own act regulating dredging and filling of coastal salt marshes. A realization clearly emerged from these regulatory efforts and studies that coastal management problems could not be resolved with a local and piece-meal approach. A national effort, accompanied by comprehensive efforts by states, was necessary.

In 1969 a coastal zone management bill was introduced in the federal Senate, followed shortly by legislation on the same subject from the Nixon administration. These proposals were debated and amended over a period of three years with the result being the federal Coastal Zone Management Act of 1972. As a side light, it is worth noting that at the same time the drafting of a management plan for land and water uses in coastal areas was taking place, a similar effort was devoted to developing a national land use planning program. This latter effort, housed in the Department of Interior, never really got off the ground despite the fact that the Nixon administration promoted it and argued that all national land use planning, including that for the coastal zone, should be located in

Interior.[29] The Congress, on the other hand, took the position that because what regulatory machinery the federal government had for marine and coastal resources was in the Department of Commerce, the coastal zone management program should be located there. Congress won this debate and finally passed the Coastal Zone Management Act (CZMA) of 1972 with authority for implementation in the Department of Commerce.

The requirements of CZMA spell out the framework of a national, but state-centered, program of coastal land and water management. The act is permissive in the sense that it does not require the individual states to implement the act and provides no sanctions for a failure to participate. However, in a defaulting state the requirements of the act were to be carried out by the federal government. Moreover, the act does provide incentives to the states in the form of grants to support the development of a state program and, perhaps more important, includes a provision that when a state plan is approved, after full consultation with affected federal agencies, those agencies must administer their programs in a manner consistent with the state plan (a so-called "federal consistency provision"). With these "carrots" as inducement, all coastal states (including states with Great Lake shorelines) eventually participated. In developing its plan, a state is required to: define the boundary of its coastal zone; inventory its legal management authorities; define permissible uses in its coastal zone; describe and define "areas of particular concern"; describe the organization of its program; provide for public participation and intergovernmental involvement in

---

[29] The proposal from the Nixon administration for a national land use program is the closest the nation has ever come, and probably ever will come, to such a program. Representatives of the administration, in appearances before Congress, were supremely confident that such a program could, and would, be developed but it never really gained any traction. Outside of the obvious objections to any land use planning, particularly on a national basis, much of the disaffection in Congress centered in the administration's insistence that the program be in Interior. This same debate took place during discussion of the Coastal Zone Management Act with Congress clearly expressing a preference for Commerce as its location. Part of this preference stemmed from the fact that most national programs for management of marine and coastal resources were in Commerce; part of it also stemmed from a feeling that Commerce might be more inclined toward implementation of the act in a manner sensitive to development interests.

development of the plan; and carry out appropriate consultation with all affected federal agencies.

*****

Background and Passage of CAMA

North Carolina's coastal management program emerged from a period of intense discussion and study of coastal resource management issues paralleling that at the federal level. In 1969 the General Assembly passed both an act regulating dredging and filling in coastal marshes and a bill requiring study of development of a management plan for the state's coastal area and of the means for its implementation. William Turner, Director of the Department of Administration, appointed a "Blue Ribbon" panel to carry out the study. The panel was chaired by Leigh Hammond, one of Turner's assistant directors, and included, among others, members of Turner's own staff, Tom Linton, the Director of the Division of Marine Fisheries in C&D who was responsible for administering the new dredge and fill act, and Milton Heath from the Institute of Government at UNC-Chapel Hill who had drafted several important pieces of environmental legislation. There was some unseemly squabbling between Administration and C&D over which should be the lead agency in development and ultimate administration of the plan. This continued throughout Scott's administration, due largely to the fact that Turner and Scott were close and most efforts of a long-range planning nature were delegated to Administration. This friction disappeared once Scott went out of office and NER, because of its statutory authority to manage most coastal resources, became the lead agency.

Planning continued from 1969-72 and, with the aid of consultants, particularly Milton Heath, several iterations of a coastal management plan were completed. No move was made to introduce a bill into the General Assembly until the beginning of the 1973 session, the first of Holshouser's tenure as governor. A bill, the Coastal Area Management Act (CAMA), was introduced in March 1973 with William J. Staton handling it in the Senate and Willis Whichard in the House. The bill proved too controversial for action in 1973 and it was agreed among legislators, NER, and the governor's office to hold the bill and further refine it. Several hearings were held in the next few months and NER staff members and key legislators took a trip to Maine and Vermont to talk with state officials who were responsible for administering coastal zone management and land use planning legislation that had just passed in both states. Because of this new information several key changes were made in the draft bill. The definition of the inland boundary of the coastal zone based on tidal data was replaced by a criterion based on inland encroachment of salt water[30] and a larger, more clearly defined role for local government was spelled

---

[30]   The definition of the coastal area was crucial to the success of the bill. It was clear from the very beginning that counties should be used as the governmental units included in the act; no portions of counties would be included (or excluded). To avoid being unconstitutional as a violation of the equal protection provisions of the constitution, a local bill (which the coastal area bill was because it applied to only a portion of the state's 100 counties) had to establish that it pertained to a "class" defined by certain conditions that pertained there and nowhere else and that the class contained all possible counties that possessed those conditions. There was much debate among the drafters of the bill as to what criteria should be used; tidal effects, salt water, proximity to the Atlantic Ocean and coastal sounds, and even certain unique coastal ecosystems were considered. The original bill included all counties bordering on the Atlantic Ocean or on a coastal sound and used tidal encroachment on tributary rivers as the inland boundary. Discussions indicated that tidal encroachment would not stand up as there were rivers on which tidal effects had been modified by man and others on which tidal effects were observed far inland in counties that no reasonable person would accept as being "coastal." So, after considerable thought salt water encroachment, for which there were objective data, was used as the ruling criterion for the inland boundary. As I was drafting the final language for this section of the bill right before Christmas 1973 I got a call from Bill Staton during which he asked how work on the definition was coming. I told him what we had decided and he said "fine, but just don't include Columbus, because I can't handle Arthur." Fortunately, application of the salt water criterion did leave out Columbus county but I never mentioned that call or the discussion to anyone. To this day, I don't know what we would have done if Columbus was included as Arthur Williamson, its representative, was a highly influential legislator and if Bill Staton couldn't deal with him it is a certainty no one in the executive branch could have. In the final bill, counties were not named. The governor was required to name by Executive Proclamation those that met the qualifying criteria. The names of the counties included in the proclamation were added in later legislation.

out. A committee substitute was prepared and submitted by Staton and Whichard at the beginning of the 1974 legislative session.[31]

The next three months were marked by intensive debate behind closed doors in the legislature. There was strong support for the bill almost everywhere but on the coast (no surprise) and those coastal legislators who opposed it did so strongly. Some legislators opposed the bill on general principle—little could be done to change their position. Other opposition centered on the requirements of certain key provisions of the act including the composition of the commission named to oversee the program (Democrats wanted assurance that Republicans would not dominate it), on the description of "areas of environmental concern" and whether prime farmland and forest land should be included, coordination of the added regulations on coastal development, and on the sense that the proposed program was an assumption of local government authority. Those of us who supported the bill, and that included Governor Holshouser and Secretary Harrington, together with Milton Heath worked to develop language that spoke to many of these concerns; others simply could not be compromised. In the end, we felt these concerns were dealt with as fairly as possible so the whole issue boiled down to a political slugging match between supporters and opponents, most of whom were coastal legislators.

---

[31]   At almost the same time I received the call from Staton about the coastal area definition I got a call from the governor. As usual, Holshouser put through his own calls so I was caught a bit off guard. The purpose of his call was to ask me if I would draft a piece of legislation for him that treated the mountain area (he was a mountain man) in the same way we were proposing to handle the coastal area. In other words, please draft him a Mountain Area Management Act. I told him I would but that it would probably be a marginally-credible piece of work at best. The most serious problem was finding a criterion to define "the mountain area". Other serious problems centered on critical areas and certain key features of the coastal bill that did not lend themselves well to transposition to the mountains. I did the best I could over Christmas vacation and sent the bill on down to his office. My recollection is that it was formally drafted into legislative form and that it may even have been introduced. However, it is certain that it was never seriously considered and the idea has not been brought up since.

It quickly became apparent that the governor's support and his ability to deliver the Republican minority in the legislature en bloc would be critical for the passage of the bill. There were fifteen Republicans in the Senate and thirty-five in the House. If virtually all those votes supported the bill, then well less than half of the Democrats in each house needed to support the bill for it to pass. As the end of the session approached, Staton and Whichard both felt they had the votes needed for passage but it was still not a sure thing. At one point Whichard called and asked if I would attend an evening session of the House where the bill was scheduled for discussion. Whichard arranged for me to have the "privilege of the floor" which meant I could sit with him during debate. At one point a question arose about the definition of the coastal area and Whichard asked the Speaker to allow me to explain the matter. So, for several minutes, with two legislators holding a large map I had brought, I did my best to explain how the coastal area was defined. The bill was subjected to a blizzard of amendments in both houses leading one veteran legislator to say that it was the most amended bill in the history of the legislature. The bill did pass on the next to last day of the session and all of us in NER involved breathed a sigh of relief. Although the recorded margins of approval were larger, actual support of the bill was nearer twenty-six to twenty-four in the Senate and sixty-five to fifty-five in the House. There was no celebration in NER, however, as we realized that now we would have to implement the bill with all the potential pitfalls it contained.

Implementation of CAMA

The version of CAMA that passed the legislature did not differ in broad outline from the version that was submitted in early 1973. However, there were a number of changes made largely to mollify both the concern of Democrats that the program might be a vehicle for tipping political power toward the Republicans (this never even came close to being an issue in implementation) and local governments concern with state assumption of their authority. The principal features of the bill were: a scientifically-defensible definition of the coastal zone; supervision of the program by a Coastal Resources Commission of fifteen members, each having a specified background with thirteen having to reside in the coastal area; an advisory council of forty-seven persons appointed mostly by local governments[32]; a requirement that each county (or any other smaller governmental unit that opted to do so) prepare a land use plan in accordance with requirements set out by the commission; identification by the commission of areas of environmental concern (AECs) with permits issued by the state required for development in them; a requirement for coordination of permits issued for work in the coastal area, particularly state-federal permit coordination; and a sunset provision effective in 1981. CAMA was passed without funds for implementation and a large part of the funds supporting the staff and program that implemented the act came from grants to the state via the federal Coastal Zone Management Act. To continue to qualify for these funds, the state had to report annually on the status and implementation of its program.

The first act of implementation involved preparation of the list of counties included in the coastal area as defined in the act. Mindful of the possible court scrutiny of implementation of the definition I compiled a list of all possible counties and whether they bordered on the Atlantic Ocean or a coastal sound, had certain soils or ecosystems that were unique to the coastal area, and met the salt water intrusion criterion. The result was a list of twenty counties that were submitted to the governor who notified, as required, local government units that they fell under the purview of the act. Then, using a table of random numbers I assigned the various backgrounds of the commissioners spelled out in the act to specific counties and prepared the necessary correspondence for the governor to send to local government units informing them of their opportunity to nominate persons who the governor would then consider for naming to twelve of the fifteen seats on the commission. We also recommended to him names that he could consider for the three seats he alone had the authority to name and began the solicitation from local governments and state agencies of the names of persons the commission could consider in naming the members of the Coastal Area Advisory Council.

---

[32]   The commission and advisory council were relatively large in comparison with other similar bodies. Their size was a result of the need to ensure adequate representation of the various interests involved in coastal management and of the need to reassure Democrat legislators that Republicans would not control them. The size of both bodies was reduced by the 2013 legislature.

The commission met for the first time in Beaufort in July 1974 and began the work of implementation of the program. Staff for the commission was provided by NER from the Division of Marine Fisheries and from the Office of Marine Affairs in the Department of Administration; it was organized into a Division of Coastal Management in NER. Tom Linton, Director of Marine Fisheries, was named as director of the division. Linton had a small staff, but working with other members of NER and Administration the first steps were taken toward developing the guidelines for preparing land use plans and identifying areas of environmental concern. For various reasons, Linton fell out of favor with the Secretary of NER and others in the departmental administration and, within a year he left state government for a two-year appointment in coastal management in Australia.[33] In truth, he left just a few days before he would have been fired.

Guidelines for preparation of land use plans were prepared relatively quickly and local governments began the planning process. Plans were financed by small grants from the state with funds from the federal CZMA. Plans had to include statements of policy, development standards, an inventory of existing land uses, land classification according to a system developed by the commission, and an explanation of permissible land uses. Considering the low level of expertise in most local governments, and the small number of state employees available to assist, the fact that the first round of land use plans was completed by 1976 is remarkable. Everyone involved recognized the weaknesses in the initial planning guidelines and the first plans and revision of the guidelines began immediately. A second

---

[33] An amusing incident explains part of Linton's managerial problems. Secretary Harrington insisted that part of each commission meeting be set aside for public comment. At the first such session, the commission Chair asked if anyone wished to comment. The very first person to speak was one of Linton's staff, a young lady with a rather feisty disposition. Her comment was to Harrington and asked him "why no women had been named to the commission." Harrington almost bit off the end of his pipe and provided an answer that obviously didn't satisfy her. After the meeting, he cornered me and told me to tell Linton to make sure that his staff didn't provide negative comments at future meetings. I think Linton's fate was sealed right then; Linton himself probably realized he was on thin ice making the opportunity in Australia more attractive.

round of plans under the new, strengthened guidelines was completed in 1981-82.

Identification of AECs was a complex process that occurred in two phases and took slightly more than four years. The first phase, identification of Interim AECs, took place relatively quickly and involved naming of those areas essentially defined in the act (e.g., coastal marshes, dunes), and other areas that obviously fit the AEC criteria. With this interim designation available for public reaction, the commission began the difficult task of making the final designations. An early decision involved whether to name large, inclusive areas (outer banks, public trust waters) or to name more sharply defined areas. Because the wording of the act seemed to support the latter, the final AEC designations were a combination of broad areas such as coastal marshes and more narrowly defined specific areas such as inlet hazard areas (the area on either side of a migrating inlet). In all cases, the AECs designated were peculiar to the coastal area to avoid any possible court case based on a violation of the equal protection provision of the constitution. Final designations were made in 1978 and the regulatory program instituted on March 1, 1978. It is safe to say that fine tuning of the AEC concept and its implementation has continued throughout the history of the coastal management program.

With passage of CAMA, NER began the work necessary to develop the state program of coastal management required to meet approval under the requirements of the federal CZMA. This was a long, drawn-out process which continued well after I left state government in August 1976. It ultimately required an executive order and was finally approved on September 1, 1978.

By that time, interestingly, I had become a member of the Coastal Resources Commission and came to play an entirely different role in the program (see Part III). Shortly after I resigned my position in NER, Governor Holshouser called me to his office and told me that he intended to appoint me to one of the three slots designated for the governor to name. I argued that he should not do this because in my role as one of the people most responsible for development of the program I had become a lightning rod for those who wished to attack the program. He effectively told me to forget it, that he was going to appoint me. So, in the fall of 1976 I became a member of the commission and stayed a member until 1989 when I moved to the Environmental Management Commission for two years. To review the history of the coastal management program further is another story for another day. Suffice it to say that the commission and the staff members working with it met all the targets and virtually all the challenges entailed in implementing the program. Those achievements are testimony to the dedication and hard work, particularly of the staff, involved in that effort. Sometimes I felt that the staff involved didn't understand that they really couldn't save the world or at least North Carolina's coastal portion of it.

The Court Test of CAMA's Constitutionality

Everyone involved with CAMA from its drafting on understood that sooner or later the constitutionality of the act would be contested. Our drafting kept that eventuality clearly in mind and language was chosen carefully so that issues involved in constitutionality, at least to the extent we could anticipate them, were dealt with during drafting. Somewhat to everyone's surprise the first test came relatively early when, in 1977, Carteret county and several citizens of Carteret and Onslow counties, sought a declaratory judgment ruling on CAMA's constitutionality. The plaintiffs were consolidated and the case, Adams v. Dept. of NER, was heard during late August 1977 in Carteret county with a special judge chosen (Ralph Walker an ex-Guilford county attorney) to hear the case. The plaintiffs sought a declaratory judgment that the act was unconstitutional based on four contentions: that CAMA was a local act denied by the state constitution; that the delegation of authority to the commission to set guidelines for development and name AECs was vague, arbitrary, and without sufficient legislative standards; that the guidelines adopted by the commission were arbitrary and deprived plaintiffs of their property without due process of law; and, that sections of the act authorized warrantless searches.

The first of these issues was the most crucial because, if CAMA were determined to be an illegal local act, then all the rest of the program would fall. Thus, much of the testimony was devoted to it. I was called to testify and spent about an hour explaining how the coastal area was defined and how the counties involved differed from all other eighty counties in certain important ways. Plaintiff's attorney questioned me and several staff members at length and it quickly became obvious he was largely fishing for something to hang his case on and that it was unlikely he would get it from any of the state's witnesses. In fact, he did not seem terribly well prepared for trial. Our testimony was based on the thought processes that were used in drafting the act and largely centered on issues that we had discussed at length among ourselves and with the state's attorneys. The trial lasted about two and a half days and shortly thereafter Judge Walker issued an order denying the plaintiff's request for declaratory judgment and ruling for the state on every issue.

Judge Walker's decision was, by agreement of both parties, appealed directly to the state Supreme Court. In 1978 the Supreme Court, in a 5-1 decision, upheld Judge Walker's opinion. The court found that the coastal area did have unique properties and that all the counties included were all those in the state possessing those unique properties. Therefore, the act was a "general law" and that "the unique, fragile, and irreplaceable nature of the coastal zone and its significance to the public welfare amply justify the reasonableness of special legislative treatment."[34] The court further ruled that the statement of legislative findings and the criteria for defining AECs were as "specific as circumstances would allow" thus providing sufficient legislative intent to guide the commission in its decision-making. The last two claims were dismissed as not "ripe" for decision because the final AECs had not been adopted and thus no regulatory action pursuant to that authority had been taken.

The net result of the court case was a clear finding that CAMA was constitutional and that the apparatus to enforce it was guided by adequate legislative findings and statements of intent. In retrospect, the timing of the case was peculiar in that it was brought to trial before any regulatory action had been taken. Furthermore, the plaintiffs were not well served by their attorney either in his advice as to when to try the case or in his conduct of examination of witnesses during the trial. In short, the plaintiffs provided the state with an almost immediate elimination of any question as to whether CAMA was an illegal local act and whether the commission was operating with satisfactory legislative guidance. Clarification of these two points allowed the commission and staff to pursue implementation without having the specter of constitutionality hanging unresolved over their heads.

---

[34] Supreme Court Justice J. Frank Huskins in "Adams v. Dept. of NER" 295 N.C. 693 (1978).

Those of us connected with the program always felt that a case brought later, after AECs and permits were in place and being administered, would have been a sterner legal test of the act. No significant attempt has been made since 1978 to strike down any of the key provisions of CAMA.

There are many lessons to be learned from the drafting, passage, and implementation of North Carolina's Coastal Area Management Act. Some of these lessons are political and others are strategic. However, so much of what happened during the drafting and legislative debate was so strongly influenced by the uniqueness of the circumstances that existed at the time that all lessons must be interpreted with that fact in mind.

The Coastal Area Management Act could not have been conceived, drafted, and passed if the years during which that happened were not years when national and state concern with the environment, particularly that of the coastal zone, created fertile conditions for what by any standard was for North Carolina ground-breaking legislation. The late 1960s and early 1970s were a unique time in the United States. Interest in management of natural resources, land preservation, and protection of the environment were at an all-time high. This interest allowed the passage of much of what is now the core of our national environmental management and land protection legislation. North Carolina reflected this national trend with passage of the amendment to the state constitution dealing with conservation of natural resources and the State Environmental Policy Act in 1971. This was preceded by passage in 1968 of an act to regulate mining and by later passage of state legislation dealing with water pollution, sedimentation control, establishment of a state scenic river system, the organization of NER to bring resource management responsibilities into parity with those for economic development, and of course CAMA. There is also no doubt that passage of the federal Coastal Zone Management Act provided not only a legislative model for CAMA but a critical source of funding for implementation that never would have been forthcoming from the state.

It is also true that the people of North Carolina, generally, have an emotional attachment to the state's coast. Travel to the coast for holidays, at least by those wealthy enough to afford it, is a summer tradition for residents of the inner coastal plain and piedmont. Thus, the public purposes represented by protection of the beauty and accessibility of the coast resonated with legislators from the populous piedmont leading them to support CAMA almost unanimously. In addition, residents of the coast have a deeply imbedded way of life that depends almost entirely on the region's resources. Even though their inherent mistrust of governmental authority led many coastal residents to oppose CAMA, the debate over the legislation and its objectives made coastal residents increasingly aware of the importance of the coast's resources to perpetuation of their way of life. Many thoughtful residents of the coast soon came to be among the strongest supporters of CAMA.

The drafting of CAMA illustrates the extent to which it is necessary to go when seeking passage of a controversial piece of legislation. Even though passage of CAMA was in large part due to the care taken in its drafting and despite all the steps taken to deal with concepts that were new to North Carolina in the end passage of the act was, at least in the Senate, by a razor thin margin. It took at least three years of discussion within state government and numerous versions of a statute before any of CAMA's supporters felt comfortable with introduction of a version into the legislature. As pointed out, great attention was paid to the concepts in CAMA that might have been considered in conflict with the state constitution. The statute was literally written with a copy of the constitution always at hand. There is no doubt that the care given to the definition of the coastal zone allowed the state supreme court to declare CAMA constitutional. The legislators handling the act, Bill Staton in the Senate and Bill Whichard in the House, showed great wisdom in not pushing for passage after introduction in 1973. The year that elapsed during the two 1973 legislative sessions allowed for extensive public discussion of the act and revision of some of its most controversial provisions. Finally, Staton and Whichard, working with the administration of NER, showed a willingness to compromise on key provisions in a way that helped some legislators support the act and helped others who could never support it to realize that at least their concerns had been considered. Finally, the support of the governor was crucial. Despite his populist leanings, Holshouser recognized that more planning in the management of natural resources would be needed in the future than had existed in the past. His support for a Mountain Area Management Act, despite its still-born introduction in 1974 and subsequent failure to move, reflects this belief. Holshouser's ability to deliver over ninety percent of the Republican vote in support of CAMA made passage possible; without it CAMA could never have passed.

The history of implementation of CAMA following 1974 is a mixed bag. There have been genuine successes, such as a prohibition against beach hardening, accomplished in the face of some potent opposition, as well as implementation of the beach access program authorized by the 1981 legislature. Perhaps the simple fact that the machinery of CAMA is still in place and that several cycles of land use planning in the twenty coastal counties have taken place represents a major success. Despite the predictions of its opponents, nothing in the act has prevented development on the coast. The pace of development is clearly more strongly affected by economic trends than by regulatory requirements. In a few cases CAMA has managed to find itself in the position of making, and supporting, a poor decision. In the late 1980s when erosion seriously threatened to undermine the Cape Hatteras Light House the commission voted to support an effort to protect the light house with a hardened structure rather than support moving it. I voted with the commission. I think we voted the way we did because none of us took seriously that it might be possible to move a 180-foot masonry structure. However, as time moved on I eventually found myself appointed to an university committee charged by the chancellor (at the request of the National Park Service) with assessing the feasibility of moving the lighthouse. Presentations made to the committee and the guidance of several engineers on the committee convinced us that moving the lighthouse was not only feasible but also the preferred way to accomplish its long-term protection. In due course, the lighthouse was moved in less than thirty days with no difficulty whatsoever and it is now safe and sound at least 1,500 feet from the ocean.

The CAMA has had several brushes with legislative change since 1974. In 1981 the sunset provision was removed and two legislative studies were authorized. One, conducted by the Legislative Committee on Agency Review as part of a larger review of over 60 programs, recommended some relatively minor changes that were adopted in 1983. The other authorized the Legislative Review Commission to study CAMA rules and regulations and recommend changes, if any, to the 1983 legislature. No dramatic changes resulted from this study either. Perhaps the major legislative change in CAMA took place in 2013 when, as part of an overhaul of virtually all regulatory commissions, the legislature reduced the membership of the Coastal Resources Commission from 15 to 13 members and altered the backgrounds of the commissioners to provide for greater representation from coastal development and more limited input from environmental interests. It is, of course, too early to know what impact this change will have on the program. In addition, the 2015 legislature in its budget bill instructed the commission to modify its prohibition against hardening of the beach environment by allowing "temporary erosion control structures" on segments of threatened beach. It also specified that the commission "may" issue up to six permits for terminal groins at inlets and that two of these may be issued for Bogue and New River inlets.

Chapter 12

The Trans-mountain Road in the Smokies:
the Road to Nowhere

Although the issue of construction of a road in the Great Smoky Mountain National Park to settle a long-standing dispute between Swain county and the federal government was not resolved during my time in state government, we did take a stab at resolution. Thus, it is worth recounting that modest effort here. The issue was (still is) so controversial at the federal, state, and local levels and has defied resolution for so long it is also appropriate to discuss the larger issue here. It is an excellent example of how government agency interests differ and how public opinion can change during the life of an issue in such a way as to make its resolution almost impossible, at least until time has allowed a complete change in the cast of characters.

*****

The story begins way back in the early 1900s with creation of the Aluminum Company of America (ALCOA) and its construction of a smelter near Maryville in eastern Tennessee. Because aluminum smelting and production involves enormous amounts of electricity ALCOA set out to create a source of electricity in the nearby mountains of North Carolina. In 1919 Cheoah Dam and lake, the first of these generating facilities, was completed on the Little Tennessee River near where it crosses the state line; Lake Cheoah extended over six miles east (upstream) on the Little Tennessee in North Carolina.

In the mid-1920s Swain county issued bonds to finance construction of a road, NC 288, on the north shore of the Little Tennessee from Bryson City to the North Carolina-Tennessee state line. The road was built and Swain county began to pay off the bonds.

In 1933 The Tennessee Valley Authority (TVA) was created by Congress and authorized to develop the resources of the valley, including western North Carolina, for multiple purposes including flood control, navigation, and power production. In 1934 Congress passed legislation establishing the Great Smoky Mountains National Park with Tennessee and North Carolina contributing substantial sums toward acquisition of land for the park. By the late 1930s, ALCOA needed additional electricity and its search led it to apply for a permit to construct Fontana Dam and lake. In 1941 ALCOA and TVA reached an agreement by which ALCOA transferred to TVA all the land it had acquired for the Fontana Dam project in exchange for guarantees of future reliable electricity from TVA.

The beginning of World War II suddenly made the aluminum production capacity of ALCOA a matter of strategic priority. Because ALCOA could not raise its production without additional power, the Fontana project thus became a high priority for TVA. In early 1942 TVA began construction of Fontana Dam making clear that NC 288, still being paid for by Swain county, would be flooded within two years. To compensate Swain county for its lost road, TVA, the National Park Service, the State of North Carolina, and the county entered an agreement that provided 1) for a road along the north shore of Fontana Lake that would replace NC 288, and 2) that all land acquired by TVA between the then current boundary of the Park and the north shore of Fontana Lake would be transferred to the Park. Fontana Lake began filling in 1944 and NC 288 thus became no longer usable.

Once the war ended, the various parties to the agreement began to fulfill their commitments. TVA transferred about 44,000 acres of land to the Park Service and completed a mile of the new north shore road east from Fontana Dam and North Carolina completed a section of road from Bryson City west to the park boundary. One matter that later became significant was that TVA's transfer of land to the Park Service cut off access to many family cemeteries and caused others to be relocated. The plan was that the new road along the north shore of Fontana Lake would provide access to these cemeteries. In the early 1960s the Park Service began construction on the north shore road from the state road at Bryson City into the park[35], completing a six-mile stretch that ended in a 1,200-foot tunnel. At this point construction on the road was stopped by environmental problems and by

---

[35] This segment of road and tunnel are now well-known as "The Road to Nowhere" and are famous as a tourist attraction and as a monument (at least in the eyes of the residents of Swain county) to the failure of the federal government to fulfill its part of the 1943 agreement.

bitter opposition from the North Carolina Wildlife Federation. Exposure of rocks of the Anakeesta formation by construction led to creation by rain water of sulfuric acid which had obvious negative impacts on water quality. In addition, fish and wildlife interests believed that completion of the entire north shore road across the mouths of Eagle, Hazel, and Forney Creeks would destroy the value of these prime trout streams.

With construction of the north shore road at a standstill, the Park Service sought ways to fulfill its part of the 1943 agreement. At the annual Fontana Conservation Roundup in 1965 Park Service Director George Hartzog proposed an alternative in the form of a trans-mountain road from Bryson City, NC to Townsend, TN. Hartzog argued that such a road would increase tourist travel into Bryson City and thus would meet the intent of the 1943 agreement. I was in the audience for his talk. There were also many wilderness devotees present and when Hartzog made his proposal to say the audience was dumbfounded would be an understatement. Since there was strong support for wilderness designation for the Smokies and given that the proposed road would have bisected the largest remaining block of potential wilderness in the eastern United States, Hartzog's proposal was, to put it mildly, not well received by the conservation community. The result was a bitter, drawn out fight in which Swain county and North Carolina sided with the trans-mountain road and the conservation-wilderness community fought it vigorously. Eventually, the proposal was killed by Interior Secretary Stuart Udall. Proponents of the trans-mountain road raised the proposal again to Walter Hickel, President Nixon's Interior secretary, but eventually Nat Reed, an Interior assistant secretary, declared that there would be no trans-mountain road effectively killing the concept for good.

However, the 1943 agreement remained unfulfilled and with each change of administration some effort was made to resolve the issue. In 1975 Governor Holshouser and NER Secretary Jim Harrington agreed to try to resolve the matter. They conferred with conservation groups and representatives of Swain county and arrived at a ten-point agreement involving the state and the National Park Service. I attended the discussions and contributed little except an occasional reminder that none of the roads proposed up to that point should be considered part of the solution. The proposal was basically an economic development plan for Swain county.

The state agreed to prepare the economic development plan and to build connectors from Bryson City and Ela to an extended Blue Ridge Parkway. The Park Service agreed to extend the Blue Ridge Parkway from Cherokee to Bryson City[36] and to build visitor facilities at the end of the "road to nowhere." Although steps were taken to implement the elements of the plan, time ran out on the Holshouser administration and the plan died. Its death was hastened by Senator Jesse Helms' adamant refusal to accept any alternative to the 1943 agreement that did not provide better access for families in the Bryson City area to their family cemeteries located in the park. The fact that the Park Service was providing once-a-year access to the cemeteries seemed to satisfy no one including Sen. Helms. In addition, several other key members of Congress took the view that there would never be a wilderness bill for the Smokies until the 1943 agreement was, in some way, resolved.

As time passed the leadership in Swain county slowly came to the realization that the terms of the 1943 agreement would likely never be met by construction of another road anywhere. They began to consider alternatives seriously and the concept of a cash settlement to the county slowly emerged as a reasonable and feasible solution. In 1980 the Secretary of Interior supported a $9.5 million cash settlement in lieu of completing a road. In 1987 the House of Representatives passed a bill declaring virtually all the Smokies as wilderness and providing for a $9.5 million cash payment to Swain county to settle the issue. This bill was held up in the Senate by Senator Helms who, joined by then Congressman Charles Taylor, won approval in 2000 for $16 million toward construction of the North Shore Road. In 2003, after Helms retirement from the Senate, the Swain county commissioners passed a resolution calling for a cash settlement of $52 million in lieu of completion of the north shore road; this proposal for a cash settlement was later supported by North Carolina Governor Mike Easley.

No further action was taken until 2010 when then Congressman Heath Shuler, a native of Bryson City, worked with the Department of Interior and Swain county to strike an agreement that the federal

---

[36] This proposal had been advanced first by Governor Dan Moore toward the end of his term; it was never acted on.

government would pay the county $52 million, again in lieu of completion of the road. This agreement called for the money to be deposited in a specially-protected trust account with the North Carolina State Treasurer who was to make annual interest payments, which were estimated to be near $1 million, to Swain county. The Swain county commissioners accepted this agreement on February 5, 2010. At the time of signing $4 million had been authorized for transfer and another $8.8 million was to be added within 120 days. These transfers were made and a Swain county Settlement Trust Fund was established by the General Assembly in the Office of the State Treasurer and the $12.8 million was deposited in it. The remaining $39.2 million was to be paid in ten annual installments, the first of which was included in the FY2013 federal budget. However, none of the $39.2 million has yet been transferred. Consequently, in December 2013, Mark Meadows, the new Representative of the area in Congress, introduced a bill, HR 3806, which directed Congress to release the funds. As of the fall of 2014 the bill, which was supported by Shuler's testimony when it was considered in committee on July 16, 2014, had been reported out of committee but not yet acted on by the full House. A companion bill, S2744, was introduced by Senator Kay Hagen on July 31, 2014, and referred to committee. HR 3806 never was acted on in 2014 and was not re-introduced in 2015. Consequently, none of the $39.2 million has been paid into the Trust Fund. Tired of continued inaction at the federal level, on March 31, 2016 the Swain county commissioners agreed to sue the federal government for the $39.2 million owed to the trust fund. The case was dismissed in May of 2017, leaving Swain county few options other than to appeal the dismissal before the settlement runs out in 2020.

The Swain county audit report for 2010 mentions the existence of the trust fund pointing out that the interest earned from the fund is unrestricted but no portion of the principal can be disbursed without two-thirds approval of the registered voters of Swain county. Similar statements appear in audit reports for 2012 and 2013. In addition, the audit report for 2012 shows interest earned of $1.38 million, $780,000 interest in the report for 2013, and $439,000 in 2014. Presumably these interest deposits were determined to be over and above an amount necessary to ensure that the principal in the fund grew to keep pace with inflation as required by the statute setting up the fund. In 2014 the fund balance had grown to $13.64 million with $382,000 transferred out. How much longer it will be before the federal government lives up to its full financial commitment to the fund is anyone's guess. In a gesture, almost of frustration, a bill (HR260) was introduced in the 2017 North Carolina legislature requiring the State Attorney General to investigate "any legal methods available to Swain county to ensure payment" [of the $39.2 million] and report his findings by June 1, 2017. The bill passed the House, and, as of late June 2017, was in committee in the Senate.

This entire sorry episode illustrates how hard it can be, in the political arena, to meet the terms of even a clear contractual agreement, particularly when events conspire to stretch out the time involved. The 1943 agreement, struck during the height of World War II, was made in good faith and made complete sense considering the missions of the participating parties. Had conditions allowed the parties to begin to meet the terms of the agreement immediately there undoubtedly would now be a road along the north shore of Fontana Lake and it would surely be as scenically-beautiful as the Blue Ridge Parkway. The extent of damage to the trout streams it would have crossed is anyone's guess.

However, because of the war, work did not begin immediately. The State of North Carolina and TVA quickly met their obligations by constructing short feeder roads on either end of the proposed road and the Park Service also began construction on the east end of the road. However, fate in the terms of delays due to unanticipated issues associated with breeching a major rock formation allowed the politically-powerful North Carolina Wildlife Federation to rise in defense of the prize trout-fishing areas at the mouths of three major streams draining the south flank of the Great Smoky Mountain National Park. The Federation's vocal opposition essentially killed North Carolina's support for the North Shore road and left Swain county without effective support for fulfilling the 1943 contract. The Park Service's ill-conceived proposal for a trans-mountain road lacked support from anywhere but Swain county and led to a ten-year delay in efforts to find a more widely acceptable solution. By the time the trans-mountain road was finally put to death the leadership of Swain county was slowly beginning to change. Younger county leaders saw the futility of fighting for a road, any road, that would never be built and rather began to focus on the more rational solution of a cash settlement first proposed during the Holshouser administration. Were it not for the stubborn, fifteen-year plus opposition of Jesse Helms, playing his favorite role of champion of those downtrodden by the federal government—in this case persons whose ancestors were buried in the cemeteries located in the park—the cash settlement resolution would have been reached much earlier. The only real benefit of the delay in finalizing the cash settlement solution has fallen to Swain county as the amount of the settlement rose from an initial $9.5 million contained in the 1987 House bill to the $52.8 million contained in the "final" agreement of 2010. Whether this increase is ever realized, of course, depends on the federal government meeting its remaining $39.2 million obligation.

This case clearly illustrates how well-intentioned efforts (the trans-mountain road, defense of access to the cemeteries) can work to defeat other equally well-intentioned efforts toward a solution. It also shows how even the resolution of a problem, straight-forward and acceptable in its time context, can become unacceptable as times change. With all the furor that the north shore road proposal stirred up, one is left to wonder what the debate would be like today were construction of the Blue Ridge Parkway to be proposed. One is forced to the conclusion the parkway would never happen in today's environment.

Chapter 13

Bald Head Island

Bald Head Island (or more properly known as Smith Island)[37] lies on the east side of the mouth of the Cape Fear River and constitutes the spit of sand known as Cape Fear. It is bounded on the north by what remains of old Corncake Inlet; at low tide, it is possible to walk, or occasionally drive, to the island. The long and fascinating history of the island has been fully documented by David Stick in his Bald Head Island: a history of Smith Island and Cape Fear published in 1985. The history of the island relevant to my involvement in state government begins after the early 1960s when a full-blown struggle over its protection from development began. In my capacity as Chair of the North Carolina Academy of Science Conservation Committee I became deeply involved in efforts to protect the island and to transfer it to public ownership.

The island had been owned since 1938 by restaurateur Frank Sherrill of Charlotte, NC who bought it for back taxes (reputedly about $10,000) on the steps of the Brunswick county court house. Between 1938 and the early 1960s the island was used for farming (not successfully), cutting of dogwood for textile spindles, and for occasional visits and camping trips by the curious. However, in the early 1960s Sherrill, who had always maintained a desire to turn the island into a high-class development, had a proposal to do that drawn up by a Florida firm, Rader and Associates. The plan contained all the elements of developments that were common in Florida at that time: complete filling of all marshland and leveling of dunes to accommodate a huge permanent population (60,000 plus 15,000 visitors). Unfortunately for Sherrill the proposed development plan also posed serious negative environmental consequences of exactly the sort that

---

[37] Technically, Bald Head refers to the large, open sandy dune area on the southwest corner of Smith Island. The area was called Bald Head because of its bald appearance as seen from boats entering the Cape Fear River. In casual conversation, the entire Smith Island complex is often referred to as Bald Head Island. Although incorrect, that is the terminology I will use here because, when one researches the events described in this chapter they will invariably be found under "Bald Head Island" rather than "Smith Island".

were being questioned and challenged by regulatory agencies in current Florida developments—loss of important fisheries habitat, water quality degradation, and exposure of structures to the full effect of hurricanes.

Although there had been suggestions made off and on that Bald Head should be preserved for public use, the impetus to make the island a major conservation "cause" was jump-started by the Sherrill development plan. The North Carolina Academy of Science took up the matter and, joined by other organizations, passed resolutions and made public statements calling for preservation of the island. Wildlife Preserves, a New Jersey conservation organization, joined the cause and sent a representative, Sheafe Satterthwaite, to North Carolina to work full time on the issue. Approaches made to Governor Terry Sanford and members of his staff seeking state intervention and purchase of the island were met with sympathy but no action. In June of 1965, Satterthwaite and I drove to Charlotte and visited with Sherrill. He was most cordial and indicated he was not averse to having the island preserved if he was paid the $5.5 million he believed it was worth. When approached with the idea of donating the island and obtaining major tax benefits, Sherrill allowed that "he had tithed ten percent all his life and he did not owe the lord anything." In June of 1965 I gave a public lecture at the Blockade Runner in Wrightsville Beach attended by several hundred people as well as Sherrill who sat in the very front row. I made as strong a case as I could for preservation and state ownership accompanied by an excellent set of color slides obtained from a wide variety of persons with interest in the island. Afterward, Sherrill said the talk was interesting and repeated his position that he was not averse to preservation and sale to the state just so long as they "get up their money" referring again to the $5.5 million he believed the island was worth.

The issue intensified into a real confrontation in the spring of 1966. By then Dan Moore had become governor and Willie York, an influential Raleigh developer, was named Chairman of the Board of Conservation and Development, the board into whose lap the issue of Bald Head island's fate most logically fell. Although York was in favor of development, one other board member, Gilliam K. Horton, a Wilmington scrap dealer, was strongly in favor of preservation and many of the other board members professed to be open minded on the matter. When the Board of Conservation and Development was asked to make a formal statement in favor of development, preservation interests pressed York to hold an open hearing at its spring meeting in Wilmington, NC. As a part of the hearing in early April 1966 a trip to the island for board members was scheduled. Members of the board, almost all in good clothes and women in high heels, assembled on the city dock at Southport and boarded a state commercial fisheries boat to be taken to the island. I was along as a "guide." As fate would have it the weather was cold with a strong southeast wind running right up the Cape Fear River producing high swells and a rough ride. The plan was to put the board members on the island by transferring them to small boats in the river. The farther out in the river we got, the less feasible the plan looked. Finally, the skipper of the boat, assuming I was the leader of the expedition, turned to me and asked what he should do. Sensing his real fear of an accident if the transfer was tried, and based on my sense that to continue was foolish, I told him to scrub the transfer and take the guests as close in to the island as possible so I could explain what they were seeing. That is what we did. Thus, the members of the board never did set foot on the island; unknowingly, they experienced one major difficulty of developing the island--access. As an ultimate irony, Frank Sherrill and others viewed the entire aborted mission from a nearby large yacht. After its formal meeting, the board did offer a summary of its position about development of the island, stating that Sherrill was free to develop that part of the island that he owned (the corollary of this was that the state owned the marsh land and that he could not develop that) and that the state would not build a road to the island. Clearly both sides got "half a loaf" with this decision and for the remainder of Moore's term there was no more mention of the island by state government.

Until the summer of 1969 the issue lapsed into the background of public discussion. Then Charles Fraser, owner and developer of Hilton Head Island in South Carolina, proposed to buy the island and develop it in the way he had developed Hilton Head. This proposal precipitated an intense public debate between conservation and development interests and again the Board of Conservation and Development became involved. However, by this time Bob Scott had become governor and Gil Horton had been appointed chairman of the board. Horton was strongly in favor of preservation of the island and he let his views be known to Scott. In September 1969 Scott spoke to the board and in his talk seemed to favor preservation but recommended no steps to accomplish that, stating that resolution of the issue properly lay in the hands of the General Assembly. He did, however, have the State Property Control Officer, Frank Turner, make an evaluation and appraisal of the island. Seeing the political winds against him, Fraser withdrew but no formal steps were taken by anyone to take advantage of what was obviously an administration sympathetic toward preservation. The stumbling block, of course, was Sherrill's repeatedly-stated price of $5.5 million. An approach was made to the Nature Conservancy; their advice was to sit tight, just keep up the pressure on the state, and eventually some accommodation would be struck. For once, their advice was bad, at least from a preservation perspective.

In the spring of 1970 a new set of actors entered the game. A development group, Carolina Cape Fear Corporation, headed by William Henderson of High Point announced that it had purchased Bald Head from Frank Sherrill for $5.5 million and that it intended to develop it in a responsible manner using none of the marsh land and intending to connect it to Fort Fisher by a bridge and ocean highway (both requiring state assistance). There followed a bitter battle between Henderson and Scott that lasted into the 1971 session of the General Assembly. Several months into the legislative session, Scott presented a package of bills dealing with the environment. There was an expectation that he would request funds to acquire Bald Head but he did not. The truth is that Scott had more important issues with which to deal, including reorganization of state government, restructuring of the university system, and passage of a tax on tobacco products. In fact, the only significant action dealing with the island in the 1971 session was introduction and defeat of a bill to prevent the state from condemning the island. I entered state government in May of the 1971 legislative session.

*****

I certainly shared the view with many in the conservation community that now I was part of the machinery of state government surely a way would be found to bring Bald Head into state ownership. For several reasons, it did not turn out that way. First, although there was interest in the Scott administration in acquiring Bald Head there was no real enthusiasm to pursue vigorously in the General Assembly the funds to do it. Second, the position I held had very wide responsibilities and I could not focus solely on one issue. Doing so would have created the perception that the real reason I "went downtown" was to save Bald Head when that was not at all my motivation. Finally, those of us in the administration of the new NER were heavily preoccupied with bringing that department into existence; that became our primary obligation.

In the winter of 1971 Carolina Cape Fear Corporation, without a permit from the Corps of Engineers, built a pier in Bald Head Creek to provide access to the island. An application after-the-fact was made in spring, 1971, for a Section 10 (of the Rivers and Harbors Act of 1899) permit. The Corps held a hearing in the summer of 1971 and the state opposed issuance of a permit. In November, 1971, the Corps denied the permit and Carolina Cape Fear removed the pier. Nonetheless, in the winter of 1972 Carolina Cape Fear began development of the island. To get its equipment to the island, and without any landing structure, machinery was barged across the Cape Fear and landed on the beach on the river side. The barge and equipment was aided in landing by dredging an area where the barge could be landed. This work was spotted by a Commercial Fisheries plane during one of its routine inspections for violations of the state dredge and fill law. The state sued Carolina Cape Fear in Brunswick county court for violation of the state dredge and fill law. The suit was thrown out on grounds that the judge could not be persuaded that although "there was a hole" testimony showed that Carolina Cape Fear created it. During the remainder of 1972 active development continued with road construction, the initial phases of the golf course, and construction of the inn and reception center begun. Carolina Cape Fear's development plans called for work to be confined to the upland part of the island without any damage to the marshland and adjacent waters. The initial phases of development were consistent with that commitment.

In January 1973 Jim Holshouser took office and appointed Jim Harrington has his Secretary of Natural and Economic Resources. Harrington's background in development at Pinehurst and Beech Mountain gave him an innate sympathy for proposed development of the island. In addition, both he and Holshouser felt that the state had unreasonably harassed Carolina Cape Fear even when it appeared there was little way to prevent development. Accordingly, the state's new official policy toward Bald Head was to let development proceed with due care for the environment and the public interest. Because development of the island

141

had, by this time, become a fact I felt little enthusiasm to try to alter the state's new position.

In the fall of 1973 the developers applied to the Corps of Engineers for a Section 10 permit to dredge a small marina into the upland and put in docking facilities. No dredging in Bald Head Creek was proposed. By this time development had reached a point where 400-plus lots had been sold, houses were started, the golf course was completed, and a clubhouse-motel was under construction. The permit application was evaluated by the Corps based on an environmental assessment rather than a full impact statement. The U.S. Fish and Wildlife Service objected to issuance and the decision and issuance finally went all the way to Corps' headquarters in Washington, DC. Nat Reed, representing Interior, and the Chief of Engineers reached an agreement to issue the permit with three provisos: no development could occur below the high-water mark, Carolina Cape Fear Corporation must deed the east beach and certain islands to the state, and Carolina Cape Fear must quit claim deed all marshes and bottoms to the state. The Corporation agreed to these conditions. Deeds of transfer were drawn and put into escrow in Raleigh awaiting granting of the permit. Eventually, the property involved was transferred to the Nature Conservancy to hold until issuance of the permit occurred.

The conditions that were placed on the permit originated in Raleigh. Shortly after making the marina permit application, Henderson approached Harrington with a proposal that Carolina Cape Fear donate part of its property to the state as a "nature preserve." This proposal was met favorably by Harrington and me and, after further lengthy discussions, it led to the conditions that were proposed for the permit. At this stage, we both felt this represented an arrangement that, short of providing for full ownership, would provide considerable benefits to the state. Harrington stated as much in a news conference announcing the agreement and much of the state's press agreed, although conservation organizations did not. NER had to be cautious about accepting a donation that involved marshland as the state contended that it already owned it and to accept even a quit claim deed could cloud that contention. The Nature Conservancy was chosen as a credible, intermediary party to hold the gift until the permit was issued. Harrington also instructed the Division of Commercial Fisheries to make its evaluation of the permit application with consideration of any donation to the state that might occur.

Final issuance of the permit was delayed because the Conservation Council of North Carolina took the Corps to court, basing its case on procedural shortcomings and the lack of an EIS. Ultimately, the courts ruled in July 1975 that an EIS must be prepared and enjoined issuance of the permit until this requirement was met. Using the environmental assessment as a basis, the Corps began preparation of an EIS in October 1976. It was issued in late 1976, commented on, a final version was issued in September 1977, and the permit finally was issued in late 1978.

Meanwhile, development of the island continued but under a series of different owners. Carolina Cape Fear Corporation went broke in 1975 when it was unable to meet payments to its financiers, having been hit by a double blow, delays resulting from regulatory problems and a recession during 1974-75. In June of 1976 Builders Investment Group, the Valley Forge, PA financial organization holding most debt for Bald Head development, reorganized and a new group, Bald Head Island Corporation took title. By this time, I had left state government but the saga of Bald Head dragged on. The corporation was never able to make Bald Head island a success and it sought to sell its interest in the development. Jim Harrington, who had left NER in early 1976 to start a brief but unsuccessful run at the governorship, by this time had become the principal in Cambridge Properties, a firm with developments in Cary and Southern Shores, NC. Harrington was approached about purchasing Bald Head and eventually he and Walter Davis, a native North Carolinian and Texas oil multi-millionaire, purchased the development in 1979. They insisted that the land held by the Nature Conservancy be transferred to the state, which it was, and that any further development continue in an environmentally-sensitive manner. Cambridge Properties invested substantial sums in re-invigorating the development of Bald Head and by the early 1980s the operation was on a solid footing. In fact, in June 1982 I had the interesting experience of participating in a "Know Your Island" program. My talk was devoted to why I thought Bald Head should not have been developed—a curious topic given that development had long been a reality. In 1983, the development was sold yet again, this time to Bald Head Island Limited, a company owned by the Mitchell family of Texas. The residents of Bald Head, together with others have formed the Bald Head Conservancy which carries out a strong program of environmentally-oriented activities such as protecting turtle nesting areas and natural history education.

What can be learned from the long, involved story of Bald Head island? One is tempted to answer with several clichés— "you can't win 'em all" and "better to have tried and lost than never to have tried at all." Although trite, both sayings are true.

The partial development of Bald Head island represented almost the lone failure in a long string of conservation successes that occurred in North Carolina during the early 1970s. The acquisition of many new state parks (including several on the coast), saving Jockey's Ridge, the prevention of dam construction on Mills River, Crabtree Creek, the major triumph on the New River, the re-structuring of environmental protection/ management agencies into a new department, and creation of the Cape Lookout National Seashore all represent important achievements where the long-term interests of North Carolinians were protected.

Interestingly, the "loss" of Bald Head represents virtually the only case in which strategies proposed by the Nature Conservancy were not successful. If the state and the conservation community had been more aggressive during the Scott administration it is almost certain that Bald Head would now be a state park. However, there was a strong feeling that the game had been won and some event would occur that would preserve the island. That is certainly the view the Nature Conservancy held; it was the only time during our work with them while I was in state government that their judgment turned out to be fallible.

Ultimately, the outcome of the Bald Head struggle is represented better by another trite saying "half a loaf is better than none." In the end, the accommodation struck with Carolina Cape Fear Corporation essentially ensuring that nearly eighty percent of the island complex was either given to the state or confirmed as owned by the state, represented an important gain for North Carolinians. Questions of public access to the water and marshes of the island complex were removed. Furthermore, when combined with other state property near Fort Fisher, a protected estuarine complex of nearly 15,000 acres was created. The northern part of this complex is now one of four parts of North Carolina's National Estuarine Research Reserve.

Although it is unclear how much of this land and water would have been saved if the fight to preserve Bald Head island had never taken place, it is crystal clear that if Frank Sherrill had proceeded with the development plan prepared by Rader and Associates North Carolina would have been faced with a coastal catastrophe. One shudders to think of what might have happened had there been a resort settlement of 50,000 people at the mouth of the Cape Fear during any one of the recent hurricanes that have come ashore near Wilmington. The negotiations that ensured preservation of the marshland and water around Bald Head, and that confined development above the high-water mark prevented such a catastrophe.

Although I would certainly have preferred to see all the island preserved, I am at peace with the resolution of the matter. Success in politics entails a willingness to engage in the fine arts of negotiation and compromise. By its very nature, a compromise solution means that neither party gets all of what it wants. Rather, each party gets enough to satisfy itself that it can come away feeling it has "won" something despite having had to sacrifice some of its goals. All of this should be well-known by anyone who chooses to participate in the political arena. Reaching a compromise solution does not mean that one has lost the negotiations; it only means one has practiced the fine art of achieving the possible which, after all, is what politics is all about. At the time these words are being written (early 2017) it appears that few if any of our politicians at any level are either able or willing to understand this fundamental truth about politics. Our current national malaise is due in large part to the inability of contesting parties to understand that our national good depends upon reaching solutions which, although not complete wins for anyone, do take into consideration the interests of all parties and truly represent partial successes for everyone.

Chapter 14

Saving the New River

Although the struggle to save the New River centered on construction of a pair of hydroelectric dams, and could easily have been discussed with the other "dam" issues, it was so significant and involved so many important personalities both in and out of state government, it deserves a place all its own. It stands to this day as the most intense, dramatic, and precedent-setting natural resource issue ever fought out in North Carolina.

The North Fork of the New River rises in Ashe county and the South Fork in Watauga county[38]. Both forks flow northerly and join about five miles south of the Virginia state line before exiting North Carolina near the tiny town of Grassy Fork. The New is reputed to be one of the oldest rivers in the world and is thought by geologists to once have been the main river of the North American continent.[39] The river valley was used extensively by native Americans after their entry into eastern North America and significant sites proving this use can be found along the river. Although European settlers were present in the upper New River area in North Carolina in the early 1700s, the area became a backwater and permanent settlement did not begin until the early 1800s. The population of the upper New River grew slowly and retained its dependence on the fertile land for an economy that had always depended on farming and timber products. There have never been any large urban areas in the region; the largest towns remain small and based on services to the local population. This way of life persisted until well after World War II. However, events beginning in 1962 with a proposal to build a hydroelectric project on the upper New River brought notoriety and visibility to the area that it previously had not known. The struggle over whether or not to build the

---

[38]   Henceforward the name New River will be used to describe both forks and the main stem.

[39]   Much of the discussion of the New River itself and of the fight to "save" it draws on information provided by Thomas J. Schoenbaum in his book "The New River Controversy."

project is a classic example of a conflict between development and its impacts, both positive and negative, and protection and preservation of resources and, most important of all, a way of life.

*****

Although other agencies (the Corps of Engineers, Blue Ridge Electric Membership Corporation) had looked at the New River as a source of power (one proposal would actually have reversed the flow of the river from north to east over the Blue Ridge!), it was not until 1962 when Appalachian Power Company (APCO) applied to the Federal Power Commission (FPC) to study construction of a pumped-storage[40] hydroelectric facility that the possibility of a change in the river's way of life became a reality. The FPC set the process in motion in March 1963 by granting APCO a permit to study the project. In February 1965 APCO applied for a license to build a conventional pumped-storage project. This original proposal was relatively small, occupying about 20,000 acres mostly in Virginia. Both proposed dams were in Virginia about fifteen miles apart with the lower impounding 2,850 acres and the upper 16,600 acres with a peak power generating capacity of 0.9 megawatts. Because the project would have had limited impact on North Carolina, little attention was paid to the proposal except by the small number of people living along the river who would have been affected by the upper impoundment.

At this point, other actors entered the game and a series of events that radically influenced the outcome of the struggle occurred. In 1966,

---

[40] A pumped storage facility is ideally suited to topography such as the New River valley. It consists of an upper impoundment that stores water that is discharged into a lower impoundment generating power as the water flows down. Typically, power is generated at periods when demands on a power grid are greatest (peak power demand periods). When peaking power is no longer needed water is pumped from the lower impoundment back into the upper to repeat the cycle during the next period of peak demand. Small amounts of water may be discharged continually from the upper impoundment to provide base power production. The justification for such a project, however, is wholly based on satisfying peak power demand. Another feature of pumped storage projects is, because of the power used to pump water back into the upper impoundment, they use more power than they generate. The critical factor, however, is not how much power is produced but when it is produced.

water pollution control interests were in the Departments of Interior and Health, Education, and Welfare (EPA was not created until 1970). Exercising what authority these agencies had, they required that the size of the project be doubled to provide "low flow augmentation[41]" in the New River to improve water quality in the Kanawha River at Charleston, WV. This change would have increased low flow augmentation from 25,000 to 400-500,000 acre feet. Taking this new demand into consideration[42], in 1968 APCO filed a "Modified Blue Ridge Project" with radically different dimensions. The lower impoundment was increased to 12,500 acres and the upper to 26,000 acres of which over half (14,200) would be in Ashe and Alleghany counties. Generation capacity was increased to 1.8 megawatts, 1.6 of which was peak power generation. This project would have used four units of energy for each three it produced. The most critical change, however, was the number of people it would affect; 893 buildings, fifteen churches, twenty-three industrial establishments and commercial facilities, and twelve cemeteries were to be destroyed together with other negative social impacts. In addition, large recreational benefits were claimed and two state parks, one in North Carolina and one in Virginia were included.

North Carolina fought this proposal but generally without much conviction. Legislation was passed opposing the project and the attorney general intervened but there never were any clear signals given as to a state position on the proposal. North Carolina's objections largely centered on the amount of drawdown in the upper impoundment; the state sought to limit it to make the impoundment more suitable for recreation. In October 1969, the FPC official hearing the project, issued an Initial Decision granting the license for the Modified Project. Virginia and North Carolina both filed exceptions to this decision, with the West Virginia attorney general also

---

[41]   Low flow augmentation in the 1960s was an accepted method for dealing with water pollution., the rationale being that greater river flows would dilute pollution and reduce its negative impacts. The catch phrase "the solution to pollution is dilution" was used, albeit sarcastically, to describe this philosophy. Suffice it to say that the concept is no longer considered a credible solution to water pollution problems.

[42]   Then Secretary of Interior Stewart Udall is reputed to have said that his support of low flow augmentation in the Blue Ridge Project was "the worst decision he made" while he was Secretary.

taking exception based on potential adverse effects of flow augmentation on the river's sport fishery. In April 1970, the full FPC overturned the hearing officer's action and ordered further hearings. After additional hearings in July and December 1970, the hearing officer in June 1971 again concluded that, with slight modifications, the Modified Blue Ridge Project should be licensed.

The effect of this series of procedural hearings and rulings was to further delay final issuance of the license, providing the opponents time to generate additional support. Leaders of the opposition in Ashe and Alleghany Counties reached out to conservation and farm interests both locally and nationally to put together an organized opposition to the project. As the dispute dragged on, this opposition became better organized and increasingly vocal and, as we shall see, played a crucial role in the ultimate resolution of the issue. In addition, the dispute began to take on national dimensions, with newspaper accounts and television programs devoted to the Blue Ridge Project and its negative impacts on the way of life of the citizens of the upper New River valley.

At this point events in an entirely different arena were taking place that caused further procedural delays in approval of Blue Ridge and thus had a profound effect on the outcome of the dispute. On January 1, 1970, the National Environmental Policy Act became law putting into effect its requirement that environmental impact statements be prepared for federal actions that would have a "significant effect on the environment." Many federal agencies either ignored the requirement, prepared impact statements after significant steps in a project's approval had already been taken, or relied on impact statements provided by others (see Chapter 5). In January 1972, a decision in another case involving the FPC was handed down by a federal appeals court. The decision held that the FPC had erred in waiting until after hearings had been held on an electric transmission line to prepare its impact statement. Even though this ruling appeared to apply directly to Blue Ridge, the FPC decided to fight the decision as it might relate to Blue Ridge, and appealed to the U.S. Supreme Court. In October, 1972, the Supreme Court denied review, thus letting the Court of Appeal's decision stand and returning Blue Ridge to the FPC for yet another round of hearings, to occur after its impact statement had been approved. The FPC wasted no time in responding. It issued its revised environmental statement in January 1973 giving state and federal agencies time for review and comment.

During late 1972 events were taking place in North Carolina that would ultimately determine the outcome of the dispute. In the gubernatorial campaign of that fall both candidates, Democrat Hargrove Bowles and Republican Jim Holshouser had opposed the project. Holshouser was elected, becoming the first Republican governor in the twentieth century setting the stage for a complete re-thinking of the state's position with respect to a variety of issues including Blue Ridge. In late winter 1973 Robert Finch, the young man who worked for me and coordinated review of environmental impact statements for NER, brought his summary of the department's review of the Blue Ridge EIS to me. He and our agencies had found the document grossly deficient, leading him to recommend to me that NER, and the state, oppose Blue Ridge. Up to this point the state had taken no formal position on the project, simply arguing details trying to get the best possible recreation benefits for the state. After reading Finch's material, I agreed with his recommendation and took the matter to Jim Harrington, the new secretary of NER. Although Harrington agreed that on the face of it the project looked like a bad deal for North Carolina, he felt he needed more information. After meeting with representatives of American Electric Power ((AEP) APCO's parent and then the largest electric utility in the country) and the local citizens, Harrington decided that the project would indeed be bad for North Carolina and that the state should oppose it. However, he and I agreed that if the state were to oppose the project that decision should be made by the governor. After discussing the matter at length with Holshouser, he agreed—the state of North Carolina should formally oppose the Blue Ridge Project.[43]

---

[43]   At one point when I was travelling to Washington with Holshouser for a meeting on the New River I asked him why he was so strongly opposed to Blue Ridge. He recounted a discussion he had with a citizen of Ashe county during his campaign in which the man emotionally told him that the project would drown his farm and family property. This touched the populist streak in Holshouser and he said that then and there he decided to oppose Blue Ridge. As Tom Schoenbaum points out, the fact that Ashe and Alleghany had strong Republican parties and that Blue Ridge provided no power to North Carolina also undoubtedly influenced his decision.

In the spring of 1973 I summarized Finch's report to me on Blue Ridge and wrote a blistering critique on behalf of the Department. Our main points were the numerous negative impacts on the citizens of Ashe and Allegheny, the significant loss of prime farmland, the negative impacts on what was generally agreed to be one of the finest fishing streams in the state, the fact that none of the power generated would be used in North Carolina, and that the only benefit to the state would be recreation that we did not need. Our position was summarized with the deathless prose that the project produced "power we did not get and recreation we did not need." On July 11, 1973, Governor Holshouser wrote the FPC stating North Carolina's new policy of opposition to the Blue Ridge project.

In the meantime, the National responsibility for water pollution control had shifted from Interior to the newly-created Environmental Protection agency (EPA). In the spring of 1973 EPA, using its authority to deny low-flow augmentation as a component of Blue Ridge[44], prohibited low flow augmentation as an element of the project. One might have thought that this would force a reduction in size of the project but when the FPC hearing officer rendered his third decision, based on new hearings, in January 1974, he simply shifted the water that could no longer be used for flow augmentation to flood control storage and downstream fishery habitat improvement. and issued yet another recommendation that Blue Ridge be licensed.

With the state firmly in opposition to Blue Ridge, opponents of the project began to act. Leaders of the opposition in Ashe and Alleghany counties settled upon the National Wild and Scenic Rivers Act (passed in 1968) as a means to save the New River. At their urging, Representative Wilmer Mizell (who represented the counties) and Senator Sam Ervin, late in 1973, introduced identical bills into the House and Senate requiring the Department of Interior to study the suitability of the New River for inclusion in the National Wild and Scenic River System. Further impetus

---

[44]   This authority was based on an amendment to the 1972 Federal Water Pollution Control Amendments introduced by Senator Sam Ervin that prohibited any license issued by the FPC from including "storage for regulation of streamflow for the purpose of water quality control" unless it was specifically recommended by the Administrator (of EPA). As Schoenbaum also points out, Ervin had Blue Ridge in mind when he introduced this amendment.

was given to such designation when the North Carolina General Assembly, with the urging of Senator Hamilton Horton, in March 1974, designated a four and one-half mile stretch of the river from the confluence of the North and South Forks to the state line as a North Carolina scenic river. In addition, a resolution was passed requiring NER to study the suitability of the entire South Fork for inclusion in the state system. Concurrent with these actions, Senator Ervin, joined by Senator Jesse Helms, introduced a new bill into the Senate calling for study of the New as a National Wild and Scenic River; the bill easily passed out of committee and, despite strong opposition from Virginia, was approved by the full Senate in the spring of 1974.

During the hearings on the Ervin-Helms bill the Department of Interior's Bureau of Outdoor Recreation, asked the bill to be deferred. The Bureau supported Blue Ridge for its recreation benefits and thus wanted only the New River above the limits of the projects studied. At this point, Governor Holshouser took matters into his own hands and met with representatives of Interior to seek a change in the Department's position. The meeting, at which I accompanied the governor, took place in the office of Nat Reed, the Assistant Secretary under whom the Bureau of Outdoor Recreation was located, and was attended, among others, by the then director of the Bureau James Watt (later to become Interior Secretary under Ronald Reagan). Watt began the discussion by extoling the recreational value of Blue Ridge but Reed immediately cut him off with the statement "that he (Watt) apparently didn't understand that we were at this meeting to support North Carolina and its desire to preserve the New River, not to destroy it." With that Watt said nothing more and Reed went on to commit Interior to support North Carolina's position.[45] Secretary Morton later communicated this position to Senator Helms.

Despite the Senate's clearly expressed desire that the New River at least be considered for wild and scenic river preservation, the FPC felt compelled to move ahead with the license for Blue Ridge. However, the

---

[45] Again, politics entered the struggle on North Carolina's side. Rogers Morton, Interior Secretary, was to become manager of President Gerald Ford's campaign in 1976. His desire to deal positively with Holshouser undoubtedly influenced Interior's change in policy.

commissioners realized that they must acknowledge Congress' interest in preservation of the river. Thus, in a concession to Congress, on June 14, 1974 the FPC granted a license for Blue Ridge, but did not make it effective until January 2, 1975. The decision allowed thirty days for appeal; North Carolina was the only intervenor that appealed within the thirty-day limit, thus maintaining its legal standing in the case. The FPC action was based on three putative benefits: peak power generation, recreation in the form of state parks for North Carolina and Virginia, and flood control.

During the fall of 1974 the Senate bill calling for a study of the New River was debated in the House. The House Interior Committee had reported the bill favorably in July. However, before the bill could go to the floor for discussion and vote it had to be reported favorably by the House Rules Committee. The Rules Committee is an anachronism, albeit a powerful one. Despite favorable action in other committees the Rules Committee can hold a bill or give it an unfavorable report, thus denying the full House the opportunity to vote on the bill. During the late summer and fall of 1974 lobbying of the Rules Committee was intense by both sides. One of the most significant interests opposing the bill was organized labor which supported Blue Ridge because of its job-creating potential. Between intense lobbying of the entire Rules Committee and the delaying tactics of the chairman the bill was held almost until Congress adjourned in December. When the bill was finally brought to a vote, it was overwhelmingly defeated. However, the Rules Committee can be circumvented by a two-thirds vote of the full House. North Carolina congressmen persuaded the House speaker to bring the question of voting on the New River study bill before the House, knowing full well that a two-thirds majority would be very difficult to achieve. The question was considered on December 18 and, although obtaining a majority of 196-181, it failed to gain the necessary two-thirds favorable votes. Thus, congressional consideration of preservation of the New River was dead for that session.

Despite failure in Washington, preservation interests were busy on several fronts in North Carolina. The FPC had denied North Carolina's request for a re-hearing on issuance of the license, leaving North Carolina free to appeal to the federal Court of Appeals. With Tom Schoenbaum playing a major role, a brief was prepared alleging that the FPC in issuance of the license for Blue Ridge had violated NEPA in three ways: refusing to allow consideration of the river as a national scenic river, failing to consider energy conservation as an alternative to the project, and failing to disclose adequately the true costs and benefits of Blue Ridge. However, knowing that it might be well into 1975 before the Appeals Court heard this appeal, Schoenbaum hit on another strategy. He used his friendship with Ernie Carl, Director of the North Carolina Office of Marine Affairs, the person charged by the governor with coordinating state efforts to stop Blue Ridge, who in turn had a former student working at the Council on Environmental Quality, to send a letter from CEQ Director Russell Peterson to the FPC strongly questioning the inadequacy of the FPC EIS on Blue Ridge. This letter served as the basis of a request to the Court of Appeals in Washington asking for a stay of the license for Blue Ridge.

Schoenbaum hit upon yet another strategy that fall (1974). It involved a provision of the National Wild and Scenic Rivers Act that allows a governor to petition the Secretary of Interior to include a river segment as part of the national system. In making his request, the governor had to show that the river segment involved had been designated as part of a state system and that the state had adopted a management plan for the segment that would involve no cost to the federal government. Although this seemed to be a promising new strategy it had two inherent problems: it had never been used before and the four and one-half mile segment of the New designated by North Carolina was probably too small to be designated into the national system. Nonetheless, NER's recreation staff put together a management plan and, after some delays the request was submitted to the Secretary of the Interior on December 12, 1974. At the same time, Holshouser submitted a request to the FPC asking for delay in issuance of the license to allow the studies required by the Department of Interior. No one expected this request to be granted and the FPC's failure to delay the license to allow action by Interior formed the basis of an appeal to the Court of Appeals in the District of Columbia.

At this point, several efforts by opponents of Blue Ridge came to a head. The Secretary of Interior agreed to make the studies required by the petition for federal recognition of the New. Two court cases, one contesting the FPC's issuance of the license and the other contesting FPC's decision not to delay issuance of the license to allow Interior to study the state's request for designation, and the date on which the license would become valid (January 2, 1975) all played out during the Christmas holidays, 1974. The ultimate outcome of these cases was 1) an agreement by the FPC to delay the license until January 31, 1975 and, ultimately, 2) a decision by the Court of Appeals to stay the license for Blue Ridge issued on January 31.[46]

With the stay issued by the Court of Appeals, events moved back to the state and legislative arenas. In mid-January Senator Helms and Representative Steve Neal (who replaced Representative Mizell in the November 1974 election) introduced Scenic River study bills into the new session of Congress. However, the focal point of action became the request to Interior to designate the river by executive action. It was obvious to everyone that the short section of river on which the request to Interior was based would almost certainly not be adequate to get favorable action. Bob Buckner, of NER's recreation planning staff, completed the suitability study of the full South Fork requested by the 1974 legislature. His study showed that the entire South Fork did meet the criteria for designation as a state natural and scenic river. Based on his report, hearings were held in Sparta, Jefferson, and Boone in late January 1975. I chaired these hearings. There were strong expressions both from those who favored Blue Ridge and those who favored scenic river status. One of the most important outcomes of these hearings was the opportunity to explain exactly what scenic river designation would entail and what its impacts would be, particularly on those who owned land along the river. The hearings also showed clearly that those whose land was directly affected by Blue Ridge strongly favored scenic river designation whereas those from areas above the limits of Blue Ridge's upper impoundment strongly opposed extending scenic river designation to their portion of the river.

The trick became satisfying both constituencies while still expanding scenic river status so that it at least equaled the Interior Department's informal criterion of at least twenty-five miles for a river segment to be included in the national system. I sat down with our recreation staff and maps of the area to see if that could be done. We found that from where Dog Creek joined the South Fork thence downstream to the confluence of

---

[46]   This sequence of events is vastly more complicated than I have explained it here. For the fuller, and much more interesting, story see Schoenbaum's book.

the North and South Forks defined a segment that, when combined with the segment from there to the Virginia state line already designated by North Carolina, created a twenty-six and one-half-mile segment. A plan was prepared for management of this larger segment calling for state acquisition of 200-400 acres and the use of scenic easements to maintain the river in essentially its current condition. This proposal was taken to a public hearing that I chaired at Ashe Central High School on April 8, 1975 and met with general acceptance. In late April, identical bills were introduced into the North Carolina legislature to lengthen the scenic river status of the New from the Virginia state line to Dog Creek. By the end of May, the bills had passed and were signed by the governor.

The focus of effort now was directed to the Department of Interior. To protect the earlier date of submission of the request for designation (December 12, 1974), the additional river segment and management plan for it were submitted to Interior as amendments to the original. The submission of this amendment to Interior became complicated because the secretary with whom North Carolina had been dealing, Rogers Morton, moved to the Commerce Department. There ensued nearly six months when it was unclear who was Interior secretary and to whom the amendment should be directed. Finally, on September 12, 1975 Thomas Kleppe, appointed secretary three days before, agreed to support scenic river designation referring the matter to the Bureau of Outdoor Recreation for study and preparation of an EIS.[47] The 4th Circuit Court in Richmond also agreed to stay North Carolina's appeal until the Court of Appeals in Washington ruled on the case involving the adequacy of FPC's EIS.

In August 1975, a reporter for the Winston-Salem Journal revealed that important archaeological data had been gathered in very early studies of the site of the Blue Ridge project and had not been reported by APCO to the FPC. North Carolina brought another suit before the Court of Appeals in Washington seeking to show the archaeological data were "material" to the decision on Blue Ridge. The Court ordered this matter held until the state's case on the adequacy of the EIS before the same court had been heard.

---

[47] Again, what happened during the 6-month period is far more complex than can be reported here so see Schoenbaum for the details.

In the fall of 1975 it became clear that the fate of Blue Ridge and the New River would finally be decided. Cases pending in the courts were about to be decided and the issue seemed soon to be decided in Congress. The first crucial date was in mid-October when oral arguments were heard on North Carolina's case before the Court of Appeals in Washington, DC challenging the adequacy of the FPC EIS for Blue Ridge. Despite reservations expressed by the judges hearing the case as to whether several issues now being raised by the state were included in the petition for rehearing, the state's attorneys were optimistic that North Carolina's case would prevail. A second critical date was November 26, 1975 when Interior secretary Kleppe announced he would begin the ninety-day circulation period required for the draft EIS prepared for Interior by BOR. Knowing how crucial Kleppe's final decision was concerning approval of the state's application, supporters of preservation of the New and of Blue Ridge engaged in an all-out lobbying campaign. Interior's decision also became involved in the presidential primary campaign in North Carolina between President Gerald Ford and Ronald Reagan with Holshouser trying to convince Ford to support designation of the New as a scenic river as part of his campaign strategy in North Carolina. Ford agreed to do so and, in addition, he instructed Kleppe to fast-track preparation of the final EIS by Interior.[48] On March 12, 1976, the EIS was completed and distributed and the next day Kleppe announced his decision to sign an order declaring the New River part of the National Wild and Scenic River system. However, to meet legal requirements concerning circulation of the final EIS, Kleppe also announced that he would delay 30 days, until May 13, before signing the final order.

On March 24, 1976, the other critical issue was decided. The Court of Appeals issued its decision, upholding the FPC's grant of the license for Blue Ridge, revoking its stay order, and stating that the FPC could immediately declare the Blue Ridge license effective. Although the court held that the state's application to Interior for scenic river status was valid, it ruled that the river was not protected while its status was being studied. The FPC wasted no time declaring on March 26 the license for Blue Ridge to be in effect. This series of decisions required the state to act quickly if

---

[48]   The sequence of events involved here is far more complex than I imply here. Schoenbaum provides more detail and explanation.

it were to maintain any hope of validating the action Secretary Kleppe said he would take on May 13. The state initiated several legal actions, the one having the most immediate impact was a petition for a rehearing with the FPC and a motion that the FPC rescind its March 26 order. This latter request was based on a federal Rule of Appellate Procedure requiring that the court maintain jurisdiction over an issue for 21 days after judgment is entered. Because the FPC had acted within this 21-day period, which would have ended on May 14 (the day after Kleppe's declaration would take effect!) North Carolina contended its decision that the license was valid was illegal. The Court of Appeals ruled in North Carolina's favor on May 5 permitting the state to file a writ of certiorari in the Supreme Court. Any case filed with the Supreme Court at this time could not possibly be heard until the fall of 1976. Rulings on another case in the fourth circuit Court in Richmond also had the effect of delaying further legal action until the fall.

With the New now safe for a few more months, all attention was directed to Congress to obtain formal congressional designation of the New as a National Wild and Scenic River. Senator Helms and Representative Neal introduced bills designating the river and repealing the license for Blue Ridge. The House bill was referred to a subcommittee chaired by Rep. Roy Taylor, a western North Carolinian who was leaving the Congress at the end of this term. He held the bill waiting for an appropriate time to deal with it. In the Senate, meantime, things became somewhat confused when newly-elected Senator Robert Morgan, who replaced Sam Ervin, expressed concerns about the bill. This brought down a blizzard of criticism in the press on Morgan who quickly began to back pedal. The dispute boiled down to Morgan's concern that the state would zone land along the river and thus deprive citizens of the use of their property. At this point, Ernie Carl was in contact with one of Morgan's staffers and found that Morgan would back off his proposed amendment regarding zoning if he had assurances from the state that it would not use zoning differentially to protect the New. When Ernie passed that information to a group of us gathered to discuss meeting Morgan's concerns, it was quickly agreed that a letter should be written to Morgan with the assurances he wanted. But who should write it and sign it? Ernie said he (Carl) should but several of us pointed out that he, as Director of the Office of Marine Affairs, had no authority to give such assurances. Ernie responded that Morgan didn't know that, so he (Carl) was the perfect author of the letter—offering deniability for higher state officials if it was needed. Carl did write the letter and it served its purpose as Morgan, in an unimpressive statement, withdrew his objections at the Senate Interior Committee hearing on May 20. I happened to attend this meeting with Governor Holshouser and I will never forget walking to the hearing room behind a phalanx of black-suited types from AEP and APCO. I nudged Holshouser and whispered to him "we'll kick their butts today." He laughed and said "Yes we will." I doubt I have ever had a more satisfied feeling in my entire life.

With Morgan's concerns dealt with the bill easily passed out of the Senate Interior Committee and was held for action awaiting the outcome of House action. Rep. Taylor then brought the matter before his Subcommittee of the House Interior Committee. At the suggestion of Secretary Kleppe the bill was altered so that it "recognized as a national scenic river" that segment of the New River named by Interior and included language that would block construction of any FPC-licensed project from adversely affecting the designated segment. In the May 6 hearing, Joseph Dowd, vice president of AEP injected a new consideration by arguing that the license issued by FPC constituted a property right and that if AEP were denied the license it would sue the United States for $500 million. A memorandum solicited from the Congressional Research Service by Representative Neal indicated it was unlikely AEP would prevail in such a suit. Taylor quickly moved the bill out of his subcommittee to the full House Interior Committee where it was given a favorable report.

Now, the entire outcome lay exactly where it did in December 1974, before the House Rules Committee. All attention was devoted to the Rules Committee as a vote in the full house would be impossible, and a vote in the Senate essentially moot, without a favorable vote there. Lobbying by the National Committee for the New River and local citizens from the region on behalf of the bill and by AEP and labor interests in opposition became intense. Despite a New River Appreciation Day in the Senate, national press coverage, and personal lobbying by a wide array of interests that never before, and never after, came together on an issue, it was still clear that labor's position of opposition would likely prevent a favorable vote. Finally, Taylor and the chairman of the Rules Committee, Ray Madden realized that the matter had to be brought to a vote. On August 4, the Rules Committee met, with the outcome unclear at the beginning, in a tense, highly charged four-hour meeting. At the end, on a roll call vote, the bill was passed ten to six. The bill was brought to the floor five days later, and after two days of debate and despite labor's continued opposition, passed 311-73.

All that remained was for the bill to pass the Senate. At this point, even labor withdrew its opposition when George Meany sent a letter to a member of the National Committee for the New River withdrawing labor's opposition. Debate in the Senate featured statements in opposition from Virginia's senators and, among others supporting the bill, a statement from Barry Goldwater that the one vote he would like to have back was his vote to support the Glen Canyon Dam. The final vote, on August 30, was 69-16 and on September 11, 1976, President Ford signed the bill in a ceremony on the White House lawn.[49] The fight to save the New River was over, the Blue Ridge project was defeated, and thousands of people in Ashe and Allegheny counties, and their children and their children's children, could remain on their land, hopefully forever.

There are hundreds of lessons to be drawn from this long, dramatic, series of events. Several, however, are worth further comment here.

At times during the discussion I alluded to the involvement of local citizens. There is absolutely no question but that the outcome would have

---

[49] A personal note here. By the time the bill passed and went to the President I had returned to the University to teach. I got a call from the governor's office inviting me to attend the signing ceremony. The call stressed that I must respond to inquiries from the White House necessary for me to gain clearance to enter. If a call came from the White House I never got it. Nonetheless, I flew with the governor and his party to Washington and taxi-cabbed to the White House. Everyone else was readily admitted but when the guards got to me they said I had not been cleared and could not enter. At that, with the time of the ceremony closing in, Gov. Holshouser asked to speak to someone in the White House. The governor and I stood alone on the sidewalk in front of the White House waiting. I urged him to go ahead—after all, he was one of the two principals in the event—and he responded in a way I will never forget, saying "we would not be here today if it were not for you and we will wait until they let you in." Word soon came, we were admitted, and the ceremony went off beautifully. I will never forget what the governor did and said—it showed what sort of a man Jim Holshouser was.

been entirely different were it not for the efforts of literally thousands of citizens of Ashe and Allegheny counties. This involvement started with those few whose land would have been directly affected by the smaller, original Blue Ridge Project. When the project was doubled in size the number of people affected was more than doubled and it reached a critical mass where, collectively, they presented an effective case against Blue Ridge. There were, of course, many equally decent citizens who favored Blue Ridge but by the time the Holshouser administration placed the state squarely in opposition to Blue Ridge they were heavily outnumbered by those, many of whom were not affected directly by the project, who expressed a strong desire to maintain their way of life without intrusion from a major energy facility. There were also many other important figures from outside Ashe and Allegheny who became heavily involved. Eventually, the citizens of the region and their supporters coalesced into the Committee for the New River, later the National Committee for the New River. The committee provided support and assistance at every step of the fight. Its work was essential to the success of moving the bill recognizing scenic river status through the Congress in the summer of 1976. If one is looking for an example on which to model a citizen action committee one need look no farther than the Committee (National Committee) to Save the New River.

The New River struggle was one of those unique situations that made for strange political bedfellows. It united the members of the North Carolina congressional delegation, both Democrat and Republican, in a way that they united on few other issues. In addition, Jesse Helms, who was certainly not known as an advocate of conservation and environmental issues, was a major force behind legislation designed to save the New. At the state level Governor Holshouser worked closely with other state officials, particularly Attorney General Rufus Edmiston, against whom he had campaigned when Edmiston ran in 1974. Party politics, although influential in other specific cases, did not play a major role in determining who did, and who did not, support preservation of the New River.

Politics were, however, critical at the national level. The close relationship between the administration of the Department of Interior and Governor Holshouser came about because both were Republican. Furthermore, as pointed out, Rogers Morton who was Secretary of Interior until early 1975 became manager of Gerald Ford's campaign for election. North Carolina was a critical state in Ford's efforts to be nominated as there was strong support for Ronald Reagan among many state Republicans. Holshouser, however, supported Ford and his position helped obtain support for the state's position on several issues in Washington. As a sidelight, Holshouser's support of Ford cost him dearly in his relations with the state Republican party which supported Reagan and essentially ostracized Holshouser from its 1976 presidential campaign effort. This dispute marked the beginning of a long slide of the North Carolina Republican Party to the more extreme political right which came to dominate the party when it took over state government in the early 2000s.

It is obvious that the clear state position against Blue Ridge articulated by Governor Holshouser and backed by officials in NER, played a major role in helping to orchestrate activity at the state level. Holshouser's political leadership may have had more to do with the ultimate outcome of the issue than any other single factor. The fact that APCO and Blue Ridge faced a unified front of opposition everywhere it turned in North Carolina government made its job of trying to gain support in the state almost impossible. Prior to Holshouser's election no clear state position had been offered and individual agencies were free to pursue their own interests in taking a position on Blue Ridge. APCO, for example, gained support from various places in state government, among recreation interests for example, for its inclusion of a state park in its plans. With the governor's position clearly stated, the state presented a united front against the project.

It is arguable whether the state's strategy of using the state and national Wild and Scenic Rivers legislation as a means for defeating Blue Ridge was, or was not, good public policy. The intent of the Scenic Rivers bills when they were enacted was undoubtedly more to provide legislative protection for river segments with unique values than to provide a means to block development of river-altering projects. However, it seems inevitable that the potential of scenic river status to protect rivers from development would be used sooner or later for that purpose. The fight to protect the New was simply the first situation where this was the case. Whether it is appropriate for a law to be used for a purpose other than its original intent is up to the courts to decide. It was always understood, but never stated (except by the opponents), that inclusion of a segment of the New River in the national system was a stratagem to prevent construction of Blue Ridge. This was especially true of North Carolina's original proposal of a 4.5-mile segment, but once the proposal was expanded to 26.5 miles, the issue was whether the segment proposed qualified on its merits as a scenic river. It clearly did, and that being the case use of the scenic river legislation was justified. Whether such a designation would have been sought absent proposal of the Blue Ridge Project is an open question but the answer probably is no.

Chapter 15

Working in State Government

Working in state government at the level I did was a fascinating experience, if for no other reason than the variety of duties I encountered on a day-to-day basis. The issues involved ranged from trivial to extremely important dealing with such things as intradepartmental problems, interagency issues at the state and federal levels, relationships with the press, working with the legislature and responding to the governor's office. Each had its own peculiar dimensions and pitfalls. The following vignettes are a sample of "daily life" in the 1970s NER.

The Great Petroleum Discovery Fiasco

The Office of the Director of Earth Resources, Steve Conrad, who was also the State Geologist, received contacts from numerous people either reporting important finds of mineral resources in the state or asking for information that would help in making such discoveries. Virtually all the reports of mineral resource discovery when investigated proved to be without merit, although occasionally one was worth further investigation. Too many of them were from crackpots who seemed, for usually completely obscure reasons, to have some bone to pick with state government. A verbatim quote from one such letter to Steve Conrad is an example, albeit an extreme one, of these latter contacts:

> "Steven Conrad: You and Sheriff Kelly thinks you are something smart don't you! Kelly hijacked another letter I mailed at Southern Pines the other week to the Mineral Department in Washington, did he send you the letter? How would you like to know where a chunk of gold heart shape 4 ½ ft.one way and 3 ft. the other and stands 35 ft. high in the ground with 11 feet of dirt on top, it has been there ever since the flood. If you dirty mason's are interested you should try finding it, you filthy skunks. You are the dirtiest liar this side of hell, you dirty low road hell bent S.O.B. The State hasn't offered a bonus for finding oil in N.C. eh, you filthy liar. A high official in a Bank tells me you told him your self the State was offering a

million dollar bonus to the first one that found oil. Kelly and Bobette has got you dirty trash in Raleigh geared in with them on that dirty organized plot to bump me off. That is why you choose to lie like hell, the man in the Bank said there were something dam screwy about you telling me the State hasn't offered a bonus for finding oil. You see I know all about the screwy part. That chunk of gold with that old time escribing on it wouldn't be worth but about one billion. And if the man that owns the land wants it let the terd find it the best way he can. Did old Hubbard tell you that too? I still have the letter you hitch hiked over to Myrt Horness with no post mark on it and had Myrt geared up to tell me it come through mail. it has a Washington return address on it. you dirty Buzzard."

To be sure, not all letters were this personal or this colorful! However, the content of the letter concerns one resource that was frequently the subject of rumored finds—oil. In addition, when this letter was written (April 1973) the nation was approaching its first oil shortage and the issue of oil deposits and exploration was very much on the minds of state and federal government officials. The debate over whether oil exploration should be permitted off North Carolina's coast was just beginning. Add to this the fact that early 1973 saw the beginning of a new administration in Raleigh. At such times, it seems that everyone with any axe to grind with state government appears out of the woodwork seeking political support for their personal schemes.

Such was the case in late January 1973 shortly after Governor Holshouser took office. An individual (not the writer of the letter quoted above) was referred to NER together with his claim to have knowledge of the location of a major oil deposit in eastern North Carolina. Steve Conrad had already dealt with the man's claims and had concluded they were without merit. Nonetheless, eager to please anyone posing as a supporter of the new administration, the governor's office insisted that we investigate the man's claims more fully. The secretary asked me to coordinate the department's investigation and report. Conrad and I discussed the matter and decided that the best approach was to take the man up on his offer to show us in person where the oil was located and hold a full "hearing" on the site.

The claimed location was in Gum Neck, NC, on the west side of the Alligator River just to the east of NC route 94. Gum Neck is hardly a town and what there is of it is buried deep amid the pocosin forests of the Pamlimarle Peninsula. So, on a bright, cold February morning Conrad, several of his staff members, and I took off from Raleigh for Edenton. We were met at the Edenton airport, an old World War II pilot training airport, by a department staff member who drove us across the Albemarle Sound and on to Gum Neck where we were to meet the prospective oil tycoon. He was indeed there, together with a woman he introduced as his administrative assistant. Apparently, her job was to take notes of all that went on; all she ever did was lick the end of her pencil and aim it at her pad of paper. She never wrote anything. We all suspected that she might well have been more skilled at performing other duties for the oil "prospector."

There were no buildings at the site but there were a bunch of boards thrown on top of a sea of mud in the middle of which was a pipe with a U-shaped end and a valve wheel. This primitive equipment did look a bit like the equipment in a primitive oil field. Being the highest-ranking department official present, it fell to me to conduct the hearing. I noted everyone present and then asked the "oil prospector" to make his presentation. After some introductory comments, he said he would demonstrate proof of the existence of oil below the site and moved toward the valve wheel. Although none of us had the faintest idea what to expect, those who were smoking tossed their cigarettes in the mud and all of us backed off from the pipe. After spinning the wheel of the valve through a half dozen full turns, the man stepped back, obviously expecting something to happen. For a full thirty seconds, with everyone frozen and not moving a muscle, nothing happened. Then, from far down in the earth below us a sound, as of gas being expelled, emerged. It sounded for all the world like a terrestrial fart followed by a long silence. Finally, I asked what that proved and the gentleman embarked on a long, incomprehensible explanation. By the time he was done everyone had wandered off and it appeared that the hearing was over. Those of us who had come from Raleigh piled back in the car to head across Albemarle Sound to Edenton, none of us having the faintest idea what we had seen or heard.

I asked Steve Conrad to write up the results of the "hearing" for me to present to Secretary Harrington, the governor's staff, and the "oil tycoon" at his current address which turned out to be a postal box in North Hills in Raleigh. In due course, the copy of the hearing results sent to him was returned marked "box closed, no forwarding address left." Clearly, our "oil tycoon" was a fraud who had left to sell his snake oil someplace else. We never heard from, or of, him again.

Thus ended the great oil discovery fiasco of the winter of 1973.

The Undeclared War on Hammocks Beach State Park

North Carolina has some of the largest and most active military installations in the country. Since the years I worked in state government were the last years of the Viet Nam war, the state's military installations regularly conducted numerous training exercises. One morning when I arrived in the office Martha Liles told me that I had an urgent call from the superintendent at Hammocks Beach State Park[50]. When I returned his call, he told me that earlier that morning his young son ran in and said "Daddy, they are bombing your park!" When he went out to check, sure enough a Marine helicopter gun ship was flying broadside down Hammocks Beach and firing rockets into the park. After telling him I would get back in touch with him, I reported this news to the secretary. After almost biting the end off his pipe, Harrington called the governor's office and it was agreed the state should protest this obvious, very dangerous intrusion on a state park (fortunately it was late winter and the park was not in use by overnight campers). Why Harrington himself didn't go was unclear to me but he instructed me to "get down there, get the superintendent, and go to Camp Lejeune, find out what happened, and make sure it never happens again!"

So, I did as instructed. After picking up the superintendent who obviously was very nervous and not enthusiastic about confronting the Marine Corps—I wasn't much excited about it either—we drove to Camp

---

[50] Hammocks Beach State Park is near Jacksonville and is essentially adjacent to Camp Lejeune, one of two major Marine Corps' facilities on the east coast. Hammocks Beach was originally one of two state parks designated for use by blacks and its superintendent was black. By the mid-seventies the park was fully integrated.

Lejeune, presented ourselves at the main gate, and I announced to the sentry that we had an appointment with captain whose name I do not remember. After checking our story, we were admitted to the base with instructions as to how to get to the office where we were to meet. Shortly we were ushered into a room and were met by the captain and several other officers. After having the superintendent describe what happened, we were told that "the event never took place." So, I asked the superintendent to repeat what happened and to make clear that he had witnessed it himself. Again, the answer was a flat denial. Being at loggerheads with the Marine Corps, and having been given a denial of an event that clearly did happen, I was not sure what to do. Having no military background, but knowing how important rank is in a military setting, I decided all I could do was try to pull rank. So, I asked the captain if he knew who had sent me down to "investigate this matter." He said no, so I told him that I was there under specific instructions from the governor and that I was to report the results of my visit directly to him.

There ensued a long silence. Finally, the captain arose and left the room returning shortly with several other officers obviously much higher up in command at Camp Lejeune. I asked the superintendent to repeat his story for a third time and it elicited a guarded response from the officers that the event might have happened but that it was inadvertent and there were safeguards to protect against it. At that point we discussed the episode at some length and arrived at both an explanation as to what had happened and an indication as to what would be done to prevent it from happening again. Apparently, there were markers in the water intended to demark a "no fire zone" that the helicopter failed to observe. We were assured it would not happen again and, to my knowledge, it never did. I reported back to Harrington and he may or may not have briefed the governor. Despite my bluff, I never saw him about this matter. To this day, I do not know what I would have done if I had been stonewalled after using my highest card, the governor's office.

Why There's a Little Piece of England on Ocracoke Island

It is well-known that during World War II German U-boats hunted, and killed, large numbers of U.S. and Allied ships off the North Carolina outer banks. Many of the sunken ships have been located and are prime sites for underwater diving. Perhaps the most famous of these sinkings was that of the British trawler HMT Bedfordshire, one of 24 Royal Navy trawlers sent to the U. S. to help deal with the U-boat problem during early 1942. The Bedfordshire was stationed at Morehead City. During one visit to Morehead City, Aycock Brown, who was Ocracoke Naval Investigator and later to become a well-known outer banks newsman, asked the captain of the Bedfordshire, Thomas Cunningham, for several British Navy flags to use when burying British sailors who occasionally washed up on the outer banks after a sinking.

When on patrol in May 1942 the Bedfordshire was sunk by U-588. Three days later the bodies of two British sailors washed ashore and were identified by Brown as Thomas Cunningham and Stanley Craig. Residents of Ocracoke buried the two next to a small family cemetery in Ocracoke village; Brown draped the coffins with two of the British flags Cunningham had given him. Later two unidentifiable bodies from the Bedfordshire washed ashore and they too were buried in the same location. The plot came to be known as the British Cemetery and down through the years it had been carefully cared for by Coastguardsmen from the Ocracoke Station.

Roll the clock ahead to 1976. In reading through a stack of papers that came across my desk I found one outlining the events described above and containing a request from the British government that the plot be transferred so that the 4 sailors could be buried "on British soil." The request had been across several desks before it hit mine and the consensus seemed to be that "it would be nice to do this but my agency can't handle it." After some reflection, I concluded that North Carolina owed that small favor to the four men and that I could use contacts gathered in five years to make it happen. To make a long story short, after many calls throughout state government an arrangement was made whereby the Ocracoke cemetery and another of similar origin at Buxton were leased to Great Britain in perpetuity for as long as the men were buried there. It wasn't hard to accomplish this; it just took a little imagination and a lot of follow through.

The formal arrangements were not completed until after I left state government and a ceremony was held in May of 1977. I had hoped to be invited because I knew there would be a full British military ceremony and I love British military band music. No such luck. Jim Hunt was now governor and those of us who had worked for Holshouser were long forgotten. Be that as it may, the graves are now formally under the custody of the Commonwealth War Graves Commission and the men are honored every May 11 with a ceremony. The graves are maintained by the Coast Guard and local residents.

Fun on the Chowan or "How Green is Our River"

During the spring of 1972 a serious episode of water pollution occurred on the Chowan River in northeastern North Carolina. By that time NER had been reorganized long enough so that administrative oversite of Water and Air Resources, where responsibility for dealing with such situations lay, resided in NER's front office. At about the same time, we were also dealing with control of pollution from a factory in western North Carolina, a situation so serious that the steps necessary to control the pollution would likely put the plant out of business. We were hit by advocates of control and those who insisted the area could not afford the loss of jobs that would accompany closure. The facility was closed but the representatives of the company were decent enough to state publicly that NER's control measures did not close the plant and it would have been closed anyway. Not surprisingly, although Water and Air Resources had a hard time accepting reorganization, they were more than willing to turn problems like that, and the Chowan, over to the front office to handle.

The problem on the Chowan River became serious enough that it took on a life of its own. The legislature was in session and, in addition to major complaints that the "Chowan had turned green" from local interests, we heard the same from the "honorables" across the street in the legislature, many of whom fought regulation of water pollution until a case appeared on their desks. The pollution—lime green colored water that smelled bad—was in the lower Chowan where it entered Albemarle Sound near the town of Edenton. It was generally agreed that the culprit was an upstream fertilizer plant run by Farmer's Chemical, and there was pressure from industry interests and supporters not to adversely impact the plant with pollution control regulations.[51] It turned out later that some research done by one of my peers at NC State, John Hobbie, showed that there were unique underwater features at the confluence of the Chowan and Albemarle sound that acted as a partial dam causing polluted water to accumulate in the lower river thus enhancing the growth of algae.

Pressure mounted on "the state to do something" and NER clearly would have to respond; a call from the legislature got the ball rolling. Two legislators from the area, Senator Monk Harrington and Representative Roberts Jernigan, insisted that NER hold a public meeting in Edenton to explain the problem and outline what could be done about it. As Monk put it in a call to me, he wanted me "to come down and meet with a few of his friends" and talk over the problem. So, on a bright sunny day I got several of the water quality staff from Raleigh and flew to Edenton where we were met by the director of Water and Air Resources' Greenville office and driven to Edenton. When we approached the court house we saw Sen. Harrington's "friends", a crowd of at least several hundred filling the building and spilling out into the street. They may have been Monk's friends but they sure weren't ours! After calling the meeting to order, I turned the floor over to the director of our Greenville office so that he could explain why the water had turned green, what the likely cause of it was, and what (if anything) we would do about it.

It was clear from the very beginning that the staff of the Greenville office and many of the people in the audience had a history of disagreement and unpleasant relationships. At one point several members of the crowd questioned the professional integrity and competence of the director of the Greenville office. I felt compelled to interrupt and vigorously defend our staff and their work. After an hour or more of this, it became clear that we weren't accomplishing much and that what we had to offer in the way of help would not satisfy most of the attendees. So, I adjourned the meeting and we returned to Raleigh carrying with us a mason jar of very green Chowan River water which we had been asked to take with us to "show

---

[51] Remember that in early 1972 the Federal Clean Water Act, which contained the basis and strategy for nationwide water pollution control had not yet been passed. The controls that existed at that time limited the ability to control sources of pollution more narrowly than would be possible now.

the people in Raleigh how bad the problem was." We knew that Governor Scott was going to use the plane that evening so we left the bottle of water on the seat he usually used with a note that "this was from your friends on the Chowan." We never heard from him, which is probably just as well.

As a side light to this episode, a day or so later I did a radio interview in my office with Bob Farrington of WPTF, a local Raleigh radio station. With his microphone stuck in my face, Farrington asked me "who was responsible for the mess in the Chowan?" Without really thinking, I responded "Every son-of-a-bitch within the sound of my voice is responsible." We both laughed and allowed as how that quote wouldn't make the five o'clock news. However, Farrington told me afterwards that he seriously considered using it and went so far as to check with his producer about using it. Wisely, they decided not to. My point was that responsibility for a problem like that in the Chowan was wide-spread and couldn't be attributed just to the Farmer's Chemical plant. Obviously, I could have chosen better language.

Why Does Everything Exciting Happen Late Friday Afternoon

It seems as if most of the rest of the world tapers its work load off late Friday afternoon. In fact, it's well-known that releasing controversial information late Friday afternoon—too late for the early evening TV news and when the release won't hit the papers until Saturday morning—permits release of controversial information so that it will largely go unnoticed.[52]

I was working late, about 5:30 when everyone else had left, when my phone rang. On the other end was one of our marine fisheries inspectors who had been flying routine surveillance looking for possible violations of the state dredge and fill law. He was calling about a violation he did find, the news was unpleasant, and he knew he had a problem on his hands. He had spotted a dredge working for the Department of Transportation

---

[52]   As proof, I submit the announcement of my appointment to C&D. Since it was an appointment of a college professor to one of the top jobs in state government I figured it would be important news and at least mildly controversial. Not so. The news was released late Friday afternoon, was never included in the evening TV news, and appeared in a brief piece on the obituary page of the News and Observer! It helped keep my feet on the ground.

violating a permit issued to DOT for routine maintenance dredging in Hatteras inlet. The dredge was clearly working in a part of the area that had been controversial and was specifically designated as "not to be disturbed" and outside the permitted area. The inspector had confronted the dredge operator who acknowledged he was working outside the limits allowed in the permit. At that point the inspector decided he needed some backup from Raleigh and I was the only person he could raise. After explaining the situation, he asked me what he should do. I asked if he would normally issue a notice of violation in a case like this and he indicated he would but followed that with the reminder that this was a "DOT project and he wasn't sure he should issue a violation notice to another state agency." I responded that if the situation normally warranted a notice of violation which would stop any further dredging then he had to issue it, knowing full-well that the action would stir up a hornet's nest.

Sure enough, Monday morning when I got to the office, Billy Rose, the top DOT administrator, and several of his staff were waiting for me. Needless to say, they were not happy. Why did we issue a violation to DOT when they had a permit for the dredging? I pointed out that the dredging involved a clear violation of the terms of the permit and that we had no real discretion in the matter. They wanted to get their dredge back to work as passage across Hatteras inlet by ferries was virtually impossible without the dredging. I agreed to let the dredge get back to work if it remained entirely within the limits of the permitted area but that the violation would stand. That resolved the crisis for the moment but did not deal with the violation.

Eventually, the Attorney General's office was involved. They were very upset because they would have to prosecute both the violation on NER's behalf and defend against it on DOT's behalf. Their message was "please resolve this administratively." My recollection is that the case did come to court in Dare county and that it was settled with the statement that NER and DOT would resolve the issue to prevent further violations. We did that, but only after a full re-examination of the permit and clearly establishing what area was off-limits from dredging work and why.

I was never happy about the issuance of the notice of violation. However, we had, and continued to have, problems with DOT's dredging program. I'm not sure they ever really accepted that the dredge and fill act applied to them. By issuing the notice of violation we were at least able to get their attention.

The NER "Air Force"

As I mentioned earlier, NER managed the two state-owned aircraft that were used for executive travel. That wasn't the only air force NER had. In fact, the State Forest Service had more than 30 airplanes when I was in the agency. Of the 30, however, only 10 or 12 were operational. The smaller planes were used for routine forest fire surveillance and the larger were used in fire control work. The remaining planes were not flyable and were cannibalized for parts to keep the working planes flying.

One day Vic Barfield came in and told me we needed to get up with Senator Hamilton Horton who wanted to talk to us about "why NER had such a large air force." The matter had come up in a legislative budget committee meeting earlier in the day and Horton, rather than browbeat Barfield publicly in the meeting, asked to talk with him privately about the matter. I think Barfield asked me to go with him as I knew Horton fairly well.

We went to lunch with Horton that day and did our best to explain why it was important to retain all the aircraft as a means of keeping the working ones flying. During lunch, we also found out that Horton had followed up on one of NER's requests for additional personnel in the state park program with a personal visit during lunch on a prior day to the state park offices. While there he spoke with each of the women in the office and asked them what they did. One young lady (we never bothered to find out who) responded to Horton by telling him she really didn't do "much of anything, just a bit of this and a bit of that." After we had about exhausted the airplane issue, Horton described to us his visit to state parks and allowed as how we wouldn't get our requested position but rather could find some work for the "little girl who didn't do much of anything." It was impossible not to see the twinkle in Horton's eye while he broke this news to us.

The Hovercraft

One of the more complex coastal issues we dealt with was access to the Currituck county outer banks. Currituck county had resisted being incorporated into the Cape Hatteras National Sea Shore when it was created—a concern that too much of the outer banks would be controlled by the federal government with consequent limitations on development. By the early 1970s there was no access by road beyond Southern Shores and there had been very little development in the southern Currituck banks area. The two small villages of Duck on the south and Corolla farther north consisted of a few homes. There were two old gun clubs, Whalehead and Pine Island, the Currituck lighthouse, and a narrow strip from sound to sea near Duck used as a firing range by Navy jets from Oceana Naval Air Station near Norfolk.[53] To the north just south of the Virginia-North Carolina state line some low-quality development, involving marsh channeling and ocean-front houses, had begun. Access was from Virginia Beach to the north down the banks with passage into the development marked by a giant rubber figure of a woman in a bikini, a classy welcoming sign. Thus, most of the Currituck banks were still a nearly wild example of what the unsettled outer banks were like.

By the 1970s access to Currituck banks rose to a level where it could not easily be ignored. Although there was some pressure from local and development interests to build a bridge across the sound, there was no support in the Holshouser administration for this alternative. The issue for NER was to determine if there was an access alternative that might

---

[53] I had a scary personal experience with the firing range. In the early 1960s Bill Woodhouse (NCSU soils professor) and I accompanied a National Park Service ranger on a tour of the largely uninhabited Currituck banks. We drove by jeep to the state line and back using the existing road along the sound side and driving on the beach. Just north of Duck on the sound-side road our pleasant drive was interrupted by a sudden roar and two small explosions. The ranger yelled "was there a red flag flying" and I responded, "there was an old pair of red long johns on a pole back there" to which he responded with an expletive and "we are in the firing range and they're firing!" As quick as possible, given the narrow sand road, he turned and headed out in a hurry. As he was turning I looked out in the sound and saw a jet come out of its turn over the sound, head directly for us, and fire two rockets—a scary sight. They exploded with two small thumps (they were not fully armed) behind us in the dunes. We got out of the range in a hurry, not to return until we counted the jets and concluded they all were headed back to Oceana.

be relatively inexpensive and without significant negative environmental impact. However, we were not actively looking for an answer.

Enter the Hovercraft, a vehicle that skims just above the surface of land and water, is driven by a large propeller, and rides just above the surface on air-filled cushions. Hovercraft had been used extensively in the British Isles and at one time were a major source of cross-channel transport for people and cars. Although they are now (2017) not widely used in the United States, at one time they had promise for public water transportation. It came to NER's attention in early 1974 that one of the British hovercraft would be visiting the United States on an exhibition tour. We immediately contacted the sponsoring British agency and arranged for a stop in North Carolina to give us a hands-on experience with the craft's potential in the mixed shallow water-marsh-low sand bar environment of Currituck sound.

On the arranged day in spring 1974 several of us from NER flew to Manteo and were taken to the great sand bar on the north side of Oregon inlet where the craft was to meet us. It was a beautiful day so we were not alone at the inlet. There were several folks fishing; in our suits and ties we stood out. At the appointed hour the craft appeared from the north about half a mile off-shore. It turned ninety degrees to head directly for the sandy shore where we were waiting. The craft was impressive to say the least—it was bigger than a torpedo boat by a good bit and with its huge propeller whirling and kicking up spray it made a great deal of noise and commotion as it came through the surf and up on the beach. On its tail was emblazoned a large Union Jack. While the craft was coming ashore one of the women who was fishing near us watched the whole performance intently. When the craft was fully ashore she turned to us and asked "That ain't one of ours, is it?" to which I replied "No ma'am it ain't, but it does belong to one of our friends" while pointing to the Union Jack. That seemed to allay her concerns about an alien invasion and she went back to fishing. When the craft had settled on shore and idled its engines, the front opened up like a huge jaw and our group all entered. The jaw then closed, the craft powered up, backed off the shore, turned out to sea, and headed to the channel through Oregon inlet. I would have given anything to hear the conversation among the fisherfolk as this was going on.

Once we had navigated through Oregon inlet we turned southwest and headed across Pamlico sound. The craft cruised at about 40-50 miles an hour (my estimate) with a very smooth ride. The only issue we encountered was a request from the crew to keep a watch for the stakes that marked the location of fish nets—apparently objects like could work havoc with the air cushions on which the craft rode. The young British crew members were very pleasant and forthcoming with information about the operation of the Hovercraft, the various situations in which it had been found to be useful, and specifics of its operation. Our trip to Beaufort took several hours and ended when we came on shore, again riding from the water directly across a low beach onto sandy land. All in all, it was a very impressive performance.

Unfortunately, the Hovercraft did not appear to be a realistic solution to the question of access to Currituck banks. Data showed that it was very costly to operate, both in terms of fuel—which it apparently used as if it were going out of style—and maintenance. Furthermore, it did not have a large enough capacity to hold a significant number of passengers or their vehicles. To provide a realistic means of access across Currituck sound, North Carolina would have needed a small fleet and their cost, which proved to be high, made that impossible. So, we had a wonderful, once-in-a-lifetime trip on a unique form of water-land transportation but when all was said and done we were not any closer to resolving the question of state-funded access to Currituck banks. In all honesty, that did not bother any of us as we really had no interest in providing access at state expense so that development of Currituck banks would be made easier.

As matters unfolded in subsequent years, southern Currituck banks were extensively developed. The state finally provided access in the form of a road from Southern Shores, first to Duck and ultimately along the sound side to Corolla where it now ends. The Southern Shores-Duck-Corolla area is now intensely developed. An interesting feature of this development is the construction of very large single-family homes which are rented for family or group vacations; in 2017, a unit is being constructed as a single-family dwelling that consists of five separate structures with connecting passages and a capacity of forty-eight persons! Completion of that project is being contested. The Pine Island and Whalehead Clubs and Currituck lighthouse still exist but each is surrounded by other development. The Navy bombing range at Duck was closed and, in 1972 was transferred to the Army Corps of Engineers. In 1977, the Corps opened a coastal processes research station and pier on the tract; they are still active. The area north of Corolla up to the remnants of the first development just south of the state line remains largely undeveloped. The bulk of the land and water are part of the State Estuarine Reserve to the south and the 4,570-acre Currituck National Wildlife Refuge to the north. These two tracts effectively block continuous south to north road access.

Dealing with the Press

One of the important duties of a position at the level I held was regular interaction with the press. I always looked on this as an important, if not essential, part of my job. Furthermore, by being open and forthright with the press it was often possible to have coverage reflect accurately our positions or views on an issue. My relations with News and Observer and local TV reporters were generally good and usually it was a pleasure to help them develop a story and to make sure "our" views were correctly reflected in their stories.

Most of my dealings with the press were one on one discussions or short interviews for TV. The full-blown press conferences were left to the secretary! One exception to that rule took place during my first year and dealt with the problem of mercury pollution in the lower Cape Fear River. Discovery of elevated levels of mercury in river water, fish, and fish-eating animals led to strong expressions of concern as to the possible sources(s) and whether it was a potential danger to humans. No obvious local sources for the mercury had been found and the working hypothesis was that the observed levels were derived from rock strata through which the Cape Fear flowed upstream. There seemed to be no danger to humans unless they regularly ate large quantities of fish from the river.

Our PR man, Steve Meehan, felt that NER needed to make public statements about what appeared to be the origin of the mercury and the possibility of danger to humans. Steve cooked up a press conference and I was tabbed to do the explanation based on written material that he and I had prepared. When time for the conference rolled around, the meeting room on the third floor of the Administration building, where our offices were, was full of reporters and TV cameras. I began reading my prepared statement which, toward the end, involved a tedious explanation of the phenomenon of bioaccumulation of pollutants in animals and humans and how much humans must eat for a dangerous level of mercury to build up in their organs. The examples we used were fish in the river eaten by raccoons which in turn might be eaten by humans and how much must be eaten for a human to be endangered. This seemed a straight-forward way to explain an important biological phenomenon that underlay many concerns raised about pollutants, particularly those in water.

About half-way through my presentation, when I reached the part about fish and raccoons and humans, I noticed several TV crews picking up and leaving, followed shortly by about half of the rest of the room. When I finished barely a quarter of the original roomful remained. After a few desultory questions, Meehan mercifully ended the press conference and the few remaining reporters left. When we were alone, I asked Meehan if I was that bad and if the presentation was poorly done. Meehan smiled and said "no, when you reached the part about water and fish and raccoons and humans, most of the people thought we were putting them on." In other words, no one took what I had to say seriously—most thought it was a spoof.

Meehan and I had another experience a couple of years later that taught me a painful, but valuable, lesson in dealing with the press. We were walking out of a legislative hearing on proposed amendments which would have seriously weakened the state Environmental Policy Act. I turned to Meehan and said, "those SOBs are going to cut the guts out of that statute." No sooner had the words left my mouth than I realized a reporter from the N&O was walking beside us. I turned to him and said, "that wasn't for publication" to which he responded, "but you didn't say that" implying that he felt free to report it. Realizing that the appearance of the comment in the paper next day would damage NER's and my relationships with that legislative committee, Meehan and I talked about what to do. We agreed that an apology was the only proper response and when I mentioned the episode to Secretary Harrington he agreed.

The next morning not only did the quote appear in the paper but it was in the headline to the article! I walked over to the legislature, went into the committee room, and asked the chairman of the committee if I could have a minute or two at the beginning of the meeting to apologize. He graciously granted me the time and I offered the committee a full apology and assured them my comment was made in haste without thought. That ended the matter as far as both everyone was concerned. I learned from that experience a cardinal rule of dealing with reporters—expect them to report everything you say unless you tell them in advance what you are saying is not for publication or attribution. Forget that rule at your own risk.! The episode also showed the value of an admission of error and an apology. Far too often government officials or agencies, when caught in an error, seek a way out by attempting an explanation that clearly is fabricated and, in the process, simply compounds the error. The mistake then takes on a life of its own. How much simpler, and more straightforward, it is to simply admit error and move on. By apologizing as I did the matter quickly became a non-issue and had no further impact on my relationships with that legislative committee.

Speaking Engagements—the Rubber Chicken Circuit

One of the important parts of my job was public speaking. Having been a college teacher and having taught a lecture class of over 350 students in General Botany and well over 100 in Ecology, I was comfortable speaking before audiences. The talks I gave almost always fell into three categories: explaining our department's programs, promoting our department's programs, and presentations on current environmental issues. Generally, I enjoyed these speaking engagements but when two or three occurred in the same week it got tiring, particularly when I had to outline what I was going to say on the way to the talk, and didn't get home until midnight. Usually audiences were receptive to what I had to say but occasionally I ran into a lukewarm, or even hostile, audience. When that happened, I just did the best I could and chalked the episode up to experience.

I was almost always asked to provide some information about my background for the person who would introduce me. I learned the bitter way to provide only the very essential information at the very first talk I gave after taking the job. The talk was to the State Soil and Water Conservation folks and without thinking much about it I provided the resume to the introducer that was part of my personnel file at the university. The introducer got up and endeavored to introduce me by reading my resume. After he got to the organizations to which I belonged, he quit and said "it looks as if this man has been a member of every organization in the United States except the NAACP and the Ku Klux Klan!" The first thing I did when I got back to the office was red-line about ninety-five percent of the stuff in the resume and ask Martha to type up what was left. That's what I used from that point on.

Most of my talks were in the Triangle area or close enough to drive. However, occasionally one would be far enough away and was important enough to warrant use of a department plane. One such talk was in January 1975 and involved participation on a panel discussion in Charlotte about land use planning. At the time, I was mentoring a young man from Colgate, Dan Stuart, who was down for the month on a work-study assignment, and I invited him to go on the plane with me. Weather in North Carolina in January can be pretty iffy and the day we had to go to Charlotte was really iffy—windy, cold rain, and low ceiling. Our pilot, Earl Gower[54] informed us that he was pretty sure we could get to Charlotte but getting back was another story. I told him we'd cross that bridge when we got to it and we took off. The flight down wasn't too bad but the panel discussion didn't amount to much so the evening seemed pretty much a loss. When we left Charlotte, Earl said he wasn't too sure we could land in Raleigh—in fact, he said he already had an alternate airport, Jacksonville. I said Jacksonville wasn't too bad, but when he said he meant Jacksonville, FL, I knew we were in for a bad time. Apparently, the entire east coast was closed in and planes were having to take what they could get to land wherever they could. By this time the weather was getting worse and we were bouncing badly. Nonetheless Earl finally announced that Raleigh had given him clearance to land and we did make it home. Dan Stuart asked me after we landed if "it was always like this." I think he had enough of flying in a small plane in bad weather that night.

Dealing with the Legislature

While the legislature was in session we usually had dealings in the building at least once a week and often more frequently than that. Barfield and I regularly discussed our dealings with the legislature with each other and with the secretary. Occasionally, we were given instructions as to what position to support or how to deal with an issue but usually we used

---

[54] I only rated one pilot; agency secretaries and the governor rated two. Earl was the man who died of a heart attack at 39 two months after I left state government.

our judgement based on what we knew NER's interests were and what our position would logically be.

During 1971-76 the legislature was dominated by Democrats as it had been for the previous seventy-plus years. All legislators were important but some were much more important than others, especially when it came to certain matters such as budgets, which Barfield always handled, and to specific pieces of legislation on which we wanted their support or which we opposed. We cultivated our relationships with those key legislators carefully and tried to provide them with the information they needed to promote a specific piece of legislation, or to influence the outcome of debate over a bill. During my time working with the legislature I felt that most legislators, when push came to shove, had the best interests of the state uppermost in their thinking. The atmosphere of rank partisanship that characterizes today's (2017) legislature did not seem to exist then. In fact, there were senior legislators who I would feel comfortable describing as statesmen.

Individual episodes reveal what it was like to deal with the legislature. The episode I discussed earlier about making the decision to promote trade with the Peoples Republic of China was one such case. Another one occurred during debate over the Coastal Area Management Act. One of the most contentious pieces of the act was the structure of the Coastal Resources Commission, the body created to oversee the program. The model used in drafting the act was entirely consistent with past North Carolina practice. A commission of fifteen was proposed with twelve of the appointees having backgrounds directly related to management of the coast and three at large. In the version of the bill that passed three of the members were appointed at the discretion of the governor and the other twelve appointed from among nominations made by the coastal counties. Early drafts of the act had allotted a larger number of positions, five to seven as I recall, to be appointed at the governor's discretion.

The number of discretionary positions allotted to the governor became a major sticking point with several key Democrat legislators. Their concern was that because of the Republican governments in several of the coastal counties a Republican governor might be able to "pack" the commission using his discretionary appointments and selecting nominees from Republican counties. Although those of us promoting the bill felt this was a far-fetched concern, we still had to respond to it as the votes of certain key legislators hinged on the final wording of that provision. Finally, we decided to change the wording to only five to be appointed at the governor's discretion and a draft reflecting that change was circulated in the legislature. One key senator balked at five and Jim Harrington and I went over to explain why five was a "magic" number that satisfied Democratic concerns about commission "packing" yet provided adequate discretion to the governor. After listening carefully to our explanation, he thought for a bit and finally said "that sounds alright to me, and what you say sounds fair, but if it is proposed by a bunch of Republicans, there must be something wrong with it. I can't accept it." So, Harrington and I left and on the way back to the office decided that if it meant passage or defeat of the bill, we would drop back to three. The senator accepted three and ended up voting for the bill. In our discussion, Harrington and I agreed that in the long run the matter about which we were arguing would probably never become an issue. There were other far more controversial matters that would determine success or failure of the coastal management program. It is quite probable that the senator's concern with the number of gubernatorial discretionary appointments was something tangible he could use as a proxy for his general concern with the program and that if he could prevail on that point then voting to support the bill would not be as difficult. Neither Harrington nor I felt we had compromised away anything important to accommodate him; it turned out we were right.

In dealing with legislators it was essential to develop a relationship such that, although they might not like the ideas you espoused, they could at least trust what you were telling them. Unfortunately, it just isn't possible to develop that relationship with every legislator. The day after I appeared on the floor of the House with Representative Whichard to explain parts of the Coastal Area Management Act, the House took up debate on the bill. I had worn my Colgate maroon sport jacket to work that day and decided to go over to the House for a few minutes and listen to the ensuing debate from the gallery above the floor. At one point, a representative from the mountains, who strongly opposed CAMA and was making his case, pointed up to the gallery where I was sitting and thundered that "if we pass this bill, then Yankees from Cornell University will be coming to North Carolina to tell us what we can do with our land." I would have enjoyed the notoriety if he had only gotten my college right!

Not all relations with the legislature were adversarial. In fact, we worked closely with several legislators in developing legislation in which either they or we were interested. In at least two cases, this collaboration involved trips to other states. Perhaps the most productive of these trips was to Maine and Vermont and involved several key legislators, members of the department, and others involved in the development of land use legislation. The purpose of the trip was to consult with persons in both states who had either played a key role in passage of land use legislation or who were involved in its administration. In the case of Vermont, we were able to visit at some length with the governor who had been a major player in passage of Vermont's statewide land use bill, the first such program in the country. Several of the concepts contained in Maine and Vermont's programs surfaced in our coastal area management act. Furthermore, the uninterrupted time for conversation during the flights up and back allowed development of agreement on certain key features of the coastal act and on the need for a state-wide land use planning program. Although a state-wide land use bill was introduced into the legislature in 1974 no action was ever taken on it and the concept died, never to be revived.

Another trip involved a visit to a recycling facility in southern Ohio. In the early 1970s recycling was hardly on national or North Carolina's radar—it had been given no serious consideration by anyone either in the executive branch or the legislature. It was generally accepted, at least at that point in time, to be economically infeasible; to be implemented on anything more than a trial basis would be impossible. The trip was to Portsmouth, Ohio, as I recall. The weather on the day of the trip was about as bad as it could get for flying—freezing rain, sleet, and snow all the way from Raleigh to Ohio and back. Nonetheless, a group of about a dozen of us, including several important legislators, took off and endured a white-knuckle flight to Ohio and landed on sheet ice at the edge of the Ohio River. The visit was to one of the first large-scale recycling plants in the country. We saw solid waste being handled and converted into usable product—in fact, I still have a picture of two legislators peering intently at a handful of some recycled glass. On the return flight, there was much discussion of the desirability of instituting such a program in North Carolina but it took fifteen to twenty more years before municipal recycling in the state's big cities caught on.

Chapter 16

Did My Background as an Ecologist Influence
My Work in State Government?

Since my training as an ecologist and scientist, and my willingness to express opinions reflecting that training, strongly influenced my being hired into state government, it is interesting to reflect on whether the results of my work reflected my background. In an earlier chapter (3) I commented that, based on my first few months, it appeared that my work mostly seemed to require knowledge and skills other than those related to ecology per se. Looking back on the whole body of work, would the answer be different? Was my work in an administrative/governmental/political environment really influenced by my background in ecology? Did my background influence my decisions and the way I handled issues or were other factors involved?

It is certainly true that I viewed the world through "ecologically-tinted" glasses, as it were, and I am certain that view did influence how I approached the issues with which NER was faced. The nature of this "tint" is perhaps best expressed by Barry Commoner's four laws of ecology: "first, everything is connected to everything else; second, everything must go somewhere; third, nature knows best; and fourth, there is no such thing as a free lunch." To this I will add a fifth: "nothing can continue to grow forever". There are more sophisticated explanations of ecology but these are sufficient to explain the way in which I viewed the issues with which we were faced and the decisions I made about them.

In a purely ecological context, applying the principle that "everything is connected to everything else" means that a proposed action must be considered in light of its impact on the environment in which it will occur, in short, application of the environmental impact assessment principle. The rule that "everything must go somewhere" is fundamental to a competent assessment of the impacts of discharges of pollutants into the environment. "Nature knows best" doesn't mean simply leaving nature alone. It means that an understanding of how natural systems work is fundamental to understanding how to manage them. "There is no free lunch" means that we cannot carry out grandiose schemes of development without expecting to incur costs in terms of environmental damage and sometimes those costs vastly outweigh the benefits; we must understand the sometimes hidden, but nonetheless real, costs of development. They are there and we ignore them at our peril. The belief that "nothing can grow forever" made me inherently skeptical of the view that continued growth was not only possible but desirable. Few in government ever seemed to question the consequences of continued growth and whether the state's economic and environmental systems could sustain it.

A discussion of some of the projects with which we were involved will illustrate how these principles played out.

The issue that most immediately led to my move to NER was expansion of Raleigh-Durham airport. Together with a small cadre of other vocal opponents of an expansion that would overfly much of Umstead State Park, I pressed a view of the uniqueness of much of the park (in the context of the rapidly-growing Research Triangle area) and the fact that overflight of the park would destroy many of its values as a park. I had become quite familiar with Umstead through using it as an ecological teaching site. There were few sites like it in the Triangle and it deserved protection on ecological grounds if none other. It was not that I was opposed to expansion of the airport; the department I worked for had already stated that it supported expansion. It was the location chosen that was the issue. That location was chosen as being the only one that was economically feasible without considering the costs of damage to the park. As is often the case, when it became clear the original expansion plan had too many negative impacts, further analysis showed that other possibilities were not only feasible but probably more desirable.

Another example involving Umstead park further illustrates. Early in my tenure I was approached by a consultant who was designing a major sewer expansion for western Wake county (my home county). His plan was to run the sewer line directly down the valley of Crabtree Creek through the middle of the park. This valley was not only the wildest, most natural part of the park but it was also very deep and narrow in places. The proposed sewer line would have done great damage to the area through which it would go. In dealing with this problem my response was simple—I invited the consultant to meet me in the park and we could look at the environmental consequences of the proposed route together. After walking a considerable part of the proposed route, it became clear that the proposed work would be both an engineering and environmental disaster. The proposal was killed right there and the sewer was routed outside the Park. In this case a simple demonstration of the environmental implications of the proposal killed it before it ever became public. Undoubtedly it would have been killed anyway but the visit to the area involved saved an unnecessary public confrontation.

Perhaps the best example as to how my ecological background influenced my work is the Coastal Area Management Act. My contributions to it and my work in helping pass it reflect my understanding of coastal ecology. Some key sentences from the legislative findings introducing the act illustrate:

> ...."North Carolina's most valuable resources are its coastal lands and waters. The coastal area, and in particular the estuaries, are among the most biologically productive regions of this State and of the nation. Coastal and estuarine waters and marshlands provide almost ninety percent (90%) of the most productive sport fisheries on the east coast of the United States. North Carolina's coastal area has an extremely high recreational and esthetic value which should be preserved and enhanced.

> ....the coastal area has been subjected to increasing pressures.......... Unless these pressures are controlled by coordinated management, the very features of the coast which make it economically, esthetically, and ecologically rich will be destroyed. The General Assembly therefore finds that an immediate and pressing need exists to establish a comprehensive plan for the protection, preservation, orderly development, and management of the coastal area of North Carolina.

> In the implementation of the coastal area management plan, the public's opportunity to enjoy the physical, esthetic, cultural, and recreational qualities of the natural shorelines of the State shall be preserved to the greatest extent feasible; water resources shall be managed in order

> to preserve and enhance water quality and to provide
> optimum utilization of water resources; land resources
> shall be managed in order to guide growth and development
> and to minimize damage to the natural environment; and
> private property rights shall be preserved in accord with
> the Constitution of this State and of the United States."

These words are extremely important as they state the legislative purpose for the act. They would frame legal debate about why the act was passed and what the legislature's intent was in passing it.

Although I alone did not write these words, I contributed extensively to writing them. Other features of the act also reflect my ecological perspective. One of the most important of these is the definition of the coastal area. We knew from the very beginning that the coastal area had to be defined in a way that both established it as a unique part of North Carolina (to avoid making it an unconstitutional local act) and in terms that were clear and quantitative enough so that there would be little argument as to the area to which the act applied. Using political boundaries simply would not be sufficient. My knowledge of coastal ecology allowed me to weigh the various alternatives and finally to decide that the defining criterion would be based on inland penetration of salt water as the definition of "coastal area" makes clear:

> "Coastal area" means the counties that (in whole or in
> part) are adjacent to, adjoining, intersected by or bounded
> by the Atlantic Ocean (extending offshore to the limits
> of State jurisdiction, as may be identified by rule of the
> Commission for purposes of this Article, but in no event
> less than three geographical miles offshore) or any coastal
> sound. ....

> "Coastal sound" means Albemarle, Bogue, Core, Croatan,
> Currituck, Pamlico and Roanoke Sounds. For purposes of
> this Article, the inland limits of a sound on a tributary river
> shall be defined as the limits of seawater encroachment on
> said tributary river under normal conditions........."

That the definition stood scrutiny by the state Supreme court says that the work was legally, as well as ecologically, sound.

A critical part of CAMA was designation of areas of environmental concern, areas within which development could be regulated. Again, although the portions of land and water that eventually fell into this category were influenced by the thinking of many, I played a major role in enumerating the areas specifically included in the act. Obviously, my background in coastal ecology heavily influenced my thinking. In fact, some of the areas included were environments in which I or my students had done research; consequently, we were painfully aware of the impacts of unwise development in them.

The composition of the Coastal Resources Commission reflected my views of the need for a body composed of persons with backgrounds reflecting as nearly as possible each of the major groups with interests in the coastal area. Only in that way would all the relevant information be fairly evaluated when development issues were discussed. To me this meant backgrounds not only in coastal development and engineering but also knowledge of the way coastal land and water systems interacted and the impacts of development upon them. The commission, as defined in the original act, had representatives not only of development and engineering but also of fisheries, wildlife, and coastal ecology.[55] My view was that each relevant interest should have a seat at the table when decisions were made about coastal development.

My long involvement with Bald Head Island, which came to a head while I worked in NER, certainly reflected my ecological perspective of the management of coastal resources. A single trip to Bald Head early in the first summer (1959) I was in North Carolina convinced me that it was "a one of a kind" place and that development, at least as it was practiced in the early 1960s, would be both difficult and disastrous. When word of proposals for its development became common knowledge in the early 1960s, given my then position as Chair of the North Carolina Academy of Science Conservation Committee, it was important that I speak out. The development proposed violated almost every ecological fact of life in the

---

[55]   The coastal ecology position was removed and fisheries and wildlife combined by changes to the commission made in 2013.

coastal environment, would have been a catastrophe for both the island and whatever residents it had, and even for the nearby mainland. I argued this view in public and with government officials for almost ten years.

As events unfolded through the following years, the scale of proposed development was dramatically reduced, but the confrontation of development versus preservation continued as a standoff. I never lost my belief that North Carolina's best interests would have been served by state acquisition of the island but despite this belief it was never translated it into reality. It turned out that the end of the game was a negotiated arrangement between the state, the federal government, and the owners of the island that gave them the right to develop the upland of the main island, transferred control of certain other high ground areas to the state, and confirmed state ownership of all the marsh and tidelands. Although I played a small role in these final negotiations the issues involved were not primarily ecological—the need to protect marsh, tidelands, and dune systems had by that time been well established, accepted, and were an integral part of the final agreement—but more a matter of developing the legal mechanism to transfer the bulk of the island complex to the state without jeopardizing the state's belief that it already owned the marshes and tidal lands. Ecological considerations won over half the battle; settling for that was, under the circumstances, the best that could be achieved.

Establishment of the Cape Lookout National Seashore was another issue that on its face would seem to have benefited from the ecological perspective that I brought to the table. However, this was a case more of a willingness to see a difficult problem through to solution. The original thinking behind establishment of the seashore certainly considered the fragile nature of Core and Shackleford Banks and the importance of the banks in protecting Core sound and the adjacent mainland. Without saying so, the legislation creating the seashore recognized the ecological realities of the situation. But by the time NER became involved, the state had committed to the seashore in word but not in deed and our (my) job became seeing that the steps necessary to enable final designation of the seashore occurred. Persistence and a thick skin, more than my ecological background, enabled me to help see creation of the Cape Lookout Seashore through to reality.

My ecological perspective contributed in varying degrees to my administrative attitude toward the several dam projects that came to a head during my tenure at NER. Approval of New Hope (later B. Everett Jordan) was far advanced by the time I joined NER and consequently I had little involvement with it. Falls Reservoir was so charged politically and was dealt with at a level well above mine so that I also had little to do with it. My attitude toward the projects I did influence, Mills River, Crabtree Creek, and the New River, was conditioned not only by ecological considerations but also by my view that in two cases the displacements these projects would impose on existing occupants of the area to be dammed were a strong social injustice. These projects were all justified by analyses that showed that the economic benefits, almost always to interests outside of the area directly affected (New River being a prime example), were greater than environmental costs and the social disruption associated with removal of residents of the impacted area. I simply viewed these social equities differently, chose to act consistent with my view, and exerted strong effort to kill the projects and to convince my administrative superiors to do the same.

This is not to say there were no ecological concerns with these projects; there certainly were. Mills River would have usurped the headwaters of a mountain stream in the same way numerous other headwaters had been usurped by TVA. Crabtree Creek was a case of flooding the most ecologically-unique part of a state park to provide protection for ecologically-unsound floodplain development outside the park. In other words, the integrity of a possession of all the people of North Carolina was to be sacrificed for the economic gain of a few Raleigh developers. The New River project would have substituted flatwater, lake habitat for a free-flowing river, was justified originally as ameliorating pollution problems in the lower New and Kanawha by dilution of flow with water from the flood pools behind the New River dams, and was energy-inefficient because it would have used 4 units of energy for every 3 it would produce. I would have been comfortable opposing these projects on these environmental grounds alone but when the social injustice associated with them was added to the equation my determination to oppose these projects increased.

My commitment to increasing the size and scope of the state park system certainly was rooted in my ecological views of the importance of protecting significant areas of natural environment, important natural features, and nature-based outdoor recreation opportunities. It was clear to any thinking person in the 1970s that North Carolina was on the verge of explosive population growth with its accompanying urbanization. If we did not act then, the opportunity to protect many of the most desirable areas would quickly disappear. I had first-hand experience with some of the areas we protected having studied in them or taken students to them so I knew the significance of many of the areas we sought to save. In other cases, I accepted the arguments made by our planning staff and by local citizen's groups, most of which contained at least a small core of qualified natural historians. The question of social equity also arises in the case of park acquisition since some areas had to be condemned. In the case of parks, however, each proposed acquisition was promoted by a strong local support group and in virtually all cases there was strong local agreement with acquisition for park purposes, including agreement from most of the affected land owners. Accordingly, we worked in concert with local interests in practically all cases. In other cases, we could work out acquisition agreements that diminished negative impacts on residents of the area.

Before ending the discussion of the influence my background as an ecologist had on my work in state government, there are two further questions to discuss. First, how does one influence policy from within a government agency? Second, what is the proper role of ecology—or of any science for that matter—in government policy-making? These are issues that warrant another book. My comments in this context cover what are the most obvious responses to these questions.

How one influences policy from within a government agency begs a complicated answer. However, the answer can be boiled down to the simple statement, "be sure you have a seat at the table where issues are discussed and decisions are made." A corollary is that the seat should be at a high administrative level; the higher the administrative level the greater the opportunity to wield influence. Few card-carrying ecologists have ever occupied a truly high position in government. Stanley Cain as Assistant Secretary of Interior in the 1960s, Ron Pulliam as Director of the

National Biological Survey in the 1990s, William Martin as Commissioner of Kentucky's Natural Resources Department also in the 1990s, and Jane Lubchenko as Administrator of NOAA in the first Obama administration come to mind.

I got my seat at the table when I was hired into a high-level administrative position in C&D/NER. Although the responsibilities of the position I was hired into were vaguely-defined when I was hired, with time and reorganization the position evolved into one in which involvement in virtually all the department-level decisions was expected. Therefore, whatever influence I had in the decisions that were made could reflect my view of the issues. This does not imply that each decision was made in accordance with my views—certainly not—but it does imply that I had the opportunity to ensure that the ecological dimensions of a decision were fairly represented as the final decision was shaped. This principle boils down to a simple example. I was asked once how "you influence policy?" Half seriously I responded that one needs to be sure to have a seat on the airplane when the secretary flies to make an important presentation. In other words, be the last person he talks to before he publicly commits himself and/or his department to a position. Although this trivializes the principle, it emphasizes that one's ability to wield influence is directly proportional to how close one is to the place were policy decisions are made—to the seat of power.

This does not imply that lower-lever administrative positions in an agency cannot wield much influence on agency decisions. Obviously, important decisions are made at all levels of government. Important decisions and policies are often shaped from the bottom up with the numerous inputs of staff members, who frequently have different perspectives, shaping the result. By the time the need for a final decision rises to the level of the agency head, the often-competing alternatives have been shaped and selected by staff input. If lower level staff members have an ecological perspective then hopefully one or more of the alternatives considered at the agency level will reflect that perspective.

The role of science in general and ecology specifically in government is to inform the decision-making process—in the case of ecology, to make certain that the ecological consequences of decisions are clearly laid out and explained to decision makers. Ideally, all factors that inform a decision are given equal weight in the process. However, government is not the ideal world and alternatives that are considered are often badly at odds with one another.[56] Nowhere is this statement truer than with economic development proposals that entail serious environmental consequences. An example in which ecological considerations were given a weight coequal to economic factors comes from development of the coastal management legislation. The basic stimulus for the legislation was the damage that poorly-conceived and poorly executed development did to the coastal environment and the fear that if this pattern persisted many of the values, both economic and environmental, of the coast would be lost forever. Critics of the early drafts of the legislation argued that it was an "anti-development, ecology bill" that would prevent any further growth of the coastal economy. As debates over the bill continued, mechanisms were incorporated that would establish which natural systems required the highest degree of protection and a process by which development could be allowed but only in a way that did minimal damage to those systems. Salt marshes had been well-documented by extensive ecological research to be central to the productivity of estuaries and to be systems highly susceptible to damage from development. North Carolina had established that minimizing salt marsh destruction was a state priority through the language of its dredge-and-fill law. The coastal management program early-on incorporated this principle and no significant destruction of salt marshes has occurred since the program was established.

Despite this example of a decision that balanced economic and environmental considerations, actual practice is usually not that reasoned. In a capitalist society such as ours, economic considerations usually carry the greatest weight in deciding issues. It is far easier to grasp the immediate economic impacts of a decision than it is the ecological or social impacts. We have developed mathematical values, such as the cost to benefit ratio, that seem to quantify a subjective decision and can lend weight to deciding an issue in favor of economics. We have limited ability to express ecological and social considerations in a similar way. Often, economic benefits in terms of jobs, increases in the tax base, and higher standard of living are valued against impairment of natural systems or destruction of

---

[56]   Recall that the final structure of NER selected during reorganization was intended to minimize this outcome. In practice, it did not realize that intention.

a way of life even when negative impacts are starkly obvious. The case of the New River is an example. The Federal Power Commission over and over decided that peak power generation was more important to society than the natural systems of the New River valley or the way of life of its inhabitants. In a rare example that defies the rule, Governor Holshouser, NER, and most citizens of the New River valley weighed the evidence and decided otherwise.

Often, the importance of ecological considerations becomes more obvious when the issues are evaluated in terms that ask, "what are the consequences of a wrong decision?" It may be clear what economic benefits will be foregone, but the ecological results are often difficult to quantify in meaningful terms. The disrupting of a food chain or the accumulation of toxic substances in the sediment of a river can be shown to be highly likely, but "so what?" "So what" does not become obvious until the fish in that river have accumulated biological toxins in quantities that will damage them and make them dangerous to be consumed by humans. "So what" becomes obvious again when poorly-treated chemical discharges into ground water make adjacent well waters unfit for human consumption. "So what" suddenly becomes immediate and personal.

As I write this (mid-2017), the global population is faced with the grand-daddy of all "so what" questions—climate change. There is clear evidence that climate is changing and the consequences of that change—different weather patterns, sea level rise, migrations of plant and animal populations—also seem clear. The evidence also suggests, through an understanding of atmospheric chemistry and its interaction with sunlight, that the causes are man-made. Societies around the globe are struggling to decide if the negative impacts of climate change are great enough, and important enough, to warrant actions that will force change in well-established patterns of economic behavior. Some governments have decided that the consequences of a wrong decision—business as usual as we now know it—are potentially so serious that such actions are warranted. Other governments, sadly our own current one, reject that course of action. That rejection raises the dilemma faced when one set of considerations—in this case the impact of climate change on humanity—becomes so great that considerations related to reducing the threat of climate change should be paramount. Society now seems faced with such a dilemma.

To sum up, the role of ecological considerations in decision making is to provide an integral part of the environment-economy-society decision process. The role of the ecologist in government is to assure that, at whatever level he or she works, final decisions reflect ecological input. Ecological considerations may not always prevail, but they must always get a fair hearing and balanced consideration.

So, having said all that, I can make the case that my background as an ecologist did have a strong influence on my work in NER. However, there were other abilities that proved to be equally important to whatever success I had. Without these other abilities, I doubt seriously I could have been influential.

Perhaps most important of these traits was a willingness to listen— to pay attention to what is being said, particularly by your adversaries. Apparently, I have that trait. I always tried to listen carefully to what was being said, and how it was being said, to get a clear picture of the issue and argument under discussion. Being a careful listener also creates a sense in others that you care about the speaker and what he or she is trying to tell you. If I disagreed with what was being said, I did not interject that disagreement into the discussion immediately—that would have created a sense that my mind was clearly made up and that further discussion was futile. Being a good listener may be one of the most important traits that a public servant needs to have.

Other traits that I had that were important to success in administration sound trite when they are spelled out. The ability to organize and multi-task were critical. Too often one would find oneself thinking out some critical issue only to be interrupted by the telephone or by a visitor who could not be ignored. It takes mental dexterity to move from one issue to another without loss of the sense of either issue. Meetings are an essential, and terribly time-consuming feature of administrative life. Apparently, I have a knack for chairing meetings (gracious knows I did enough of it so I should have learned something!) as occasionally I heard someone say after a meeting "he runs a good meeting." Most people would consider that being damned with faint praise! The secret centered on a few simple ideas. Always sit in the middle of the table, never at the end. Being at the head of the table created a sense of importance that wasn't necessary—one's position and title should do that job. I made sure there was an agenda, tried to stick to it, injected some humor when it was possible, and never left a meeting without some form of closure. Even after the most rancorous and chaotic meetings I would try to wrap up by saying something like "what I hear us saying......" That offered attendees the chance to differ—they might have "heard" differently—and it gave me the chance to frame the outcome in a way that reflected my goals for the meeting. In other words, when there was no real consensus on an outcome, I would frame one mixing the threads of what I had heard together with the results that I had hoped would come from the meeting.

Finally, a reminder here of something I stressed in other contexts. Always tell the truth so that the people with whom you interact know that they can trust what you say or what you will do. Telling the truth doesn't necessarily mean baring your soul to the world and revealing every iota of truth. It's fine to tell only part of a story if the part you tell is true. Nothing can destroy your effectiveness quicker than gaining the reputation of being one who dissembles, particularly on difficult issues. Being known as a person whose word is always "good" lends one credibility, and credibility is of great value in the political environment.

I discovered one thing about myself while working in NER—I am a political animal. By that I do not mean I am a politician—in fact, I stayed very far away from partisan politics while in office and never have run for elective office. What I do mean is that I have a knack for working out solutions to complicated problems that will satisfy most of those with a stake in the problem. This involves a willingness, when it is necessary, to compromise and to accept something less than what one might have hoped for. As Bismarck said, "politics is the art of the possible." It is not a sign of failure to negotiate and accept a resolution that does not reflect all one wants—that is quite often the necessary reality of a situation. On the other hand, there are times when it is necessary to accept no less than a solution entirely acceptable from the point of view of your agency's interests. Knowing when to compromise and when not is essential in a political context.

Although whatever success I had did reflect my ecological background, it also was due to some innate abilities I had that allowed me to adapt to, and be successful in, an environment very different from the university. As it turned out, those talents also allowed me to be involved successfully in several other important public service positions and in an administrative position at the University.

Another important outcome of my work in NER was establishment of a precedent that, because of the complex technical nature of NER's work, there should always be someone in the secretary's office competent by background to deal with those issues. It need not always be an ecologist; enough of NER's work involved disciplines other than ecology so that expertise in other disciplines was highly appropriate. In fact, for over thirty-five years after I retired one or more persons in the secretary's office did have such a background. In at least one administration, the secretary himself met those criteria! That precedent was broken badly in 2012 when at least one assistant secretary with an expressed agenda to diminish the agency's regulatory reach was appointed. Fortunately, he did not last long. However, the reduction in scope of the agency's authority in 2015 changed the department so dramatically that the qualifications for those serving in the secretary's office no longer resemble those of the NER of the 1970s, 1980s, and 1990s.

Chapter 17

Reflections on the History of NER Since 1976

When I began this chapter I intended it to be something entirely different. I had become frustrated with the changes in what was NER as I knew it in 1976 and with the loss of public support the agency had experienced. Thus, the original intent of this chapter was to explain the changes that had taken place in NER, why they were unwise, and why as the state's environmental protection agency it merited more public support. As I wrote this apology, I began to realize that the changes that had taken place reflected a natural evolution of the department in response to political and social change and because of inherent problems associated with its the original structure. In short, the changes were in many ways inevitable; for the department not to have changed would have been remarkable, given the malleable state of government agencies as the winds of political and social change swirl about them. Thus, this piece became an explanation of how and why the old NER changed since 1976, the causes of those changes, and what they mean for the future of natural resource management at the state level, at least in North Carolina.

The North Carolina of 2017 is vastly different, socially and politically, from that of the 1970s when I worked in state government. The "environmental" movement, which began its full flowering in the early 1970s, has matured and dealing with environmental issues is now a major function of virtually all government agencies and at all levels of government. In North Carolina, complex regulatory programs in coastal management, water and air pollution control, erosion control, solid waste disposal, recycling, and hazardous waste management, to name just a few, have been implemented and have become fixtures of state and local governments. Implementation of these and other similar programs has introduced a new level of government regulation of activities that prior to the 1970s had been minimally regulated. In many cases, new regulations had to be developed for management activities that were complex and often with limited available scientific understanding of the systems and processes being managed. These regulations sometimes resulted in delay or elimination of projects with significant political support, resulting in the projects and the programs involved becoming highly controversial.

Furthermore, environmental regulations had the potential to constrain the use of private property. These forty-five plus years of regulation have provided enough time for development of a backlash reaction to environmental protection measures. This backlash has sometimes been based on legitimate differences of opinion or on complex equity issues, but more often it is a result of an important political "ox being gored." Whatever the reasons, management of environmental programs is now an almost unremittingly contentious process that serves as a lightning rod drawing controversy to regulatory agencies.

North Carolina has undergone a political sea change since 1970. North Carolina then was a one-party state with Democrats controlling both houses of the legislature and the governorship. Despite the election of Republican Jim Holshouser in 1972 Democrat Jim Hunt followed him for eight years, with eight years of Republican Jim Martin's administration followed by eight more years with Hunt. Democrats continued firmly in control of the legislature until 2000. However, in the early 2000s the major change in North Carolina politics began with a significant increase in Republican membership in the legislature. Although Democrats occupied the governor's office through 2012, the legislature became more heavily Republican. A series of political scandals during the 1990s and early 2000s involving Democrat officials further diminished public confidence in that party's ability to govern. The Senate remained Democrat through 2010, but the House was split evenly in 2002; by 2010 both chambers had Republican majorities. The 2012 election ran heavily Republican with the GOP gaining both the governorship and veto-proof majorities in both houses.

The agendas that Republican majorities brought with them when they took control of the legislature in the 2011 session emphasized, among other things, three areas of significance to environmental management programs: tax cuts, down-sizing and re-organization of state government, and reduction in "burdensome" regulations, particularly those related to environmental protection. With the election of Republican Pat McCrory in 2012, the administration of state agencies shifted to Republican control and, as might be expected, new management reflected the agendas of the new governor and the legislature. As might be expected, the state's environmental management agency became a target for implementation of the agendas of the legislature and governor. In fact, one of the new assistant secretaries in the environmental agency had been a legislator known for having a target aimed at the Archdale Building (where the agency was located) painted on his office window. Objectivity with respect to environmental programs was hardly the order of the day in North Carolina state government from 2012 on. Nonetheless, environmental issues, particularly management of coal ash storage ponds, demanded a regulatory response. That response was, at best, controversial, and few have been satisfied by it.

*****

The length of time between the creation of NER in 1971 and the time that this is being written in 2017 (forty-six years) is the same as the forty-six year period between creation of C&D in 1925 and its movement to Natural and Economic Resources in 1971. Given the major social and political changes since 1971 it is not surprising that the department that exists today bears little resemblance to its 1971-74 structure. In fact, there is probably a greater difference between the environmental department of today and its progenitor of 1971 than there was between the original and final versions of C&D.

When the legislature created NER in 1971 it consciously decided to create a large, "super agency", one that combined all natural resource and economic development functions, rather than leaving those programs in several separate agencies. In short, it chose an expanded version of the old C&D model. The premise inherent in this choice was that the large agency would maximize opportunities for intra-agency coordination that would replace inter-agency disagreement. Furthermore, it hoped that this model, by its similarity to the C&D model, would centralize political support for all its constituent programs. The years that followed NER's creation have provided a period of trial to determine if the legislature's choice would work. History has shown that it did not. The question, of course, is whether the model was inherently unsound or did it fail because of unpredictable external events. As I shall explain, the answer is some of both.

Natural and Economic Resources in its original structure lasted only until the aftermath of the 1976 election. Jim Hunt, in his first gubernatorial campaign, made an issue of the fact that economic development programs did not receive the emphasis they needed to grow the state's economy because they were buried in a department whose duties and agencies were heavily oriented toward natural resources and environmental protection. At Hunt's request, in 1977 the legislature moved all economic development and tourism promotion functions from NER into the Department of Commerce. Natural resources, environmental protection, and community development functions were not moved and the new department was named Natural Resources and Community Development (DNRCD). This combination of responsibilities fitted the interests of the then-secretary, Howard N. Lee, and several of his successors.

The department remained with this alignment until 1989 when a profound change in its structure and authority took place. For years there had been confusion concerning the authority of DNRCD and the Department of Health and Human Resources relating to various aspects of water pollution, including water treatment facilities, septic tanks, and pollution of shellfish waters. To clear up this confusion, the 1989 legislature (Session Laws 1989- 727) renamed the Department as the Department of Environment, Health, and Natural Resources (DEHNR) and transferred the Health Services, Waste Management, Radiation Protection, Water Treatment Facilities, and Shell Fish Water Protection programs of the Department of Health and Human Resources into the renamed department. At the same time, the Division of Economic Development, Community Assistance, Community Development, and Employment and Training together with the Board of Science and Technology and the Park, Parkway, and Forest Development Commission (all remnants of the original Office (Division) of Industrial, Tourist, and Community Resources in NER), were transferred to the Department of Commerce. The net effect of these changes was to remove almost completely the "community assistance" functions of the old NER and replace them with regulatory programs from Health and Human Resources. It also created a department even more heterogeneous and complex than its predecessor.

These changes transformed what had been a department with mixed regulatory and community assistance functions to one that was, except for its forestry and park and recreation programs, strongly regulatory in nature. The 1989 reorganization legislation also repealed the statute creating a "Board" for the department. Collectively, the changes had the further effect of reshaping forever the department's constituencies beginning, in turn, a change in the way the legislature and citizens viewed the department. Deleting the department's board also solidified the change that Roy Sowers had predicted would occur if Conservation and Development were split—the loss of any possibility of unified political support.

The Budget Act of 1997, recognizing that the entity created in 1989 was unworkable, made further changes in the department by returning many of its public health-related functions to the Department of Health and Human Resources and renaming it the Department of Environment and Natural Resources (DENR), the name it bore until 2015. Wording in the Budget Act also instructed the secretaries of the two departments involved to develop a memorandum of understanding to cover coordination of the areas where the two departments shared functions, reflecting the fact that the changes made in 1989 never fully resolved the overlap in program authority between DEHNR and DHH.

In 2011 the legislature finalized several changes that had been discussed for several years by shifting the Division of Forest Resources and the State Soil and Water Conservation Program to the Department of Agriculture and Consumer Services. Forest Resources staff and, more important, forestry's external constituencies had come to view the program as a more-or-less ignored function of DENR and felt that their mission could be better realized if they were aligned with agriculture programs. The same views were held by the Soil and Water staff and its constituencies in the agriculture community. Furthermore, staff members of the forestry and soil and water programs strongly supported this move.

For unclear and unexplained reasons, the 2015 legislature, responding to a recommendation in the governor's budget legislation, in its own budget act moved all recreation and visitor-oriented programs (state parks, the zoo, the aquariums, and the Natural Sciences Museum), the department's few remaining service functions not related to a regulatory program, into the Department of Cultural Resources, creating a new Department of Natural and Cultural Resources. This move completed the progressive reduction of North Carolina's unified natural resource management agency from an entity with, in theory, the capability for unified management of natural resources and economic development with both regulatory and service functions, to a purely regulatory agency. In fact, the legislation[57] to effect these last changes acknowledged this by renaming the Department as the Department of Environmental Quality (DEQ).

In retrospect, it was inevitable that the Department of Natural and Economic Resources would not survive as originally constituted. No institution of government can be expected to survive nearly fifty years without some change. The vicissitudes of politics and the winds of social transition are powerful agents of change. As painful as it is for someone who was instrumental in the birth of the department to admit, it is clear in retrospect that it contained the seeds of its own destruction. Several factors have contributed to the systematic conversion of the agency from one with overarching responsibility for all the state's natural resources and economic development to one with a narrower focus on regulation as a tool to maintain environmental quality. Some factors were inherent in the model chosen for the department and others related to external social and political changes between 1976 and 2015.

One reason that the original Department of Natural and Economic Resources did not survive had to do with the difference between its structure and that of its predecessor Department of Conservation and Development. I have pointed out that C&D, which combined conservation and development and served as the model the legislature chose for the new department, succeeded in large part because its supervisory body, the Board of C&D, consisted of politically-influential people who generally supported all the programs of the department and served as a means for connecting citizens to those programs. It would be naïve to suggest that all twenty-seven members of the board were equally supportive of all programs. However, when the board acted as a full board, all members voted to approve, or not, proposed actions and programs coming from each departmental division. This vote of the board provided a political "stamp of approval" for an action and lent it stature in front of the legislature and the public.

The Board of Conservation and Development was created together with the department in 1925. It typified a long-standing North Carolina tradition that governmental authority was too important to leave in the

---

[57] Session Laws 2015-241 14.30(a)-143.30(ttt).

hands of bureaucrats alone; its exercise must be overseen by citizens themselves. This tradition was exemplified by the numerous boards and commissions attendant to all major programs of state government and it generally functioned well, providing a means for direct citizen access to and oversight of government agencies. Although board and commission duties were often advisory there were numerous cases where a board or commission exercised statutory authority. Although agency heads and board members were generally all appointed by the same governor, differences could arise between agency heads and their attendant boards or commissions, sometimes centering on "who ran the show" but more often on important policy issues. This was certainly true in Conservation and Development during the 1960s with strong-willed Board Chairmen J. Willie York and Gilliam Horton frequently differing openly with agency heads Dan Stewart and Roy Sowers. It is no wonder that the "care and feeding of the board" became an important function of upper level agency administrators in all departments. Despite the awkwardness these differences could create, a board composed of knowledgeable and politically-influential private citizens generally provided a strong source of political support for agency programs.

How to deal with the great number of boards and commissions scattered through state government became an important issue in government reorganization. The nineteen principal departments specified in the reorganization legislation each consisted of a collection of previously independent or quasi-independent agencies whose authorities were transferred, either wholly or in part, to the chief officer (secretary) of the new agency. In so doing, the legislature in almost all cases re-defined the structure and authorities of the transferred agency. When the Department of Conservation and Development was created in 1925 its "control and management" were vested in a seven-person Board of Conservation and Development that included the governor and other defined state officials. The board controlled the work of the department and could make rules and regulations. It, rather than the governor, appointed a director who had "charge of the work of the department under supervision of the board." Although by 1971 the board had increased to twenty-seven persons appointed by the governor, none of whom were sitting government officials, it retained its original statutory relationship with the director, i.e. the statutes still specified that the board "controlled and managed" the department. As might be expected by this time the director in practice ran the department; nevertheless, the board exercised authority and was far from an advisory body.

The reorganization legislation of 1971-74 that created the Department of Natural and Economic Resources, hoping to continue this beneficial relationship, specified that there was to be a Board of Natural and Economic Resources. However, the language called for a board very different from the old Board of Conservation and Development. The majority of the new twenty-five member board consisted of the chairmen and an elected member from many the department's commissions and councils with just ten members-at-large appointed by the governor. Furthermore, the duties of the board were to "consider and advise" the secretary on any matter that he "may refer to it." In other words, the board no longer had a strong connection to citizens at large and it no longer had any authority whatsoever in running the new department. The powers and duties of the department were conferred on the secretary. Although a board was initially appointed after NER was established it seldom met and its meetings were perfunctory. Eventually, it was deemed so useless that the statute creating it was deleted by the 1989 legislature thus ending (ignominiously, by reference!) the long-standing tradition of direct citizen input to the department.

It is true that NER and its successor agencies house several commissions (e.g. Environmental Management, Coastal Resources) and that in most cases these are comprised of private citizens (often meeting statutorily-prescribed criteria). The legislature has delegated authority to these commissions to develop and enforce most of the regulations governing the department's key regulatory programs. However, each of these commissions is dedicated to a specific statutory responsibility and none has a department-wide mission or vision. Thus, there is an absence of a body of citizens appointed to provide input to, and support for, the department as a whole. The close relationship between the department and its board, assumed by the legislature when the department was created, never materialized. Although certainly not the reason the department failed in its original configuration, it is surely a contributing factor.

The sheer complexity of NER in and of itself created several serious problems and proved to be a fatal flaw.[58] First and foremost, the complexity of the department made it difficult to realize the goal of coordination among management of the various resources and thus negated the first legislative assumption in structuring the department. The belief that placing programs in the same administrative unit would foster closer cooperation among them proved to be an impossible dream. The scope of interests in the original NER and its successors DNRCD and DEHNR was simply too great. When the department was created in 1971, the position of Assistant Secretary for Resource Management, the position I held, was created to facilitate intra-departmental coordination. In practice, this did not happen as too much of my time was spent on managing departmental involvement in issues that transcended the interests of individual departmental agencies and, in some cases, even the department itself. As time passed, additional assistant secretary positions, with clearly-defined responsibilities, were established, thus creating administrative compartmentalization rather than integration of agencies.

Another result of the department's complexity was the significant differences in perspectives, objectives, and constituencies of its various programs. The wide array of departmental programs simply prevented equal attention to each. Furthermore, each of the department's programs had its own sphere of influential constituents. From the very beginning the economic development program and its supporters expressed frustration over the time and attention that the secretary necessarily had to devote to high-priority environmental programs, such as the expanding water and air pollution programs, the millions of dollars spent to grow the state park system, and establishment of the coastal management initiative. The criticism was that the state's economic growth was limited by the

---

[58] Part of this complexity goes back to the widely-different nature of the major departments reorganized into NER. However, part of it derives from the fact that the legislature, to remain under the "nineteen new departments" called for in the constitutional amendment authorizing reorganization, put several programs in NER because they literally could not find any other place to put them. When Barfield raised a question with legislators as to why this or that program was put into NER, the answer he often got was "we couldn't figure where else to put it, and besides, we know you will run it well." The management problems that created eventually came back to haunt NER.

divided administrative attention given to economic development within the new department. Feeling that it would never be given the attention it deserved in its new home, economic development staff members and their supporters made the program's needs felt, not only within the department but undoubtedly in the 1976 gubernatorial campaign, the first following reorganization. Expansion of a Department of Commerce with economic development as its top priority became inevitable when Jim Hunt espoused it. Similar perceptions, and realities, of internal neglect within the department eventually led to the 2011 move of the North Carolina Forest Service and the Soil and Water Conservation Program to Agriculture and Consumer Affairs. An inability, or unwillingness, to make those programs a high departmental priority eventually led to their departure for perceived greener pastures.

If it proved difficult to manage the wide array of programs included in NER and even its successors DNRCD and DEHNR, it was even more difficult to find persons to serve as upper-level administrators who had the background and knowledge to deal with programs ranging from economic and community development to pollution control. The department's secretary was clearly a political appointment selected for various reasons, none of which necessarily included technical knowledge of resources and their management. He (all have been men so far) necessarily brought with him a limited knowledge of the scope of the department's responsibilities and a unique set of instructions from the governor as to how the department was to be run and what its emphasis was to be. These may or may not have covered the full range of interests of the department. Several secretaries have brought closeness to the governor as a major qualification; several others had strong environmental or community development qualifications and thus credibility with their constituencies, and several others had no identifiable interests within the department. Deputy and assistant secretaries, with more narrowly defined scopes of responsibility, were intended to create the necessary breadth in departmental administration. Although these lower-level administrators might have been able to bring about coordination among the units that reported to them, the ultimate responsibility lay with the secretary.

Finally, perhaps the most important factor contributing to the changes in the state's natural resource agency was the increasing scope, complexity, and administrative demands of the department's regulatory programs. To make a long story short, between 1974 and the late 1990s a wide variety of regulatory programs came to dominate the department and necessarily required the close attention of the secretary and his assistants. This growth of regulatory programs was a response both to North Carolina legislative initiatives and to federal mandates from the Congress. When NER was created in 1971 the old Department of Water and Air Resources brought its water and air pollution control programs, limited in scope as they were, into it. The only other significant regulatory programs in the department at that time were the dredge and fill program in marine fisheries, the enforcement of mining regulations by the mineral resources agency, and the wildlife and inland fisheries regulation programs of the Wildlife Resources Commission. Although these were important programs with significant impacts in defined areas, they did not have the wide-spread impact of water and air pollution control.

It is hard to overstate the impact that passage of the National Environmental Policy Act, passage of the Clean Air Act, and creation of the Environmental Protection Agency all in 1970 and passage of the Clean Air and Clean Water Act and Coastal Zone Management Act in 1972 had on NER. Each of these programs established standards at the federal level but delegated implementation to the states. Substantial funding accompanied the delegation pending, of course, demonstration by the state that it had the appropriate statutes and administrative capability to carry out the responsibilities of these programs. Meeting these demands required additional personnel, a new administrative apparatus, and entirely new regulations as well as close and constant attention from the departmental administration. The requirements of the federal and state coastal zone management programs required an entirely new administrative unit and regulations. Further new mandates, such as hazardous wastes, buried storage containers, and solid waste management and their associated federal mandates added new complexity and required additional staff. Incorporation in the late 1980s of health-related functions such as septic tanks, restaurant sanitation, and clean drinking water had a similar effect (who would expect to find the secretary of a natural resources department as the enforcer of bathroom handwashing regulations!). By the 1990s, the work of the department was overwhelmingly involved in these regulatory programs. These regulatory programs were in many ways the public face of the department and in a very real way shaped the department's public image. Internally, the management of these regulatory programs served to further diminish administrative and public attention to the department's other important resource management programs including forestry, mineral resources, and state parks.

Because of the major changes in the department's emphasis and effort, the Department of Environment and Natural Resources (as of 1989) became primarily a regulatory agency with all the negative baggage that implies. Clearly, it is now viewed that way by the legislature. Since the 1980s there have been regular legislative efforts to chip away at that authority or to find other ways to limit its application. One means of limiting regulatory authority has been to subject regulations proposed by the department to progressively greater review and modification. Using amended requirements of the Administrative Procedures Act (first passed in 1973), mechanisms for review and approval of regulations have been made more extensive. These reviews confer greater authority to request change, or further review, of proposed rules on persons often relatively-poorly informed about the details of a regulatory program. Some of these legislative constraints on executive branch authority were appropriate and ensured public input and important review. Other changes, however, seem to constitute legislative infringement on the powers of the executive branch and have been put in place primarily to impede and make more difficult enforcement of legislatively-mandated actions.

Another means of limiting the department's regulatory authority has been to enact into statute not only limitations on the scope of enforcement of laws designed to protect natural resources and the environment, but also their substantive requirements. An example is the legislative derailing of a set of water quality protection measures for Jordan Lake and their replacement with the "experimental" solar bees. Despite demonstration of the failure of "solar bees" there are still no water quality protection measures for the lake in place. All the legislature accomplished was more years of inaction during which water quality in Jordan Lake continued to decline.

One can judge that the department's relationship with the legislature recently has been, to put it mildly, not healthy. In the last several legislative cycles, the cry from the legislature is to "do away with burdensome regulation." The crux of the issue is whether the concern is with the "burdensome" nature of regulation or with the substance of the regulations themselves. If the concern is the former, then it is reasonable to expect the department to make a good-faith effort to explain the regulatory process as clearly and concisely as possible and to offer the regulated community assistance in its efforts to meet regulatory requirements. If, on the other hand, the concern is with the substance of the regulations—the technical requirements of the regulations and what is regulated, why, and how--then the problem becomes infinitely more complex. The agency must be certain that the science and technical rationale behind its regulations are sound and that the proposed regulations are necessary to protect public resources and public health. If "doing away with burdensome regulation" means softening the regulations to the point where they are meaningless, then the results of legislative intrusions are more than merely mischievous. They pose threats to the long-term health and well-being of North Carolinians and to the ability of the state to prosper.

I view the new DEQ as a department without an obvious constituency. In that regard, it resembles the Environmental Protection Agency on the national level. The regulated community views the department's programs as restraints on growth and takes every opportunity to inform the legislature of this. Because its regulatory programs must be administered with a view toward the political consequences of regulatory decisions, the environmental community also does not generally have a positive view of the department. Citizens generally do not think much about the department except when they need its regulatory protection. The department has a constituency only when environmental problems arise that demand action and/or regulation and then the constituency that appears consists primarily of those directly affected. Once the issue is resolved one way or another that constituency usually dissolves and disappears. In short, the history of DEQ illustrates the political principle that executive departments that "do things for people" generally have more popular support than those with a primary mission of "doing things to people."

If DEQ remains constituted as it is now, this problem will continue to exist. It is highly unlikely that the current DEQ will ever be reorganized to include politically more popular programs. There seems to be no real solution to its current political whipping-boy status other than a concerted

211

effort by the department to make its regulatory programs more "user-friendly"—not less substantive but easier to understand and comply with—and redouble its efforts to explain why what it is doing is so critical to the future of the state, its environment, and ultimately, its citizens. The role of the secretary is critical. Whoever holds that difficult job accepts, among all the positions' duties, the responsibility of speaking for the department, explaining its work, and helping build for it a positive image in the minds if the legislature and the public.

Postscript to Part I

I remained at NER through August 1976. Although I continued to believe in the department's work, I sensed that it was time for me to leave. When a new issue or problem hit my desk, I realized that my thoughts were more and more "to whom should I send this" rather than "how should I handle it", a sure sign I should move on.

After leaving NER I returned to NC State, but not to the Department of Botany. During my absence interest in ecology increased and Botany filled my position and added another to handle the increased student interest. The department really did not need another ecologist. Furthermore, the School of Forest Resources had undergone rapid growth and had added several new positions. The dean and faculty wanted to develop a position in natural resource and forest policy, a position they felt that, given my experience, I could fill. Thus, I joined the Forestry faculty in September 1976 and remained there until my retirement in early 2001. In late November 1979, because of the untimely death of the department head, I was named Head of the Department of Forestry, remaining in that position until July 1994

References

Adams. D. A. 1993. Renewable Resource Policy: the legal-institutional foundations. Island Press. 557 pp.

Addresses and Public Papers of Robert W. Scott, Governor of North Carolina, 1969-1973. Memory F. Mitchell, ed. Div. of Archives and History, Dept. of Cultural Res., Raleigh. 1974. 770 pp.

Addresses and Public Papers of James Eubert Holshouser, Governor of North Carolina, 1973-1977. Memory F. Mitchell, ed. Div. of Archives and History, Dept. of Cultural Res., Raleigh. 1978. 676 pp.

Biennial Reports of the Department of Conservation and Development, 1924-1970.

Christensen, Rob. 2008. The Paradox of Tar Heel Politics. The University of North Carolina Press, Chapel Hill. 351 pp.

Gantt, Charlotte R. 1974. The Reorganization of the North Carolina Department of Natural and Economic Resources: A Case Study. Unpublished research paper, Dept. of Political Science, Univ. of North Carolina, Chapel Hill. 122 pp.

Mallison, D. J., S. J. Culver, S. R. Riggs, J. P. Walsh, D. Ames, and C. W. Smith. 2008. Past, Present, and Future Inlets of the Outer Banks Barrier Islands, North Carolina. White Paper, Department of Geological Sciences, East Carolina University, Greenville, NC. 28 pp.

North Carolina Manual. 1973. Office of the Secretary of State, Raleigh, NC. 913 pp.

Position paper dated April 1, 1971, by Mercer Doty, Director of the State Government Reorganization Study, titled: Proposal for a Single Department for Natural Resources and Economic Development.

Sawyer, Ann L. 1981. Fifty Years of North Carolina State Government. Popular Government 46(3): 4-10.

Schoenbaum, Thomas J. 1979. The New River Controversy. John F. Blair, Publisher. Winston-Salem, NC. 195 pp.

Stick, David. 1985. Bald Head: a history of Smith Island and Cape Fear. Broadfoot Publishing Company, Wendell, NC. 143 pp.

Wager, Paul W. and Donald B. Hayman. 1947. Resource Management in North Carolina. Inst. For Res. In Soc. Sci., Univ. of North Carolina, Chapel Hill. 192 pp.

Part II

The Committee of Scientists—1977-1979, 1982

Since its creation in 1905, the United States Forest Service has been widely regarded as one of the most professional and trustworthy agencies of the federal government. The positive image of the forest ranger portrayed in the Boy Scout manual was one that most boys grew up with in the first half of the twentieth century. The agency enjoyed the trust and admiration of the clear majority of Americans. A large part of this positive public image stemmed from what the Forest Service did prior to World War II—protect and nurture forests on public lands. Protection from forest fire, mostly in the west, and restoration of forests on degraded lands, mostly in the east, were the agencies primary missions.

All this changed after World War II. Wartime needs had placed heavy demands on private timberlands in the west. To keep a flow of timber available to industry, primarily in the Pacific northwest, the Forest Service substantially increased the allowable cut on National Forest land. In addition, it permitted much more intensive management practices than it had previously allowed. Clearcutting and timber type conversions over tracts many hundreds of acres in size were common in the northwest. Large acreages of old-growth timber that had previously escaped logging were harvested and replaced with rapidly-growing early successional species, again particularly in the northwest. When questioned, the Forest Service justified these practices as being, in its professional judgement, acceptable.

At the same time, individual incomes, family mobility via the automobile, and leisure time increased, all combining to put greater demand for recreational uses on the National Forests. During the late 1950s and early 1960s non-timber forest users raised questions about the aesthetic and environmental impacts of Forest Service timber harvest practices. To resolve these conflicting uses (and users) of the National Forests, Congress enacted the Multiple Use-Sustained Yield Act in 1960. The language of the act was, however, vague and seemed to promise everything to everyone and did not resolve the conflicts among uses. Furthermore, there was no mention of wilderness in the act. By the early 1960s protection of wilderness had become a national issue to which Congress responded by passing the Wilderness Act in 1964.

This conflict over the purpose of the National Forests and the allowable management practices on them was but one specific example of the broader debate over national policies with respect to the environment and resource management that flowered during the late 1960s and early 1970s. Passage of the National Environmental Policy Act in late 1969 added yet another Congressional directive to those with which the Forest Service had to comply. It took a 1975 court case involving clearcutting on the Monongahela National Forest in West Virginia to bring the issues confronting the Forest Service to a head. In Monongahela, a federal district court ruled that clearcutting was inconsistent with other legislative directives under which the Forest Service operated, specifically the Organic Act of 1897 which required that trees to be harvested must be "individually marked and designated." This ruling effectively banned clearcutting. Additional cases expanded this ruling to about fifty percent of National Forest lands effectively putting the Forest Service out of the timber harvest business.

Thus, in the winter of 1976 Congress was faced with a critical situation where some sort of definitive action was necessary—and this during the run-up to the 1976 election. Congress could have taken the easy route and enacted a provision that would have legalized clearcutting. Instead, at the prodding of several well-respected, veteran members of the Senate, it undertook to develop legislation that would provide the Forest Service a framework within which to deal with the multiple, often conflicting management demands on the National Forests. The result, after about six months of intense debate, was the National Forest Management Act of 1976 (NFMA) which passed literally on the last day before Congress adjourned prior to the election. Seen in broad perspective, NFMA did not resolve conflicting management issues; rather it established a planning process which, with required public input, would provide a means for resolving management conflicts. The hope expressed by members of the Senate was that this process would "get the Forest Service out of the courts and back into the woods."

One of the unique features of NFMA was a requirement that a "Committee of Scientists" be appointed to oversee and comment on the regulations the Forest Service had to develop to implement the act. This committee, unfortunately, was referred to as the "wise man committee" during Senate debate on the act. Even though the section of NFMA that was the committee's purview contained the language dealing with the most controversial timber management/harvesting guidelines, the paragraph describing the Committee of Scientists provided no real guidance as to how the members should be selected or how they should conduct their work.

After the dust of debate and the election settled, late in the fall of 1976 the Forest Service turned to the National Academy of Sciences to advise it on how the committee should discharge its duties and, in addition, asked it to suggest names of persons qualified to serve. The Academy provided its report to the Forest Service in the late winter of 1977. By this time, a new administration (that of Jimmy Carter) had taken over Washington and a new set of upper-level administrators had been appointed in the Department of Agriculture. As fate would have it, the man appointed as the Assistant Secretary of Agriculture with responsibility for the Forest Service was Rupert Cutler. Cutler was strongly identified with environmental interests, especially wilderness. I had known him since the mid-1960s when we had worked with each other in efforts to prevent construction of a trans-mountain road in the Great Smoky Mountains; we continued our contacts while I worked in state government.

At this point, a matter that seemed distant and of little more than academic interest to me—by this time I had returned to the University to teach and do research—suddenly became very personal and very important. In mid-April, I received a call from Cutler. After pleasantries, he told me that he wanted me to serve on the Committee of Scientists and furthermore he was going to suggest me as chairman. I had never heard of the committee and barely grasped what he was talking about, except that he stressed that this was a high-visibility job, that it would be time-consuming, and that the work would be of great value to the Forest Service. I told Cutler I would serve if asked, thinking that because of my low visibility in the forestry community it was unlikely I would be selected.

How wrong I was! In late April I received a formal letter stating, subject to my acceptance, that I was to be the Chairman of the Committee of Scientists and that our first meeting was to be in Washington on May 24-26, 1977. At this point the gravity of what I was about to become involved with began to sink in and I started to wonder why I had been chosen and how I would discharge my duties. In retrospect, I believe I was nominated by a fellow member of the College of Forestry at NC State, Ellis Cowling, who was a member of the National Academy. I have always suspected Cutler suggested me as chair because of my experiences in state government dealing with similar kinds of land planning issues and because he and I generally agreed on environmental issues. All of that is speculation, as I never made any effort to find out the particulars of my nomination to the committee and choice as chair. I was, of course, familiar with the debate over Forest Service management practices that had gone on for over ten years but I certainly didn't grasp the nuances of the issues. Furthermore, I began to speculate on how I, as chairman, with my limited forestry background, could do a credible job of managing the work of the committee and how I might respond if my credentials were challenged publicly. One of my first responses to this speculation was to join the Society of American Foresters, reasoning that I could always respond to challenges that I was an SAF member—of course, by the time of the first meeting I would have been a member less than a month!

Our first meeting was held in the Department of Agriculture building just south of the Mall and Smithsonian where my father still worked and where my sister and I as small children had spent many hours. My fellow committee members were all present. They were an impressive group with impeccable credentials: Thadis Box, Dean of the College of Natural Resources, Utah State University, a range management specialist; R. Rodney Foil, Dean of the School of Forest Resources, Mississippi State University, forest management and silviculture; Ronald W. Stark, graduate dean and coordinator of research, University of Idaho, forest pathology; Lucille F. Stickel, director of the Patuxent Wildlife Research Center, U. S. Fish and Wildlife Service, fisheries and wildlife management; Earl L. Stone, professor, Department of Agronomy, Cornell University, Ithaca, NY, forest soils; and Dennis E. Teeguarden, professor of Forest Economics, University of California, Berkeley, forest economics. [Stickel was replaced as fisheries and wildlife specialist after the first meeting by William L. Webb, professor emeritus, New York State College of Forestry, Syracuse; it was believed that Stickel resigned because the time demands of the assignment were too great given her current job, although I never confirmed this.] The early part of the meeting involved explanation of what would be required of us and how a group such as ours must conform to the various rules and regulations of the department and federal government. We learned we were to be paid

$100/day for our service (specified in the enabling legislation) and our per diem expenses would be covered either by direct payment by the Forest Service or by remuneration based on expense accounts.

On the second day, we began to deal with the substance of our assignment through a lengthy discussion of NFMA, the thinking behind the act, and the Forest Service's views of what some of the requirements meant. I can truthfully say I came away from the discussion with no more than superficial familiarity with our duties and the conflicts swirling around some of the controversial parts of the act. Unwisely, I had stayed with my parents (who still lived in Washington in the house where I grew up) which meant that I did not have time to go to dinner with the other committee members. I regretted that. Our agenda for the summer of 1977 was laid out; it consisted of a meeting in June in Boise, ID, a week-long late July trip to the panhandle of Alaska, and an August meeting in Denver. Considerable stress was placed on the time commitment we were making; the National Academy had indicated that a twenty-five percent time commitment would be required and that proved to be conservative, at least for me. Although most of the discussion was led by Cutler, Forest Service Chief John Maguire and the person who was to be our primary contact in the Forest Service, Rex Hartgraves, also played major roles. Hartgraves was the newly-named director of the Forest Service Land Planning staff (consisting of him, Bill Russell, and their assistant Joyce Parker). Hartgraves proved to be an excellent choice and much of what success we had is owed to him. Despite strong differences of opinion on several issues of procedure and substance all committee members came to respect Hartgraves and benefited greatly from his assistance.

Discussion also began on some of issues with which we would have to deal in the next few months. Not the least of these was the breadth of the committee's purview. The NFMA specified that we were to "provide scientific and technical advice" to the secretary [of Agriculture] in carrying out the purposes of the section of the act that dealt with the most complex forest management issues. The National Academy report recommended that the committee deal with the entire section devoted to forest planning broadly rather than just with the portion involving certain specific forest management issues. Cutler charged the committee with this broader assignment. However, discussion revealed sympathy among committee members for an even broader purview dealing with all NFMA; this matter was not resolved at the first meeting.

The meetings in Boise and Juneau, Alaska, amounted to chances for the committee members to become familiar with each other and with the Forest Service, its staff members who were to work with us, and particularly in Alaska to get a first-hand, on the ground, introduction to some of the more vexing management issues. We visited Ketchikan, Petersburg, Juneau, and Glacier Bay, traveling throughout the Alaska panhandle by plane. The planes were old Grumman Gooses, capable of landing on water (usually) and land. They were noisy, uncomfortable, with metal seats and no cushions but they afforded us up-close views of some of the most spectacular scenery southeastern Alaska had to offer. The five-day trip not only gave us a sense of Forest Service management problems but also gave committee members a chance to get to know Rex Hartgraves better.[59],[60] The rapport developed on that trip persisted through the entire two-year work of the committee. When the plane on which I flew into Ketchikan landed, almost the first thing I saw was that virtually every vehicle had at least one bumper sticker with the message "no more Wilderness!" Although wilderness per se was not our principal concern those bumper stickers did drive home the message that environmental concerns were viewed differently in Alaska than in the lower forty-eight! We held one public meeting in Juneau at which many local interests expressed their views on Forest Service management in Alaska. Late in the hearing a strapping, native Alaskan, took the floor and began to tell us why designation of more wilderness was unacceptable to Alaskans. Dennis Teeguarden was sitting next to me and whispered in my ear "tell

---

[59]   Hartgraves suffered from severe disc trouble in his lower back and flying in the Gooses was terribly painful for him. He toughed it out with pain killers. We learned later in our relationship with him that he had a small daughter with cystic fibrosis. After several of our trips he went directly to the hospital to relieve his wife. Given the short turn around expected on putting ideas expressed at our meetings into regulatory language, Hartgraves lived under extreme pressure all while he worked with us. His daughter died a year or so after the committee completed its work.

[60]   In the fall after our meeting (1977) one of the Gooses we flew in crashed into the side of one of the fiords we flew up, killing all occupants.

this guy to sit down--we aren't here to talk about wilderness." I put my hand on Dennis' knee and told him to go run if he wanted to (he was a regular runner) but that "I was going to sit there and listen as long as this guy wanted to talk—I wasn't about to tell him to sit down—he was a lot bigger than me!" Several of the events of that Alaska trip are still clear in my mind—eagles as numerous as crows in North Carolina, glaciers, and a 727 landing on the gravel runway at Gustavus (the airport for Glacier Bay National Park) with dust and gravel flying everywhere. That runway has since been paved!

The August meeting in Denver brought to a head several of the issues that had surfaced at our first two meetings. The meeting was ostensibly to discuss the matter of non-declining, even-flow, one of the most contentious timber harvest issues facing the Forest Service. Teeguarden came armed with materials on the subject as did several Forest Service staff members. The discussion was long, complex, and much of it was well beyond my grasp. No decisions were reached but the committee did agree that it wished to expand its purview to all of NFMA. Dealing with this issue was the first disagreement we had with Forest Service staff. One high-level staff member argued that we should confine our work to comment on the planning procedure and not deal with substantive issues such as non-declining, even-flow, the issue discussed at much length at the Denver meeting. Dennis Teeguarden became so upset over this attempt to circumscribe our work that he openly threatened to resign— whether he was serious or not we never knew. The rest of the committee strongly disagreed with this narrower view and I ended up writing a letter to Chief John Maguire arguing that there was no real difference between the planning procedure and the technical substance that the regulations required and that competent regulations could not be written pursuant to one part of NFMA without considering other portions of the act. Since it would have been difficult to prevent us from dealing with the entire act if we had arbitrarily chosen to do so, Cutler and Maguire intervened and from that point on our work encompassed all of NFMA.

Our next meeting in Minneapolis represented a turning point in our work. The meeting consisted of several Forest Service employees from all branches of the agency providing us comment and opinion relevant to the content of the regulations.[61] The longer we talked the less substance relevant to our charge emerged and it was easy to sense a growing frustration among the committee members. Furthermore, nowhere did the discussion deal with how the regulations would be structured, a matter we all felt strongly needed to be settled to provide order to our discussions. Without this framework, we could not begin to make useful input toward meeting our charge. In reflecting on the Minneapolis meeting, I think all of us came to the same view—that the Forest Service itself was groping for a way to structure the regulations; they had provided us no framework because they had none! Before leaving Minneapolis, and during the month before our next meeting I and other committee members relayed our frustration to Rex Hartgraves.[62]

When we met in San Francisco in late October it appeared that the Forest Service planning staff had had an epiphany, as a framework and concept for the regulations was proposed and discussed. At this point another change in the committee's modus operandi took place. We changed from mere commentators on material proposed by the Forest Service to more active participants. In specific cases where input was meager or non-existent we began to draft regulations ourselves. This role was never envisioned for the committee but it was necessary if we were to make progress toward development of the regulations. There was no dearth of proposals from the Forest Service for language dealing with the most heavily-debated timber management issues, such as marginal lands, timber harvesting guidelines, circumscription of clearcutting, timber harvest scheduling, and soil and water protection. Little language, however, was provided for such resource areas as wildlife management, range management, recreation, and the complex issue enshrined into law in NFMA and the Endangered Species

---

[61] One of the participants was a Forest Service geneticist that I had in the very first class in ecology that I taught at NC State. I don't believe we had seen each other since.

[62] To structure the committee's work effectively, and to talk privately with Hartgraves and other Forest Service staff members about issues related to our work, I made it a regular habit to fly to Washington in between each of our meetings. These visits were very helpful but they meant that I had at least thirty-six trips related to NFMA, rather than just the eighteen regular meetings, during our two-plus years of work.

Act, biological diversity. Shortage of working material in several of these areas led us to take advantage of outside help to provide language from which at least to begin discussion. For example, Dennis Teeguarden had two of his students (both Forest Service employees on study leave) prepare versions of the regulations that we used in our discussions and another committee member enlisted several graduate students to prepare language for the recreation resource; that language persisted only slightly changed through to the final draft. The lack of substantive input from several critical areas of resource management raised serious questions in the committee's minds about the administrative attention given those resources by Forest Service management. To us, it became clear that the agency, at least at that time, was a timber management first operation, confirming for us the commonly-held criticism of the agency.

A word about the conduct of our meetings is appropriate. From the very beginning we had been instructed by Cutler and the Forest Service that our meetings were to be fully open to the public and, subject to the discretion of the chair, participation of members of the public was appropriate. I was quite comfortable with this stipulation, as I had considerable experience from my time in state government in running public meetings and dealing with the difficulties of public input. Several committee members were concerned that the open meeting format might constrain free discussion of ideas and concepts, that it might discourage the kind of "thinking out loud" that had to be done to think (and talk) our way through complex concepts. Everyone quickly realized that the open meeting format was beneficial as it made clear to any person in attendance how we and the Forest Service were working our way through the job of developing the regulations. There were no secret, behind the scenes accommodations struck. After our first several meetings, I realized that we were not attracting many observers and those we had attracted were primarily from the timber industry. Realizing that if this continued, public participation as it was reflected in comments made during our meetings and in the minutes, would be heavily biased, I called several national conservation organizations and suggested that it might be important for their opinions to be reflected in the attendance at our meetings. From that point on, at least one "environmental" representative was present at every meeting. In fact, two of the most faithful attendees at our meetings were Doug McCleery[63] representing the National Forest Products Association and Julie MacDonald representing the Sierra Club Legal Defense Fund. Both made important contributions to our work.

With a framework in hand, discussions continued through the fall and winter of 1977-78 with meetings held in Atlanta, Phoenix, Biloxi, Dallas, and back in Washington. During this time, most of the drafting work was done by the Forest Service with largely editorial input from the committee. By July 1978, the Forest Service had completed a draft of the regulations and it proposed to issue the draft in the Federal Register during the summer. The legislation creating the Committee of Scientists required that "the views of the committee shall be included in the public information supplied when the regulations are proposed for adoption." Since the committee had not had an opportunity to review this proposed draft at any length, and because it contained new language and ideas not fully discussed with us, the committee felt unable to do the necessary technical review in the short time available in the summer and refused to publish any comments when the draft was published in August. There was pressure on us—some commentators felt we "had to comment" and that we were violating NFMA by not doing so. Nonetheless, the committee held to its position and the first draft of the rules was published in the Federal Register on August 31, 1978 accompanied only by a short note from me explaining why there were no comments from the committee.

During the fall of 1978 two public meetings were held in Washington at which public comments on the first draft were made. I attended both meetings but other committee members did not. All of us felt that our job now was to do the detailed analysis and critique of the first draft and to begin the job of preparing a formal report on our views. At meetings held in Denver, Seattle, Sacramento, and Houston we continued a detailed analysis of the draft and, in areas where our thinking differed from that of the Forest Service, we proposed our own language. Most of one of these meetings was devoted to discussion of new proposed language

---

[63]   When Ronald Reagan became President in 1981, McCleery was appointed to the Undersecretary of Agriculture position that Cutler held during the Carter administration. McCleery eventually joined the Forest Service and completed his career there.

prepared by a special Forest Service task force on silvicultural practices; much of this material was included in the next draft of the regulations. At several of these meetings we found that proposed language to deal with an issue was either deficient or non-existent. When we could not come up with language of our own, occasionally language provided by members of the public attending the meeting was used to stimulate discussion.

After our December meeting in Sacramento, the committee charged me with overseeing preparation of a draft of our report. Each member provided input in his area of expertise or in areas with which he had special interest. I edited and assembled the material, wrote necessary language in areas where we needed comment, and prepared a first draft of the full report. This work was very time consuming and was done on an electric typewriter—very slow in comparison to what could have been done now on a computer. I did have permission from the Forest Service to use and pay one of our NC State Department of Forestry secretaries; she did the final typing of the first draft of the report. My recollection is that this work consumed a good bit of my Christmas vacation in 1978. Obviously, this work went with the job of being committee chair. It also reflected one of the habits that I had developed when I worked in state government (chapter 16, part I): to ensure that a report said what I felt it should say I wrote its initial language myself. It was not a case of inflicting my views on the committee. I was simply using the opportunity to provide initial language that I knew I was comfortable with and which seemed to me to reflect the committee's discussions.

A word here about my relations with the committee members. As I said earlier, I regard the six of them as extremely competent, diligent, and thoughtful professionals and a thorough joy to work with. The seven of us developed a rapport and respect for one another that was remarkable. There were few, if any, personal disagreements among members. There were, of course, professional differences of opinion but these never hindered our work. A good bit of this undoubtedly was because each of us was a professional "one of a kind"—there were no duplications of professional expertise. Thus, during discussion we tended to defer to the member with the greatest expertise in each area. This created the danger of permitting one person's views to go unchallenged but the give and take of open discussion and the additional expertise of Forest Service staff members minimized such professional deference. I deliberately never became close to any one of the members; as chairman I had to maintain an attitude that valued each member's input equally and to ensure that no member ever felt the chair favored one member's opinions over another's. Every evening after meetings and before dinner we gathered in a member's room for a drink. The discussion usually was a free-flowing rehash of the day's work. I did not drink as I had become almost allergic to alcohol while I worked in state government. Rather than drink, I sat and listened to the conversation and the views, opinions, and prejudices that were freely expressed after lubrication with a drink or two. By doing this, I felt I could get a reasonably good feel for where individuals, and the committee stood regarding the major issues facing us. That knowledge was of great help in summarizing our work and allowed me to feel comfortable with the language used in the early drafts of our report.

The committee's final report was submitted on February 9, 1979. It contained not only a critique of the Forest Service draft published the previous August, but also an entirely new version of the regulations drafted by the committee. In areas where the committee differed with the language the Forest Service proposed, or where no language on a given subject was included in the first draft, the committee's proposed regulations incorporated its own new recommended language. This report met our statutory obligation to make public our review of the proposed regulation. It was published in the Federal Register, together with the Forest Service's second draft of the regulations, on May 4, 1979. Thus, interested parties had available both a draft of the regulation that we recommended as well as a second draft proposed by the Forest Service. The framework of both proposals was basically the same; differences lay primarily in the details of planning related to specific management practices and in the more specific language the committee proposed for dealing with certain issues such as biological diversity and maintenance of viable populations of vertebrate species.

During the time between submission of the committee draft in February and publication of the committee report together with the second draft of the proposed regulations in May, Hartgraves and his staff had incorporated many of the committee's recommendations together with new some material into the second draft. Committee members reviewed the second draft, provided me with their comments that I incorporated into a supplemental final report. At the committee's final (we assumed!) meeting in Asheville, NC, on June 20-21, 1979 we reviewed and revised our supplemental report and said what we thought would be our final good byes. The supplemental report was submitted on August 17 and the Forest Service published its final regulations on September 17, to become effective October 17, 1979, just about a year past the two-year deadline specified in NFMA.

When the committee members left Asheville, we assumed our work was done, leaving the Forest Service to implement what we had helped it create. In the two years and five months the committee and Forest Service worked together we created an entirely new planning process where none had existed before. Of course, each of us was keenly interested in how the proposed process would work when applied to real life management situations on the National Forests. Teeguarden continued to be involved in implementation of some of the timber harvest proposals but to my knowledge none of the rest of us had similar experiences. I did give many talks, mostly to Forest Service employees about the regulations, how they were developed, and the origin of some of the more controversial requirements. I got very mixed feedback from these talks. In some cases, I talked with Forest Supervisors and persons of similar rank who were well into the planning process and who appreciated being given a framework within which to determine how to manage the resources entrusted to them. In other cases, reactions were less than enthusiastic and I could sense the frustration of agency personnel who had no real sense of how to implement the new planning process. Most of the talks I gave in the two years after the committee disbanded were devoted to explaining what some of the requirements in the regulations meant and how the committee arrived at the language in the regulations.

One of the most interesting assignments I had was to participate on a keynote panel on "Land Use Allocation: Processes, People, Politics, and Professionals" at the September 1980 SAF meeting in Spokane, WA. My talk was, frankly, nothing new and was completely overshadowed by one given by John Crowell, a timber company executive from the Pacific northwest. I was a bit perplexed as to why Crowell's talk was given so much attention because the views it presented were what one would expect from a timber company representative and hardly spoke to the topic of the program. Only later at the meeting I learned that it was widely rumored that if Ronald Reagan were elected President that November, Crowell would be appointed as Assistant Secretary of Agriculture with responsibility over the Forest Service. I recalled then that the committee had indirect input from Crowell via Doug McCleery and that some in industry were not at all happy with the direction the regulations had taken.

Ronald Reagan was elected in November 1980 and, sure enough, John Crowell was named Assistant Secretary of Agriculture with Doug McCleery brought on as his Deputy Assistant Secretary with direct oversight of the Forest Service. These appointments set in motion the machinery that insured that the committee's assumption that it would never meet again would turn out to be wrong. One of the first moves of the Reagan administration was to appoint Vice President George H. W. Bush as chair of a committee charged with eliminating unnecessary and burdensome regulations. The NFMA regulations fell squarely in the cross-hairs of the Bush committee. Consequently, McCleery and the Forest Service staff began an effort to modify the regulations. Specifically, their attention was devoted to clarifying economic analysis, revision of the non-declining, even flow requirements, a general softening of the demands for analysis of the impacts of management on wildlife populations and biodiversity, and a reduction in the overall length of the regulations. It has never been clear to me exactly who drafted the changes; Forest Service staff members must have been involved but later events showed that they did not really agree with the changes. The proposed revisions were published in the Federal Register in February 1982. These proposed changes brought down a fire-storm of protest, almost all from the environmental community, with thousands of comments, largely representing a knee-jerk reaction from the environmental community, deluging the Forest Service. It is perhaps indicative of the sensitive nature of the proposed changes that they brought forth so much comment, even though the impact of the regulations on forest planning was largely unknown at the time. Planning was only in the earliest stages of implementation, only a few National Forests had begun the proposed planning process, and hardly anyone had any real understanding of how the planning requirements would be executed and play out in changes of on-the-ground management. Nonetheless, these protests became so widespread that the Forest Service, Crowell, and

McCleery were forced to respond, and they did so by calling back the Committee of Scientists to assist in evaluating the changes. For political reasons, we could not return as the "Committee of Scientists"; we were brought back as a "panel of experts."

There is some debate as to how Crowell and McCleery envisioned the role that the committee would play. Some felt that the committee would be "used" to dignify the proposed changes. McCleery contended that the purpose was to give the regulations and the proposed changes a thorough review that would help the credibility of the changes. I am inclined to accept McCleery's explanation at face value with the proviso that another equally important purpose was to deflect the fire storm of protest into a dispassionate forum that would allow full public discussion of the proposed changes. All members of the committee agreed to return and we convened in Washington in the late spring of 1982. In a meeting between the committee members and Rex Hartgraves the night before the meeting, Hartgraves showed us a version of the regulations, done by his planning staff, that was different from the proposed revisions published in the Federal Register. Hartgraves purpose in doing this clearly was to tell us that the Forest Service really didn't agree with many the proposed changes and to suggest to us what it would like to see come out of our review. Hartgraves intended to use this version as the basis for recommendations as to how the Forest Service proposed to change the regulations. It was never clear to me how much Hartgrave's superiors knew what he was planning to do. I'm sure Chief Maguire did but whether Crowell and McCleery knew was never clear to me. I always thought what Hargraves did was gutsy; if what he did had been fully understood, I suspect he would have been fired or at least banished to the back waters of an obscure National Forest. Interestingly, there never has been any mention of the meeting with Hartgraves in any of the material that has been published in the discussion of the proposed 1982 revisions of the NFMA regulations. The only written description of how the revisions were handled by the Forest Service is in a paper Hartgraves contributed to a symposium on the Committee of Scientists published in 1992[64] and it is understandably vague on the details of how the revision process was handled within the Forest Service.

---

[64] Hartgraves in Symposium on the Committee of Scientists, For. Hist. and Cons. 36(3): 125-128. 1992.

The meeting at which we reviewed the proposed new regulations was fascinating for a variety of reasons. We were arrayed around a table in the front of the room, a format never used in our previous meetings. I did not chair the meeting; it was chaired by a Forest Service member whose name escapes me. There were interesting role reversals: Rupert Cutler sat in the audience; John Crowell and Doug McCleery sat with the committee. We went through the regulations change by change, discussing each and the rationale for it. In most cases, discussion eventually turned either to the draft language Hartgraves had shared with us or to the original language, or something close to it, so the net result of our review was that the regulations were left pretty much as they had been before the changes proposed by the new administration. We did accept some changes particularly in the area of determination of "viable populations" of vertebrates and biodiversity.[65] The meeting lasted a day and a half; when we said our goodbyes and left Washington it was indeed for the last time. We never met again.

In all that has been written about NFMA and the planning regulations, there has been very little comment about the committee per se and its role in the process. Several articles have been written[66] commenting

---

[65] The only time during all the committee's service that our mutual commitment not to deal as individuals was broken because of this discussion. Well after we had left Washington I received a letter from one committee member confessing that he had unilaterally gone to staff members after the first day and suggested language that he personally favored and which had not been discussed on the floor or with the committee. Either he withdrew his proposal or the Forest Service chose not to act on it as it never appeared in our discussions during the second day of the meeting. That he felt compelled to confess what he had done to me is a measure of the strong bonds of mutual respect that had formed between the committee members.

[66] S. E. Daniels and K. Merrill, For. Hist. and Cons. 36(3):108-116. 1992; A Symposium on the Committee of Scientists, various authors, For Hist. and Cons. 36(3): 117-128, 1992; B. S. Pasko, Lewis and Clark Law School 32 Env. L. 509.

on the work of the first Committee of Scientists[67] but that constitutes about all the assessment of our work that has appeared in print.

These commentaries are generally critical of the committee's work. Although the criticisms vary based on who brings them, they generally boil down to several key points: whether we were co-opted by the Forest Service, that the planning process didn't work because the regulations were too complex and not clear enough, and the enormous amount of agency time and manpower they forced the Forest Service to devote to planning rather than on-the-ground management. Although these criticisms have some validity, I feel they need further discussion.

In evaluating whether we were co-opted by the Forest Service, it is necessary to look again at the genesis of the committee. The committee was created by an act of Congress, not by the Forest Service. The intent of Sen. Metcalf of Montana in proposing the committee ("wise men" in the words of Sen. Metcalf) was that it would be independent of the Forest Service and would "look over their shoulders" as they developed the regulations. The statute specifically forbids Forest Service members from serving on the committee. The seven members were chosen by the administration of the Department of Agriculture (Rupert Cutler specifically) from thirty-three nominees presented by the National Academy of Sciences. Critics argue that the National Academy itself has a record of bias toward business interests and therefore was not an unbiased source of nominations. Never having seen the full list of nominees, it is impossible to assess this criticism. Judging from the widely different philosophies of the members selected as well as their backgrounds and professional experience, that bias is not apparent. The language creating the committee also specified that the "views of the committee shall be included" when the regulations are proposed for adoption. In specifying the purpose of the committee, its freedom from Forest Service membership, and requiring publication of its views, Congress did as much as it could to insure a review independent of the <u>direct</u> influence of the Forest Service.

---

[67]   The Forest Service convened an entirely new second Committee of Scientists in the late 1990s to assist in review and revision of the regulations. No members of the original committee served on the second. The work of the second committee is beyond the purview of my discussion of the original committee.

It would be naïve to argue that the committee was not influenced in its work by the Forest Service. It is true that it provided what staff we had, that it influenced the flow of information to the committee, and that it "wined and dined us" at our meetings and on field trips. Nonetheless, the committee did not accept many proposals from the Forest Service on controversial issues without extensive discussion and showed an ability to deal independently with many issues. An example comes from the debate over maximum clearcut size that took place in the fall of 1978. The act suggests that there should be more than one limit by calling for establishment of "maximum size limits for areas to be cut in one harvest operation." A Forest Service task force debated this matter and proposed to us that one size (forty acres) should apply to all clearcuts nationally. In our discussions, we unanimously agreed that there was no biological or other basis for the forty-acre limit, We proposed, and the final regulations included, a range of clearcut sizes depending on forest type and geographical region, i.e. closely following the wording of NFMA. It is, of course, possible that the Forest Service wanted a range of sizes in the regulations, and that the task force proposed a single size knowing that the committee would not accept it and would opt for the range of sizes the Forest Service wanted all along. Although such Machiavellian tactics cannot be discounted I believe the totality of the record and the content of the final regulations show a high degree of independence on the part of the committee. In the last analysis, those who want to believe we were co-opted will always do so and no amount of evidence to the contrary will dissuade them.

An interesting twist on the question of co-option arises from suggestions as to what might have motivated committee members to accept appointment.[68] The suggestion is that we might have accepted appointment because, as professionals, we had a strong desire to influence the direction of federal forest management and that we perceived appointment as an opportunity to exert an influence on Forest Service management that independent professionals had, up to then, never been afforded. In other words, the lure of being able to influence decision-making caused us eagerly to accept the assignment and this, in turn, could lead each of us to believe, when we finished, that we had done something important for our

---

[68]   This argument is raised in Marcus' paper in the Symposium on the Committee of Scientists (For. Cons. Hist. 36(3): 117-128. 1992).

profession and society. This in turn would lead us to an overly generous conclusion as to the quality and value of our work. I cannot speak for the others but to some extent this observation pertains to me. I have always had a streak of "Don Quixote" in me and I have accepted several assignments out of a belief that through them I could influence society for the better—obviously by seeing my beliefs and knowledge put into action. This feeling may indeed have much to do with my belief that the work of the Committee of Scientists was, overall, a success.

One critic[69] has argued that the very independence that has been cited as preventing the committee from being co-opted by the Forest Service in fact made it wholly dependent on the Service. This argument stems from the fact that none of the committee members had any significant experience with the Forest Service culture and management style. The Forest Service could feed us only those issues it wanted us to deal with and prevent us from dealing with others, and thus our independence made us their captives. My experience says that this criticism in not valid. However, it is true that, because of our lack of familiarity with Forest Service internal management and tradition, none of us on the committee could anticipate fully, or even perhaps partly, the operational impact of our proposals, thus contributing to difficulties with implementation of the planning process.

Yet another reason why the committee's work has been deemed a failure is that it strayed from the work for which scientists are qualified, that is, defining the technical dimensions of an issue. It is argued that science should confine its contributions to explanation of the outcomes to be expected from implementation of a series of alternatives. Rather, the nature of the work confronting the committee and the job of crafting a set of guidelines for making policy decisions inevitably led it into development of policy itself. The extent to which this is true results from the fact that Congress never clearly articulated the policies that were needed to guide the value-laden decisions required in forest planning and to guide the development of a process to lead to those decisions. It has never been clear to me what requirements in the regulations constitute "setting policy". Perhaps the regulations themselves can be considered a policy-setting document. I do not think this is true. What the regulations do is describe

---

[69]   Luke Popovich in the above cited Symposium.

a process that, with public input, allows the Forest Service to propose a series of alternative courses of action with explanation of the consequences of each. If adoption of the regulations itself constitutes a policy decision, then perhaps the committee was guilty of "setting policy." That is too much of a stretch for me.

Finally, a major and widely-voiced criticism of the committee's work is based on what the outcome of that work—the planning regulations themselves—has been. Because of their sheer volume, complexity, and in some cases lack of specificity, implementation of the regulations proved difficult. The size and complexity of the regulations reflected the difficulty of the issues they sought to resolve. Our interpretation of the words in NFMA led us to believe that the regulations needed to be detailed and specific with respect to meeting certain provisions of the act. The lack of specificity is, in large part, a result of imprecision in the language of NFMA. It is not a tightly worded, carefully thought out, statute, a result of the time pressure and conflicting demands Congress endured during debate on the act. No doubt some of this was unwittingly carried through to the regulations.[70]

Although ten years after the adoption of the final version of the regulations in 1982 nearly all National Forests had completed a plan, virtually all of those had been contested, and some had been the subject of administrative hearings and/or court cases. Thus, the objective of "getting

---

[70] Jim Giltmire, one of several congressional staff persons who worked on the act, told a story that explains some of the internal inconsistencies in the act. After a conference committee meeting, where the House and Senate versions were being integrated, was breaking up, Giltmire realized a key provision had been left on the table. Calling this to the attention of one of the Senate conferees, he was told as the Senator left for another meeting to "put it where it belongs." Many of the inconsistencies in the act are a function of the fact that the final version was an amalgamation of House and Senate bills that each sought to resolve the issues before Congress in quite different ways. The conference committee was up against a hard deadline—adjournment for the November election—and it thus made some quick decisions regarding inclusion of certain provisions without having time to be sure the results were internally consistent. The guidelines for standards to be met in the plans are a hasty blending of House and Senate versions with no effort at integration.

the Forest Service out of the courts and back in the woods", for which the framers of NFMA hoped, was not realized. In addition, there is no doubt that implementation of the regulations has been very expensive, both in dollars and staff time. None of these outcomes should have been a surprise as the committee, at the close of its final report, warned that the planning process would be "costly and imperfect." Nonetheless, when National Forest managers found themselves involved in what seemed to be an endless process that took time away from their field management, there was understandable frustration.

Although these problems were real, one must realize that the completion of the committee's work simply represented the first step in the evolution of a process for resolving management conflicts that would, with the benefit of experience, go through many more iterations. If any step in the development of an agency process is imperfect and requires further refinement, can that step be regarded as a failure? That would be analogous to regarding the first generation of computers as failures. Yes, they were limited in capability, were awkward to use, and were expensive but they were not failures. They simply served as one step in the long process of development of the sophisticated machines we have today. So it is with forest planning. The committee's effort assisted the Forest Service to develop, where none existed before, the first steps in a new planning process. Congress and the various groups with interests in National Forest management would certainly have liked an immediate, clear process for resolving contentious management issues as the result of NFMA. The issues are too complex and too value laden for this to have happened. Until Congress itself can articulate a clearer statement of national policy than can be found in a planning act, the issues will remain and the Forest Service will still have to struggle with them.

Outside of my service in state government I always regarded service on the Committee of Scientists as one of my greatest contributions to society. Despite the criticisms leveled at its work, the committee made a major contribution to the Forest Service and to forestry generally. Service on the committee also gave me a degree of credibility in forestry that I did not previously have. Very shortly after the regulations were first adopted in the fall of 1979 I became, because of the unexpected death of Bill Johnson, the Head of the Department of Forestry at NC State. That job put me in wide contact with other forestry programs and further allowed me to understand the field better. My experience in state government administration made the duties associated with that academic position easier to grasp and easier to manage. Although I probably would have become head of Forestry had I not served on the Committee of Scientists, that background made my appointment more credible in the eyes of other forestry programs. I went on to several significant elective positions in the Society of American Foresters, served on several of its national committees, was named a Fellow in 1984, and in 1999 was awarded the Gifford Pinchot medal, one of the Society's two most prestigious awards. It is doubtful that last would have happened had I not chaired the Committee of Scientists.

Part III

The Coastal Resources Commission —1976-1989, and the Environmental Management Commission —1989-1991[71]

---

[71] There is some duplication between this section and Chapter 11 dealing with CAMA, particularly in the paragraphs describing the court case. As pointed out in the Preface, I feel this duplication is necessary to provide a full narrative and explanation.

My longest continuous involvement in public service was as a member of the North Carolina Coastal Resources Commission (CRC) established by the Coastal Area Management Act (CAMA) of 1974. I served from 1976 to 1989, having been appointed by Gov. Jim Holshouser, and reappointed by governors. Jim Hunt and Jim Martin. Although my tenure was long, the work involved was not as intensive as my service in state government or as Chairman of the Committee of Scientists. Nonetheless, time spent on the CRC was not without stress and numerous difficult decisions. I probably could have continued on the CRC for at least another four-year term had I not been asked by Governor Martin's staff to move to the Environmental Management Commission (more about that later).

As pointed out in Chapter 11, my appointment to the CRC began almost immediately after my tenure in state government ended. Governor Holshouser asked me to his office and told me that he planned to appointment me to one of the seats allocated to gubernatorial appointment and not requiring residency in the coastal area. Holshouser rejected my argument that baggage I brought from my involvement with passage of the act might compromise his appointment and my ability to serve. I was appointed effective September 1976, and was sworn in together with the other members of the second round of CRC appointees.

The CRC was a body of fifteen persons, thirteen of whom filled positions with qualifications described in the enabling statute, e.g. coastal engineer, fish and wildlife background, etc. Thirteen also had to be residents of the coastal area (as defined in the act). All but two were chosen by the governor from among nominees presented by the twenty coastal counties. I filled an at-large position named by the governor himself. As a staff member of NER I was one of several who advised the governor as to his selections; the final choices were his alone. I remember being impressed two years earlier by the final selections made for the original commission. The nominees from coastal counties were virtually all highly capable persons and the governor's selections from among them were good. Most commission members had strong ties back to local government as might be expected and appropriate, as one of the important thrusts of CAMA was to place a high percentage of the responsibilities established in the act—land use planning and certain types of permits--on local governments. The weaker members of the original commission were simply not re-appointed when the second round of appointments was made in 1976.

Recall here my earlier explanation about the role of commissions in North Carolina state government. The North Carolina General Assembly historically has been unwilling to bestow regulatory authority directly on bureaucrats appointed by the governor. Its philosophy has been to reserve the exercise of such power to bodies composed of ordinary citizens, usually referred to as commissions, or occasionally boards. The statute creating such a body confers regulatory authority and the responsibility for approving the ground rules (regulations) under which regulatory authority is exercised on the commission (or board). Throughout the first two-thirds of the twentieth century appointments to these bodies were made exclusively by the governor with few qualifications spelled out in the creating statute. However, as regulation became a progressively larger part of government, the General Assembly began to specify the qualifications (background) of commission members. Furthermore, the General Assembly began to reserve the right to make some appointments to itself. This trend began with just a small number of appointments made by the General Assembly but the number of reserved appointments has grown progressively until the majority of some commissions now is made up of legislative appointments.

This trend reached its zenith when in the 1980s the General Assembly appointed several of its own members to the Environmental Management Commission. Three other commissioners (all NC State University faculty members) sued contending that appointment of legislators to commissions violated the separation of powers principle of the constitution. Lower courts did not find the practice to be unconstitutional. However, the case was ultimately heard by the state supreme court which reversed the lower courts and held that service by legislators on executive branch commissions was indeed a separation of powers violation (State Ex Rel. Wallace v. Bone 286 S.E. 2nd79(1982)). This decision undoubtedly played a key role in leading to greater number of commission members being chosen by legislators. The commission form of administering regulatory programs has, generally, served North Carolina well and regardless of method of appointment commissions generally show considerable independence in making decisions.

The CRC that I joined was still feeling its way into its job and there were many important decisions yet to be made. Although initial land use planning guidelines had been approved by the commission, land use planning at the local level was far from complete, and the commission had yet to deal with designation of Areas of Environmental Concern (AECs) where the commission's regulatory authority was to be exercised. These matters consumed almost all the time of the commission and its staff for the first several years I was a member.

Developing the guidelines for land use plans was essentially a first-of-its-kind effort by North Carolina state government. Although numerous local governments, particularly the state's large cities and counties, had been developing such plans for years, no state government agency had undertaken such work[72] and virtually none had been done by coastal municipalities. The effort took place in several stages, each requiring the approval of the commission. Planning guidelines approved by the commission in late 1974 specified four areas to be treated in each plan: statements of goals, objectives, and policies; data regarding population and economic trends and identification of valuable resources; a land classification system; and recommendation of interim areas of environmental concern. An important decision made early in this process involved establishing criteria to be followed by counties when exercising the authority conveyed in CAMA to delegate preparation of a plan to a city within a county. Preparation of land use plans represented an entirely new activity for virtually all coastal counties and municipalities, and in some cases, it was difficult to get local government authorities to respond and participate. In one case, a county had failed to respond to any communications from the staff and commission. When a staff member finally contacted the chairman of the county commissioners it turned out that all communications relating to planning were in the bottom drawer of his desk in the garage he ran. When asked why he didn't respond, his answer was "I didn't understand what those letters were about so I saved them and figured if they were important someone from Raleigh would contact me." Someone did!

---

[72] The Community Assistance staff in NER had assisted local governments with development of land use plans but none of these involved the complexity inherent in such plans for coastal counties.

Land use planning began in January 1975. Originally, land use plans were to be submitted in late November 1975. Although the General Assembly extended this date by six months, the commission required that draft plans be submitted on the original date. Those plans were then reviewed intensively by state agency personnel and finally by the commission; particular attention was given to AECs. Federal agencies were invited to participate in this review and some did. Review comments were discussed with persons responsible for each local plan and plan revision was begun. Final plans were submitted by fifty of fifty-two participating local government entities in late May 1976; the commission prepared plans for those two localities that refused to submit. After review by the commission in June 1976 all plans were either approved or returned for minor changes. The last local plan was approved in January 1978.

The other major initial duty, definition of AECs, was far more controversial as these were the areas where the commission's regulatory authority, together with that of several other state agencies, was to be exercised. CAMA required that the designation of AECs must take place in two steps, the first involving identification of interim AECs followed later by final designations. Initial designation of interim AECs was done based on recommendations made by the secretary of NER (I was involved in that process) in February 1975. His proposals were based on the results of six public hearings held on the coast in September 1974. The commission did not accept fully the Secretary's recommendations, particularly the one that involved designation of the entire outer banks, and remanded them to its staff for further refinement. In May 1976, after an additional public hearing, the commission designated Interim AECs and the requirements associated with them went into effect August 1, 1976.

I have gone into so much detail concerning the early steps in implementation of CAMA to show how much work had been accomplished before I joined the commission in September 1976 just two years after its creation. Considering the significant impact of the requirements of CAMA, and the limited experience of staff assigned to the Coastal Management Program, to this day I remain impressed with the work that was done in the two years after CAMA's passage. It is a testimony to the work of a small number of dedicated NER employees and to the first set of commissioners that this work was done in such an expeditious fashion.

The first major decision in which I participated was the designation of final AECs. Staff work centered around analysis of the types of development proposed in Interim AECs based on notice submitted when such work was undertaken as required by CAMA, refinement of technical descriptions of AECs, and recommendations concerning permissible uses in them. Designation of some AECs was clear cut—there was little argument about what a salt marsh was. Others were more difficult and in some cases boundaries were the subject of disagreement. In one discussion of the buffer zone around coastal sounds, there was no agreement on the two limits proposed—fifty feet versus 100 feet. Someone suggested that since seventy-five feet is half way between the limits being discussed, why don't we go with seventy-five feet. That limit was chosen and it remained in force for years. In January 1977 based on staff recommendations the commission proposed amendments to the AEC requirements of the state guidelines for the coastal area.

During the next few months, staff members visited with local governments to obtain feedback on the AEC proposals. Using this information, the commission refined its designations and use standards and took them to public hearing, one in each of the twenty coastal counties. I attended several of these hearings; at one there was an amusing exchange of "views" with one crusty old coastal resident. During the question period, he rose and asked "I want everyone here who is from Raleigh to stand up", whereupon a sizeable majority of the audience stood up. Then he asked "everyone who is standing and who doesn't favor this proposal, sit down." Only 2 or 3 people sat down prompting his final comment "See, that's the problem with this program; it brings its own crowd." I suspect his views coincided with those of many coastal residents—it was major change taking place too fast to assimilate and seemed dominated by the heavy hand of Raleigh. On June 22, 1977, after the results of all public hearings were known, the commission adopted the definition of, and development standards for, each AEC.

With the final definition of AECs and development standards the permit program began. CAMA differentiated between permits for minor development and permits for major development. The authority to issue minor development permits, under CAMA, could be assumed by a local government if its plan for implementation of this authority had been approved by the commission. Since virtually all local governments chose to issue minor development permits, one of the commission's duties, in addition to approving its own plan for issuing major development permits, was approval of these local implementation plans. This work, together with involvement in the training of local government officials in the permit process, occupied much of the commission's time after designation of AECs. Permit issuance went into effect in the summer of 1978.

After this first crush of important actions and decisions, the commission settled down to a regular pattern for its meetings. They were held four to six times a year, virtually always on the coast, beginning on Wednesday afternoon, continuing all day Thursday, and half a day on Friday. The commission members were assigned to committees where much of the work was done; these usually met Wednesday and Thursday afternoons. Thursday and Friday mornings were when the commission met as a quasi-judicial body, approving rules and regulations and hearing appeals from permit decisions. As might be expected, the commission had its "social life." For the first few years I was on the commission, there was always an open house in a motel room hosted by a member who ran a very well-known restaurant, the River Forest Manor, in Belhaven, NC. He always brought large amounts of fresh seafood with him and his room was always jammed with eager eaters (and drinkers). It was a treat to look in the trunk of his car and see what he had brought with him. Unfortunately, he had a serious problem with alcohol and his health consequently was not good. After this gentleman passed from the picture his place was taken by the then chairman of the Advisory Committee [Bill Gardner, aka "The Dancing Bear"] who also could put on quite a spread.

The commission had its share of important citizens and characters —anyone familiar with state boards and commissions will know that this is true of all such bodies. One of the better-known members of the original commission, and one with whom I served several years, was David Stick of Kitty Hawk. Stick is a well-known historian, particularly of the outer banks and North Carolina coast; a visit with David Stick was a real treat for any history buff. He was a strong supporter of an improved system of managing coastal resources, but his view of how that should be accomplished was not always the way CAMA played out. It seemed that he felt the program was too bureaucratic and by his choice he did not remain a commission member long. The first chair of the commission was Tommy Eure from Morehead City. He did an excellent job but as he resigned his position after several terms, I did not serve long under him. The chair of the commission for most of the time I was a member, was Parker Chesson, the president of the College of the Albemarle in Elizabeth City. I had Parker in one of my graduate ecology classes in the early 1960s and we became good friends during our time on the commission. He ran meetings well and, as they say, no "fights broke out." Several times, however, we ran into procedural snarls that required heroic measures to resolve. During one meeting, we became so tangled up in parliamentary procedure that we had to resort to Roberts Rules of Order. Unfortunately, no one in the room had a copy and we had to send a staff member to the Beaufort town library to charge out a copy! Another time, late one Friday morning, everyone felt we had resolved a permit issue and, since it seemed no more votes would be necessary, a member left early. Unfortunately, the issue was not resolved and another vote was required. Even worse, we had lost our quorum due to early departures. This required a staff member to call the local highway patrol office, give them the missing member's license number, and ask them to flag him down and tell him to return to Morehead City. Until he returned, the rest of the commission remained in "recess"; upon his return, we resumed discussion of the item of business and completed voting on it.

When the issuance of permits began, the commission's work gravitated heavily toward review of permits and hearing appeals of permit denials (appeals for both minor and major development permits were heard by the commission). Permit hearings were quasi-judicial in nature and usually involved at least one attorney on the part of the appellant plus the staff member(s) and attorneys from the Attorney General's office who had dealt with the permit application. In practice, many hearings on permit denials were heard by a single commission member acting as the "hearing officer." After hearing testimony from the appellant and state and/or local officials involved, the hearing officer prepared a set of "findings of fact" and "conclusions of law" together with his/her recommendations. These were then brought to the full commission for final decision.

Service as hearing officer was an interesting and sometimes challenging duty. Often a case was relatively simple and there really was little to do but uphold the issuance or denial of a permit. I chaired several permit hearings, no two of which were similar. The venue for one was the Beaufort county court house in little Washington. The only room available was the actual court room and, as hearing officer, I had to sit in the judge's chair. Consequently, those testifying in the case seemed compelled to refer to me a "your honor" much to my amusement. Another much more complex hearing took place in Raleigh in the Archdale Building where the offices of the Division of Coastal Management were located. That hearing involved a highly controversial application for a development that had the potential to pollute the waters of a coastal sound thus impacting the local oyster fishery. In addition to attorneys for the appellant and the commission's own staff, there was an attorney from a state-wide environmental organization. As I recall the hearing went on for nearly two days and was marked by pointed exchanges between the parties which required refereeing on my part. Several of our exchanges became quite heated and I recall having to urge both sides to speed up their presentations and to stop making sarcastic comments. I recommended denying the permit but I believe it was subsequently altered enough so that the commission decided to approve it. Despite my heated exchanges with the attorneys, the lady representing the environmental organization gave me a wolf's head (artificial, not real!) for Christmas!

The commission's hearings on permit actions were quasi-judicial, meaning that the same standards that would apply in a court of law were applicable except that greater latitude was allowed in the introduction of evidence and in the questioning of witnesses. The commission's actions had to be consistent with legal procedure as the record of its actions in a case were used as the basis of appeals to the courts. We were always admonished by our attorneys to be consistent with good legal practice and not to allow testimony that would be inadmissible in court or resort to decisions that were clearly inconsistent with good legal practice. Although we tried very hard to adhere to these standards there were times when it became difficult. This was particularly true in cases involving granting of, or rejecting, a variance from our standards[73]. Because granting of a variance invariably

---

[73] Allowance for issuance of a variance from the commission's rules was written into CAMA; a variance is a decision that allows an action that is against the intent of a rule or regulation. A variance ruling must always be accompanied by a statement of explanation as to the reason(s) for granting the variance.

involves subjective judgements, it was important to specify the grounds on which the variance was being granted or denied in the motion to approve (or disapprove). I remember one case involving an elderly woman who was applying through her lawyer for a variance to allow restoration of a walkway over saltmarsh that served as her only access to tidal waters. The variance had been denied on grounds of damage to tidal wetlands but no one was happy with this strict application of the rules. A motion was made to grant the variance but it was quickly pointed out that without a reason for the variance it was not a permissible motion. Since lack of access to the water creating a hardship was the issue involved, the motion was amended to state that to prevent extreme hardship to the woman a variance should be granted. That satisfied our legal obligations and we all felt that justice had been done—within the commission's leeway to act!

From the very beginning of drafting CAMA there had always been a question as to whether such a statute would be constitutional.[74] The major issue was whether it could be deemed a local act and thus unconstitutional on grounds that it violated the equal protection clause of the constitution. There was sufficient precedent from North Carolina zoning law that an act that affected only a portion of the state might be constitutional if the geographic area to which it applied constituted a "class", i.e., it applied to situations that occurred only in a defined area of the state and the criteria used to define the class clearly included all areas of the state that could qualify for inclusion. A great deal of thought went into the criterion finally used to define the "coastal area"; several criteria were considered. As pointed out earlier, I wrote the final definition that was based on counties bordering salt water or bordering water into which salt ocean water intruded. Although this definition satisfied those of us who wrote the act, we had no way to know whether it was indeed legally sufficient until it had been ruled so in a court of law. Thus, there was always a concern that CAMA would be tested in court—the only question really was when.

I had always expected the test of CAMA to come in conjunction with denial of a permit and that it would center on the legality of the permit process as well as the legality of the criteria used to deny the permit with

---

[74]   See also the similar material in Chapter 11.

the question as to whether CAMA was a local act a second complaint in the suit. My expectation proved to be incorrect as the first test of CAMA involved first its constitutionality—was it an impermissible local act—as well as other subsidiary issues. The case (Adams v. N. C. Department of Natural and Economic Resources) was brought in district court in Carteret county and heard in late summer 1977. The plaintiffs raised four issues: that CAMA was an unconstitutional local act, that CAMA was an unlawfully-vague delegation of legislative authority to the commission, that the CRC's regulations were arbitrary and deprived plaintiffs of their property without due process, and that CAMA authorized warrantless searches and regulatory takings. A special trial judge, Ralph Walker, who was from Greensboro and who had considerable knowledge of zoning and urban law, was assigned to the case. After a three-day trial, he ruled against the plaintiffs on all counts, finding that CAMA was not a local act, that the criteria in the statute were sufficiently precise (were not a vague delegation of legislative authority), and that the third and fourth counts were not ripe for decision as no regulatory actions had yet been taken. The Supreme Court allowed a motion to bypass the Appeals Court and heard the case directly. The trial judge's findings were upheld in a 5-1 decision. This case seems to have resolved the question of CAMA's constitutionality as no other cases have been raised since concerning that issue.

I felt that the attorneys for the plaintiffs made a serious mistake by bringing the case too soon—there was not sufficient history of actions under CAMA to constitute the basis for a case. Furthermore, the lead attorney was not well prepared and did not do a good job of representing his clients. The trial had its amusing moments, especially when one of the state's major witnesses had to leave the courtroom to get material he was supposed to introduce into evidence that he had forgotten to bring with him! Fortunately, his office in Morehead City was close by and he retrieved the material in time. I was on the stand for perhaps two hours and most of the questions to me concerned the boundary that defines the coastal area—whether it was precise enough to include all of the areas that could possibly be included and whether any of the areas that the General Assembly excluded should really be included.[75] Naturally, I was somewhat apprehensive when my testimony began as the plaintiff's attorney had a reputation for badgering witnesses, but after the first fifteen minutes of questioning it became pretty clear to me that he was really on a fishing expedition, just throwing out questions in the hope one of them might "draw blood." At several points, I asked the judge if I might expand my answer, knowing full well that what I might add would weaken the meaning of the answer I had given.

In thinking about how I would explain the decision on the criterion for the boundary of the coastal area, I had in the back of my mind the discussion I had over the phone at Christmas time 1973 with Sen. Bill Staton, the Senate manager of the bill. He asked me what criterion we had decided on and I explained the wording to him. His response was "fine, just so long as it doesn't include Arthur [Williamson, a cantankerous senator from Columbus county] because I can't handle him." Fortunately, the criterion I had chosen did not include Columbus county. None the less if anyone had learned of that conversation a case might be made that my choice was determined by a need to avoid a confrontation with Williamson. That would have been very helpful to the plaintiff's argument that CAMA was a local act! My response on the stand would have explained that the call from Staton and his comments about Williamson came after I had decided on the criterion for demarking the coastal zone. Nevertheless, the content of the conversation might have helped the plaintiff's case. Fortunately, the plaintiff's attorney never came even close to that point in his questioning. When the trial was over all of us were relieved and had a reasonably optimistic view of the outcome. That optimism proved to be well founded and subsequent legal tests have been of specific actions under CAMA rather than of the statute itself.

I was also relieved to get home after the trial as I had begun my trip to the trial with a three-day meeting of the Committee of Scientists in Denver, CO. I left Denver in mid-afternoon of the day before I was to testify

---

[75] Opponents of CAMA in the General Assembly were fully aware of the "local law" issue and concentrated on changing slightly the impact of the definition of the coastal area enough to make that a potential point on which to attack the statute if it passed.

and flew home via Oklahoma City, Atlanta, and Jacksonville arriving in Jacksonville after 11 PM where I was met by one of the state's attorneys and driven to Beaufort. The trial had begun that day so he briefed me on what had gone on and how the testimony had unfolded. It's a good thing I was only in my early forties when my involvement with state government and CAMA took place; the schedules we kept in those days were brutal.

Although the CRC was faced with a continuous flow of proposals for development of one sort or another along North Carolina's coast, several projects stand out because of their broader significance. Perhaps the best example of this involves the Cape Hatteras lighthouse. Ever since the 1930s the lighthouse had suffered periods when it was threatened by erosion only to have the pattern of sand movement shift and, for the moment, reduce the threat. However, in the 1980s a pattern of erosion developed at the lighthouse that, if continued, would undermine its base. There is no structure that is more important to the outer banks than Cape Hatteras lighthouse. Indeed, its symbolism for the outer banks and the residents of Dare county cannot be overstated. Despite several efforts at protection, such as groins and beach nourishment, the erosion continued. If not interrupted it clearly was a threat to the long-term stability of the lighthouse and, somehow, had to be managed. A movement to "Save the Lighthouse" gained steam in North Carolina and even nationally. Such diverse political figures as Jesse Helms and Jim Hunt signed on as supporting protection of the lighthouse. As might be expected, the initial proposals for protection were structural and involved construction of a concrete and steel revetment around the base of the lighthouse. In the late 1980s no other method of preservation was seriously considered although a suggestion that the lighthouse be relocated was, at the time, not considered to be a workable and "safe" alternative. Relocation was never considered a solution by residents of the outer banks; they could not envision how a structure that tall could be moved without it falling. In fact, the idea was locally ridiculed. Efforts to approve the protective barriers gained support and numerous entities were asked to "sign on." The matter did come before the CRC during the last year I was a member. At a meeting on the outer banks we were subject to a hard sell by proponents of saving the lighthouse and I voted with the rest of the commission to support construction of the hardened barriers. At the time, I was not proud of the vote as it was more a "go along to get along" gesture and did not reflect my conviction (and the commission's) that the barriers not only would not work but, in the long run, would doom the lighthouse to becoming a concrete island in the surf—and later in the ocean. However, at that time no alternative seemed to exist and a vote against would have been considered a vote against saving the lighthouse.

While this was going on, the National Park Service, which had jurisdiction over the lighthouse and had the ultimate authority to determine what method would be used to protect it, was gathering information to inform its final decision. The Park Service had available a study done in 1987 by a National Academy of Sciences committee. Ten alternatives were considered and relocation was deemed the most effective. However, relocation seemed impractical and local opposition made it unpopular. Although the Park Service finally chose to support the option involving a seawall, in light of the National Academy study it continued to gather information about the feasibility of relocation.

The matter continued under debate throughout the early part of the 1990s. The Park Service made no budget requests and despite its preference for relocation a short-term structural option remained the only option "in play." However, the prospects for the structural option looked dim because shortly after I left the CRC, its staff informed the Park Service that, considering CRC policy against shoreline hardening, it would not recommend approval of another groin (which would have been the first minimal step at structural protection).

In 1996, at the urging of fellow forestry faculty member Ellis Cowling, who was a member of the National Academy of Sciences, N C. State University was asked to undertake an independent review of the Academy report on saving the lighthouse. I was asked to serve on the review committee and I must confess that I went into the work not at all convinced that relocation would work. The committee flew to Cape Hatteras in mid-December of 1996, toured the lighthouse, and talked at length with Park Service officials. One member of the committee was a civil engineering faculty member with considerable experience with the techniques of moving large structures such as chimneys. I listened carefully as he explained how it could be done and why moving the lighthouse was neither an especially difficult nor dangerous undertaking. His explanations, and discussions during the visit to Hatteras, convinced me that relocation was not only the best, but really the only workable, method of protecting the lighthouse. Our committee recommended relocation to the Park Service in early 1997 and urged the Park Service to proceed as quickly as possible to obtain funds to move the lighthouse. This affirmation of relocation allowed the Park Service to accelerate its planning and a request for funds was made to Congress. Funding was approved in FY 1998 and a contractor, Expert House Movers, was approved to do the work in the summer of 1999.

The actual moving of the lighthouse started on June 17, 1999 and on July 9 the structure was placed in its new home 1600 feet from the ocean surf. I regretted not being able to visit while the lighthouse was being moved as the whole process was a fascinating exercise in engineering. The move went entirely without incident with the lighthouse finally placed on a new steel-reinforced concrete foundation replacing the old timber and stone foundation on which the it had stood since its construction in 1870. The outbuildings were also moved and Cape Hatteras light again became active on November 13, 1999.

I go into moving of Cape Hatteras lighthouse in some detail because it is an excellent example of the evolution of a policy involving coastal management and the interplay of public pressure, science, and agency decision-making. Although the CRC played a very small role in the actual decision to move the lighthouse, the results were consistent with the commission's policy of protecting coastal resources, as much as possible, through non-structural means. The commission's vote to support the concrete and steel revetment was more a gesture of support for preservation of the lighthouse than an actual endorsement of a structural alternative. The National Park Service's slow movement to obtain funding for the revetment reflected its lack of confidence that it was the right alternative. Despite being subject to heavy local pressure to "do something" the Service's final support for relocation, and the success of the move, vindicated its actions and final decision.

My service on the CRC ended in the summer of 1989 when I was approached by a member of Governor Jim Martin's staff with the proposal that I consider a shift to the Environmental Management Commission (EMC). Why this move was proposed was never clear to me but I think the motivation was to get some additional technical expertise on the EMC—no one ever said it was a move to get me off the CRC! After consideration, I agreed to the move with the proviso that my place on the CRC be taken by

Dave Adams. This proposal was based on my belief that the CRC needed as much technical expertise among its members as possible and Adams certainly would provide that. Martin's staff agreed to this and effective the summer of 1989 I became a member of the EMC and Adams replaced me on the CRC.

The EMC is undoubtedly the most difficult North Carolina regulatory commission on which to serve. It has statutorily-delegated responsibility for regulation of water and air pollution, hazardous substances, ground water management, erosion control, and waste management. As these responsibilities imply, the commission's work involves a great deal of technical information and decision-making. Hence, the amount of material to be read, assimilated prior to meetings, and voted on, can be enormous. In addition, the EMC has quasi-judicial authorities like those of the CRC and part of virtually every meeting involves the exercise of this duty. The EMC met six times a year together with additional committee meetings meaning that the work of the commission was literally always with its members. Conscientious service on the EMC can come close to a full-time job. Although service on the CRC was time-consuming, it never reached the burden that attended being a member of the EMC.

My service on the EMC was limited to two years. During the time I was on the commission I can remember dealing with only one major issue (there were many more) and my involvement in that one led to my quick departure from the EMC. The issue involved a dam proposed by the Piedmont Triad Regional Water Authority at a site near Randleman.[76] This same site had been under consideration for a Corps of Engineers dam while I was at NER. No action was taken by the Corps until 1987 when the project was eliminated from consideration as the cost of construction well-exceed its flood control benefits. However, the Triad Water Authority almost immediately began planning for a water-supply impoundment at the site.

The EMC became involved with this project while I was a member; several of the permits it required had to be approved by the EMC. Together with two other EMC members I was appointed as hearing officer to gather

---

[76] Recall my earlier discussion of this issue in Chapter 10.

evidence and prepare recommendations for the full commission to consider as it decided if the various permits required should be issued. Throughout the hearings, it was clear that there was a strong political commitment by Triad leaders to the project. Nonetheless, there were several major questions about the project, primarily about the narrow size of the proposed buffer and, more importantly, about the possible impact of an abandoned chemical plant site very near the headwaters of the proposed impoundment. After hearing the testimony of witnesses, I concluded that there was a distinct possibility that the drinking water quality in the impoundment would be compromised and I recommended against granting the permits. After hearing the evidence, the full commission voted to approve the project; I voted against it. I can only assume I was wrong in my concern about water quality as the impoundment was constructed in the mid-2000s, water was withdrawn from it beginning in 2011, and I have read of no water quality problems occurring. When I cast my vote, I realized that was probably enough to prevent me from being re-appointed to the EMC when my term expired in mid-1991. I was not re-appointed and I shed no tears over that result. I had had enough of "commissioning" after 15 years!

One final note. In December 1990 I received the Eure-Gardner Award from the Coastal Resources Commission. The award recognized my role in leading creation and administration of North Carolina's coastal management program and my service as a member of the CRC. The award was a great satisfaction to me.

Postscript to Parts II and III

With the end of my service on the EMC, the public service part of my career came to an end. Having been away from active service in state government for over fifteen years, I was not considered for any further appointments. However, in 1995 I was asked by the secretary of Environment, Health, and Natural Resources to serve as chairman of Governor Jim Hunt's Task Force on Sustainable Forestry. Together with Fred White, a staff member of the State Forest Service, we prepared a report with many recommendations and submitted it to Governor Hunt in early 1997. Outside of being invited to the governor's office later that year to receive a plaque for this work, there was no visible result of our work.

I did serve on the initial boards of two important and very different non-governmental organizations. Tom Massengale, who through his own personal efforts, created the North Carolina Nature Conservancy (later to become the North Carolina chapter of the national Nature Conservancy) asked me to serve on his board as the conservancy was coming into being. I agreed, not knowing Massengale and feeling there was little chance his effort would come to fruition. Again, I was wrong. I served eight years as a board member and during that time we did some remarkable things. One was creation of the Nags Head Woods Preserve (Chapter 8); others were preserves at the Green Swamp and Bluff Mountain. The North Carolina chapter has gone on to become a potent force for land preservation in North Carolina. As of 2017 it has fifty-five active projects or preserves and has preserved, or help preserve, over 700,000 acres in the state. The other organization was the Southern Environmental Law Center. Again, the original director, Rick Middleton, approached me about serving on his initial board. I did so and, together with the others on the board, set in motion a highly effective organization dedicated to using the law to protect and preserve North Carolina's environment. In fact, in at least one case when I served on the Coastal Resources Commission one of the contesting attorneys in a permit case was from the Center (remember the young lady that gave me the wolf's head—it was she!).

To be truthful, I was not looking for additional work outside of the university. I had been appointed NC State's faculty athletics representative in 1990 and that, I found, took up all the creative time I was able to devote to it. But that is another story, for another day.

Cover Illustrations

(all by the author)

Upper left: Bald Head Island, aerial photo from the north, 1965, Chapter 13.

Upper right: Jockey's Ridge in winter, 1966, Chapter 8.

Upper center left: Oregon Inlet from the air, 1972, Chapter 15.

Upper center right: Cape Hatteras Light House, 1996, showing erosion, and before being moved in 1999, Part III.

Lower center left: Medoc Mountain State Park, in foreground, 1973, Chapter 8.

Lower center right: Tunnel on the Road to Nowhere, Great Smoky Mountains National Park, 1988, Chapter 12.

Lower left: Mount Mitchell, North Carolina's first State Park, 1970, Chapter 8.

Lower Right: The New River, Ashe County, 2001, Chapter 14.

Printed in the United States
By Bookmasters